T0308768

THE GUESTROOM NOVELIST

THE
GUESTROOM
NOVELIST

A DONALD HARINGTON
MISCELLANY

EDITED BY BRIAN WALTER

The University of Arkansas Press | Fayetteville

2019

Copyright © 2019 by The University of Arkansas Press
All rights reserved
Manufactured in the United States of America
ISBN: 978-1-68226-091-3
eISBN: 978-1-61075-660-0

23 22 21 20 19   5 4 3 2 1

Designer: April Leidig

∞ The paper used in this publication meets the minimum requirements
of the American National Standard for Permanence of Paper for
Printed Library Materials z39.48–1984.

Library of Congress Cataloging-in-Publication Data
Names: Harington, Donald, author. | Walter, Brian, editor.
Title: The guestroom novelist : a Donald Harington miscellany /
edited by Brian Walter.
Description: Fayetteville : The University of Arkansas Press, 2019. |
Identifiers: LCCN 2018034004 (print) | LCCN 2018043025 (ebook) |
ISBN 9781610756600 (electronic) | ISBN 9781682260913 (cloth : alk. paper)
Classification: LCC PS3558.A6242 (ebook) | LCC PS3558.A6242 A6 2019 (print) |
DDC 814/.54—dc23
LC record available at https://lccn.loc.gov/2018034004

Supported in part by Archie Schaffer III of *Thirteen Albatrosses* fame.

For Don,
the better maker (of course)

———

And for Brenda,
my improbably loving wife

CONTENTS

A Very Loud Amusement Park

BRIAN WALTER

"A methodical man, John Shade usually copied out his daily
quota of completed lines at midnight but even if he recopied them
again later, as I suspect he sometimes did, he marked his card or cards
not with the date of his final adjustments, but with that of his Corrected
Draft or first Fair Copy. I mean, he preserved the date of actual creation
rather than that of second or third thoughts. There is a very loud
amusement park right in front of my present lodgings."
—V. Nabokov, *Pale Fire*

THE FIRST MISTAKE I MADE with Donald Harington remains the most useful. Over lunch during our very first meeting, I asked him, in reasonably perfect innocence, "So, what kind of projects are you working on now?"

It was the fall of 1996, and I hadn't read any of his books yet. On this, my first trip to Fayetteville, I was seated across the table from Don and his wife in their deceptively expansive home, and I was just trying to be polite by lobbing him a flattering question. In my three decades of presumptuous existence, I had had the good fortune to dine with a number of fine fiction writers and poets who, like Harington, paid the bills with university teaching posts, and most of them, I had learned, produced scholarly and professional work along with their art. "Project" seemed like a safe term for anything my host might be working on.

Harington would have none of it. Leaning over the table, leaning into his response, leaning—it somehow seemed—right into *me*, the playfully offended writer retorted, "*'Projects'*? I don't do 'projects.' I write novels!"

Anyone who ever met Harington will understand perfectly well why I went right home and dove into *Ekaterina* to repair a glaring omission in my education. What did it mean for this tall, stooping, white-haired man with thick glasses, a voice thinned out by throat cancer, a ponderous hearing aid, and a breast-pocketful of index cards to *write novels?*

Over the course of the next thirteen years, Harington's indignant declaration of his real vocation echoed and reechoed in my mind as I read my way through his corpus, corresponded with him, visited and hosted him and his wife, wrote articles and reviews about his novels, and, finally, interviewed him at considerable length in what he clearly knew to be the last years of his life. And the pursuit of a plausibly full answer to the question of what it meant for Donald Harington to write novels has continued in the decade or so that has passed since his passing, particularly in the Harington archive housed by the University of Arkansas's Special Collections and in the computer files that were approved for this research. You now hold the result of these efforts in your hands, this first collection of nonfiction writings and interviews by someone I once nicknamed (to his great pleasure, as he later told me) the court jester of the Ozarks.

Harington's work has always appealed at least as much to the general reader (or, as Harington nominates her in *When Angels Rest,* "Gentle Reader") as it does to the literary scholar, and his own long (and frustrating) quest for success in the literary marketplace showed how ardently he courted the former, elusive quarry. An art historian and a technically uncredentialed but superbly knowledgeable (and opinionated) student of literature himself, Harington was quite at home among other scholars, of course, but it was clear to anyone who discussed his work's history with him that he would have traded all the favorable reviews and the awards he had won for the kind of sales that his friends and rivals, like John Irving and Cormac McCarthy, enjoyed. So, in preparing a volume of Harington's nonfiction that will serve the efforts of both kinds of readers, I have tried not just to provide texts that will shed more light on his many inspirations and thicken scholarly appreciation of his favorite themes, but also to provide his beloved Gentle Reader with another pleasurable Harington reading experience, a fresh and deepened perspective on the restless mind that was tied so firmly (if, for him, frustratingly) to his equally restless but tender heart. In an interview included in this volume, Harington declares his work to be primarily intellectual, "for the head," and only secondarily emotional, "for the heart," but like any of his novels, this volume of his nonfiction shows how beautifully the two collaborated in all of his creative endeavors.

The various texts that comprise this miscellany invite you to enjoy still more of the imposing learning that made Harington's novels possibly the most quirky and inventive corpus in American letters, as a reviewer once put it. But perhaps more importantly, they invite you to see that, no matter what he was writing—essays, reviews, or responses to interview questions that he couldn't hear and which were thus submitted to him in writing—Harington was always the novelist, always spinning yarns, rigging up plotlines to hook, entrance, and delight the Gentle Reader whom he loved so dearly (sometimes desperately) through the medium of his written words. Harington was an incorrigible storyteller, a loving co-conspirator with anyone who would set foot into his imaginary realms, to our perpetual enrichment as readers.

The three sections of nonfiction in this *Guestroom Novelist* commence with the eponymous essay, which Harington first wrote as a talk to be delivered at Texas Christian University and which he then, without success (in a frustrating pattern that most writers can sympathize with), tried to sell to a variety of editors. It offers an almost perfect example of his take on the figure of the writer: decades of frustration and bitterness transmuted into a generous series of love letters to fellow accomplished, worthy, but commercially unsuccessful authors, a potential rant about the fickleness of the fiction marketplace gentled and deepened into a well-researched, systematic, wryly lively gift to curious readers and gifted but lonely writers everywhere.

The themes realized so thoughtfully and with such restless love in the title essay reappear, in various guises, throughout the essays, speeches, reviews, and interviews that follow. Over and over again, Harington emphasizes and embodies the personal nature of both the writing and the reading experience, the connections between logophilia, gifted logorrhea (such as he was blessed with), and the desire for an other, a partner for both the mind and the heart. Whether he's discussing the soul-soothing comforts of his mother-in-law's chicken-and-dumplings, or taking museum directors to task for failing to realize their glorious mission, or licensing the reader's most dubious responses to a painter's most dubious portraits, Harington consistently humanizes, illuminates, and enlarges his topics as a gift to the reader, an invitation to join him in the Stay More of his imagination for respite and repast that will last a lifetime (however creatively lonely that lifetime may turn out to be).

The final text in this miscellany, "The Stay More Interviews," is (admittedly) something of a cheat. Every other text in the volume is something that Harington, in one way or another, wrote, even (it seems clear) the earlier interviews in which the deaf novelist was given the questions and allowed to respond in writing. But in the "Stay More Interviews," which I conducted over three visits to the Harington home in Fayetteville between August 2006 and June 2007, I wrote out the questions beforehand on note cards and then handed them to him (along with several on-the-spot additions prompted by his comments) one by one in person in front of the camera, purposefully putting him on the spot and denying him the comforts of his preferred medium. He was, of course, a practiced teacher and speaker, and he often slipped into stories that he had clearly retold many times over the decades, but even so, I like to think that whatever the transcriptions of those interviews lack in the polish so clear in his writing, they more than make up for with a different kind of eloquence. Our mutual favorite writer, Vladimir Nabokov, hated to give interviews and, after *Lolita* brought him enough fame to avalanche him with requests, soon began accepting only ones in which he was allowed to write out his responses to questions submitted to him prior to the actual interview; Harington, his great (if seemingly improbable) Ozarkian heir, was almost as ill at ease during our sessions, often growing tired or frustrated when Mnemosyne wouldn't deliver to him the required name fast enough (or sometimes at all), calling out for his wife's help, lamenting the bareness of the top of his white-haired head as a resource when he wanted to come up with something cleverly Haringtonian in response to my "tricky" or "creative" questions. Certainly, if he'd had the time and inclination to respond in writing, at his leisure, to my stacked deck of queries, the responses would look rather different—and that's why I wanted him (as much as possible) to answer my questions in the moment of their asking, to capture a comparatively raw record of the voice and sensibility of this most incorrigibly personal of writers.

It is in honor of that final cheat of a tête-à-tête text that I stole the title of this introduction from Harington's favorite Nabokov novel. Three paragraphs into his preface to *Pale Fire*, Charles Kinbote interrupts his straightforward technical description of recently deceased John Shade's final poem to inform the reader—completely out of the blue—that there is a "very loud amusement park right in front of my present lodgings." This bizarre observation serves up the first hint to the reader that the editor of this fiction may not stick entirely to the script, that the scholar's subjective perspective will, in fact, intrude importantly and meaningfully on the dead writer's art. In nothing did Harington more gleefully or solemnly emulate Nabokov than in the latter's insistence that "reality" itself—much less the transmuted reality of a work of art, in any medium—was entirely subjective, constructed idiosyncratically within the mind of each of us to the point that all we can really talk about are our perceptions of reality, not mere reality itself. Which means that—for Harington as much as for Nabokov—every text serves as a happy marriage broker between the author and the reader; it also means that the wise, knowing, loving reader will always, finally, welcome the author's intrusions on the text, because that's all the text really is: an intensely personal coupling through the medium of the page, the beautifully written word the ring that the inspired writer slips onto the finger of the inspired reader. When Kinbote interrupts the rote recital of mere schematic information to bring the reader momentarily into his living world, he does what Harington always insisted on: foregrounding the writer's subjective reality as the real source of interest and art and love, the most generous and authentic compact the writer can offer to the reader.

For that reason, in honor of our mutual favorite teacher of a novelist, I have also let loose a loving little Kinbote in the pages of those concluding "Stay More Interviews," a mildly mischievous antagonist of an annotator to play a bit of footnoted chess with the Nabokov of the Ozarks. Wherever he is now in the mountains above Stay More, hiking toward the remote waterfall or sitting on Latha Bourne's porch in a rocking chair or enjoying Nail Chism's authentically rustic stylings on the harmonica in some idyllic pasture, Harington's happy spirit will, I trust, forgive me for suggesting that those interviews find him, the better maker, and yours truly, his ever-grateful student, collaborating a bit like Nabokov's Kinbote and Shade to produce the intensely personal and unmistakably summative memoir that the novelist-writer, in effect, spun out in response to his project manager's playful questions.

Note on the Text(s)

The essays, reviews, and other original texts collected in this volume come primarily from two sources: (1) the Harington archive housed by the University of Arkansas Library's exemplary Special Collections, and (2) files saved on Harington's various hard drives that his widow, Kim Harington, generously shared with me. For the most part, I have (with the scrupulous help of Matthew Somoroff) silently fixed the occasional grammatical or mechanical or typographical mistake, inserted words or phrasings that Harington pretty clearly would have added if he'd seen the texts into publication himself, and regularized punctuation throughout, often by adding commas to smooth out complicated syntax. (Harington seems to have been a curiously inconsistent devotee of the so-called Oxford comma, for instance; this collection makes him much more consistent.) Where his ellipses pretty clearly indicate omitted words (and not just pauses), I have also enclosed them in brackets ([. . .]).

The one notable exception to my policy of general editorial restraint remains "The Stay More Interviews" at the end, where the transcribed recordings (of course) include no punctuation or paragraphing at all, leaving it to the editor to shape Harington's responses into readable (and hopefully appealing) prose. The editorial hand there necessarily recasts Harington from the author speaking in his own voice into (if you will) my character, a creation of the page that is (for better or worse) pretty much entirely in my control. I think Harington would certainly recognize and approve of the version of him that my editing choices offer up, but he would also, no doubt, note a few technically apocryphal flow-enablers and a collection of playful subtleties that I have sprinkled through this printed presentation of our in-person exchanges. Perhaps he would even rise to the occasion to protest one or two of them, to scold his protégé for cheek above and beyond the call of editorial duty. To this prospect, I will (as Harington would certainly have wanted me to, for he always considered me far more a character in *his* fictions than he ever could be in mine) just reply with the wry send-off that concludes Kinbote's introduction to *Pale Fire*: "To this statement my dear poet would probably not have subscribed, but, for better or worse, it is the commentator who has the last word."

I

ESSAYS, ARTICLES, AND SPEECHES

⚡⚡⚡

"EVERY WRITER WRITES," Donald Harington wrote in the melancholy prologue to his 1986 nonfiction novel, *Let Us Build Us a City*, "in expectation of love." If that claim holds true, then what kind of love did Harington the essayist, article author, and speechwriter expect from his efforts?

In many of the examples that follow, the answer jumps out pretty quickly: love for his novels. Even if his cover letter for "The Guestroom Novelist" didn't declare Harington himself the "epitome" of the guestroom novelist (see p. 24 below), it would be clear, in his generous praise for other underappreciated American novelists, that Harington is making a plea for the enduring substance and appeal of his own work, however obscure it remained (at least in the author's eyes). From another angle, "Arkansas's One and Only Hero" works to whet the reader's appetite for a book on Albert Pike, the subject of *A Work of Fiction*, Harington's still unpublished novel from the late 1960s about the soldier, mason, and Ozarks mountaineer who had so inspired him. And in his 2006 acceptance speech for the *Oxford American*'s Lifetime Achievement Award in Southern Literature, he jokingly but repeatedly reminds the audience that he has not received the remuneration he has deserved for his work, four decades and more after he published his first novel but just a few years before the final one (as he seemed already to have a sense) would appear in print. Perhaps by that point, Harington was most interested in measuring love (at least the love he still hoped to win from the greater world) in dollar signs.

If other entries in this section take up causes that (at first) seem to have little to do with inspiring the reader to love Harington's novels, it takes just a little imagination to see how Harington was using even them to woo readers to his lonely work as Stay More's determined chronicler. Most of these pieces concern themselves with Arkansas questions and matters, and in all of them, Harington's status as a native Arkansawyer, in one way or the other, crucially informs his appeal (and authority) to the reader and serves as a clever invitation to enjoy his Arkansas-set novels. At times sounding like an Ozarkian Mark Twain, Harington affected a cantankerous, playful, knowing persona, one who loathed academic puffery as much as he loved his home state, the visual arts, and language as wellsprings of the imagination. For example, in the article "Let Us Become Arkansawyers," Harington argues for the referent that he so vigorously preferred for natives of his home state, but only after poking serious fun at the provinciality of local speech habits and his own (not entirely convincing) ignorance of fancy academic words. In the subtly learned piece "Comfort Me with Chicken and Dumplings," Harington sends a son-in-law's loving thank-you note to his mother-in-law while instructing the reader in folk culinary traditions, the hillbilly gastronome who spends even more time in libraries than he does at the supper table. If he could be charged with playing a bit shamelessly to the pragmatic impulses of his fellow Ozarkians and Arkansawyers, the flattery works more subtly as a rhetorical Trojan horse, a reassurance devised to win entrance for the intellectual and philosophical arguments in which he so earnestly believed but which he didn't want to deliver in a crude, frontal scholarly assault. If he could deliver such learned pleas in terms that his fellow literate "primitives" (as Harington refers to them) in his home state would accept, then why couldn't his novels perform similar two-handed magic, having their homespun cake and eating it like the mannered scholar too?

Apart from the joys of Harington's playful work as the hillbilly scholar, veteran readers of his novels will also appreciate the glimpse afforded here, in his article "Searching for 'Cities' that Didn't Make It" (1983), into the early workings of what would become *Let Us Build Us a City*, including the reference to its original, equally biblical working title, *No Need of the Sun*. Another highlight is Harington's loving profile of painter and friend Bill McNamara, who would reappear, name intact, a few years later in Harington's tour de force of a novel, *Ekaterina* (1993). Harington continues to write cleverly about himself and his own work while doing his subject full justice in the McNamara profile, which grounds the artist's inspiration in a minutely sensual relationship with a verdant, vital mountain landscape peopled only by his few beloved intimates, erotic love grading naturally into spiritual and intellectual love. In Harington's characterization, McNamara's paintings are as personally and naturally inspired by his wife-muse and children-apprentices as Harington himself was by his Latha Bournes and young Dawnys.

Or, as he shows in the curious "first dates" essay that ends this section, as intimately inspired as he was with his own, real-life muse. In "First Dates," Harington takes himself down an old favorite memory lane, a story that he and his second wife, Kim, loved to tell as the beginning of the novelistic life they went on to live together. In this final piece, Harington's signature designs on a muse to mold (even as she, too, molds him and his work) preempt the comparatively prescriptive tone that marks several of the other entries in this group.

As always with Harington and other masters of metafiction, the reader will find it useful to read these pieces with two eyes, one attending to Harington's topic and argument but the other just as attentive to the persona he was always crafting within and through the argument: clear-eyed, loving (not sentimental), and knowing, but also hungry, sad, and even a bit wistful. Toward the latter end, the author's brief bios that appear at the ends of many of these pieces particularly stand out. If it overstates the case to say that Harington wrote the articles and other pieces here simply to remind readers that he was a novelist forever working on books related to his beloved home state, it is not at all a stretch to note the care he clearly took to keep his fellow Arkansawyers apprised of his current doings as a novelist. Harington took his responsibilities as a public intellectual very seriously, but just as clearly, his occasional pieces represented here should (in his own mind, at any rate) lead readers to his lifework as an underappreciated but deeply, even incorrigibly, personal novelist who yearned to escape the guestroom.

The Guestroom Novelist
in America

—1990—

T IS A DARK AND STORMY NIGHT. Make believe that you have never slept in this bed before. The room is familiar only because you recognize certain features—a floor, a ceiling, four walls, a door, a bed. You have taken the trouble to learn the location of the bathroom. But make believe you don't recognize other features of the room: the pictures on the wall, unremarkable, the curtains on the window, the bookcase in the corner.

Now make believe you scan the titles of the bookcase in search of support against the night and the storm. There are several *Reader's Digest Condensed Books*, a college biology textbook, a high school algebra textbook, a Gideon Bible taken from some motel. There are three consecutive years, many years before, of a school yearbook, whether high school or college is not determinable without opening them, which, make believe, you don't care to do. Nor do you care to open the photo album, the out-of-date phone book, or the twenty-four issues of *National Geographic* magazine. You need not make believe that the whole set of Will and Ariel Durant's *Story of Civilization* is here intact.

But make believe you find among this dross some things that might pass for literature: Gibbons, a Sir Walter Scott novel, a Thackeray, Margaret Mitchell, Bulwer-Lytton, Edith Sitwell, Berry Fleming, Robert Louis Stevenson, Wilbur Daniel Steele, Hamilton Basso . . .

Berry Fleming? You don't have to make believe you have never heard of him, because you actually haven't. The book has a fetching title, *The Make*

For more information about this essay's origins, see Harington's cover letter that follows.

7

Believers, and you open it and notice the publisher, Pelican, a small outfit in Louisiana, and the date of publication, 1972, a good year for neglected novels. You begin reading, and soon the night and the storm are gone.

Chances are you won't finish the novel before it's time to vacate that guestroom, but depending on your relationship with your host or hostess, you'll either ask to borrow the book, or steal it, or start looking in second-hand bookstores for your own copy.

And you'll want to learn more about this Berry Fleming, of whom you'd never heard. You'll find to your dismay that he died last September, of cancer in his home in Augusta, Georgia, but that he lived for ninety years, which Faulkner would have done if he hadn't died, and that, like Faulkner, Fleming wrote many novels in obscurity, the first one in 1927, but unlike Faulkner, Fleming never managed to emerge from his obscurity. He was nominated last year for a Nobel Prize, but the only honor he ever received was a promotion to first lieutenant in the Coast Guard during the First World War.

Fleming's few readers have noticed with surprise that he compares favorably with Eudora Welty, Erskine Caldwell, and J. P. Marquand, as well as with Faulkner, but a more recent comparison is with Pat Conroy, whose *Prince of Tides* seems florid, overwritten, and empty alongside the best Fleming novels. If you ever find Pat Conroy in a guestroom, you should fumigate the sheets.

The novelist in the guestroom, as I define him here, is that ubiquitous but lamented writer who doesn't deserve neglect, who deserves for you to make believe that you have discovered him, all on your own, although I intend to help you.

Think of the ones you've already discovered, the no-longer-living minor masters like Conrad Richter and Conrad Aiken, Gerald Warner Brace, Jack Conroy (no relation to Pat), and Wilbur Daniel Steel. Or the still-living-in-obscurity masters like Andrew Lytle, Mark Harris, W. M. Spackman, and James Still.

There are far too many of them. But that is, and always has been, the way of the publishing world. Every novelist writes secondarily for money or movies or Mother. Every novelist writes primarily for approval, for praise, for honor, for love. But the world of readers is stingy with its esteem, fickle with its favor, and short with its memory. The shelves of the guestroom, as well as the shelves of the public library and the secondhand bookshop, become a mausoleum, waiting for your breath upon the open page to resurrect the defunct author.

The true guestroom novel is not the erstwhile bestseller faded from its glory, nor the one neglected masterpiece by an otherwise famous writer, nor the classic that remains unread by its owner. Many guestrooms are populated by Sterne's *Tristram Shandy*, Proust's *Remembrance of Things Past*, and Nabokov's *Ada*, worthy works of literature although no one remembers having finished reading any of them, and no guest is ever likely to read them in your guestroom.

Nor is there room here for that mass of novelists whom the publishers quaintly identify as "midlist": the gray tribe of permanently marketable but never bestselling writers. All guestroom novels are midlist, but not all midlist novels are worthy of the guestroom.

And with one exception I must also exclude the one-shot first-and-only novel, worthy though it might be, for there are too many *Raintree County*s, too many *Pictures at an Exhibition*s, and too many *A Tree Grows in Brooklyn*s, and too many *A Gay Place*s, although I have to confess that I first discovered Billy Lee Brammer in a guestroom, and will never forget his rich humor and his elegant prose. By all other standards, Brammer should be on our list: *The Gay Place*, that Texas trilogy transparently based on Lyndon Johnson, enjoyed a fine critical reception but was ignored in the marketplace. It was reissued posthumously after Brammer's untimely death in 1978, and earned a great eventual readership. But, without arguing that it is actually three separate novels in one, it was Brammer's only book.

To limit the population of the crowded guestroom—and remember that we are still excluding hundreds of worthy novelists—we should confine ourselves to Americans. The British have even more nicely appointed guestrooms per capita than we do, and many unheralded masters—John Cowper Powys, the Sitwells, L. P. Hartley, and the guestroom novelist par excellence, Ford Madox Ford, come to mind—and the French and Italians and Spanish are just as bad as we are when it comes to neglecting their geniuses, but for the sake of our small room, let's limit it to Americans, shall we? Let's limit it, except for the late unlamented Berry Fleming, to those still living, those still susceptible to whatever encouragement or terminal cheer our notice and readership may give them.

Let's limit it to the American novelist who has published several books, who has been through the painful process enough times to give him the sense to quit, but who has not quit, who still keeps trying, against the odds, to be approved, praised, honored, loved.

He should be past forty. Guestroomer Richard Stern told me, "It's silly to name young writers under forty who have time to be in many guestrooms."

Probably the guestroomer has had more than one publisher, more likely three or more different ones (Stern has had nine, Berry Fleming had ten, but, after all, Faulkner himself had five), and probably he has never had a major review in the *New York Times Book Review*, which has a good nose for ignoring worthy masterpieces.

Probably he has never had a major book club selection, although Fleming himself had one of his novels, *Colonel Effingham's Raid*, chosen by the Book of the Month Club, back in 1943 during the lean war years, and there was a subsequent movie, starring Charles Coburn and Joan Bennett. For a brief time, at least, Fleming made a little money from that book.

Probably the guestroom novel, if it ever stirred up the hopes of its original publisher, was overprinted and undersold and remaindered, and it's easy to stock the shelves of a guestroom with books purchased at discount prices. A few years ago, I found on the bargain table a marked-down hardcover of Alexander Theroux's *Darconville's Cat*. I recognized the last name and realized he might be related to Paul Theroux, who, of course, is his kid brother, very famous, very rich, and very good. Alex Theroux has written not nearly as many novels, which haven't caught on with the mass readership, possibly because, like *Darconville's Cat*, they are extravaganzas: wild and experimental and self-consciously efflorescent. To tell you that you wouldn't be able to put down *Darconville* is wrong: it is over 700 pages and it's easy to fall asleep in places, but when you've finished it, you'll know that you've read an outrageous masterpiece. One of the few recognitions it received was from British novelist Anthony Burgess, who put it on his list of the ninety-nine greatest books of our century.

Guestrooms are also well-stocked with cheap mass market paperbacks, and while the majority of hardcover guestroom fiction is never lucky enough to be reprinted as mass market paperbacks, that may be the only form in which you can find such things as Donald Newlove's *Sweet Adversity*, the title that Avon paperbacks gave to its reprinting together of *both* of his earlier twin novels about two hilarious Siamese twins, *Leo and Theodore* and *The Drunks*, which is what they are: two chronic alcoholic brothers, Teddy and Leo, jazz musicians sharing a common bloodstream but with separate brains; both novels are written in a gorgeous bouncy prose that teeters on the edge of slapstick, silly as all get-out at times, setting you up with comic relief for the most tragic examination of alcoholism in any novel of our times. Donald Newlove is almost famous as a leading expert on drunkenness, and he has also published a nonfiction study called *Those Drinking Days: Myself and Others*, which exhaustively explores the effects of booze on our century's major writers, including himself.

The *New York Times Book Review* ignored the first novel, *Leo and Theodore*, and consigned the review for the second novel, *The Drunks*, to one of those catch-all columns in which the reviewer tries to review three or more books with the haste and myopia demanded by the task. Still, the reviewer, Frederick Busch, himself a guestroomer of good standing, managed to praise Newlove more than condemn him, calling *The Drunks* both "one of the most desperately funny books we've been given in a long time, and one of the most frightening."

The *New York Times Book Review* also relegated to one of its catch-all grab-bag columns, by the perennial sniffer Anatole Broyard, a hedging review of Janet Burroway's *Raw Silk*, which Little, Brown published in 1977. Broyard complained that Burroway "is not saying anything radically new" and dismissed it as one more woman's novel, although he admired its good lines. But the Bantam paperback edition helped to bring *Raw Silk* to the attention of a wide audience, who appreciated its examination of an unusual marriage, between an American woman from trailer park California and a British executive. Despite Broyard's caveat, the novel not only avoids feminist rhetoric but, as *New Republic*'s critic pointed out, it "provokes women's novels today as surely as Ralph Ellison's *Invisible Man* challenged the black novel a quarter century ago."

Burroway likes to think that *Raw Silk*, her fourth novel but first successful one, built the house in which she lives in Tallahassee, where she teaches fiction writing at Florida State University (of the thirteen novelists on our list, ten are teaching college in order to earn a living), and Burroway has written a popular book on the craft of creative writing, but most guestroom novels never made much money for their authors.

Indeed, the essential yardstick for inclusion in the guestroom, apart from literary excellence, is lack of monetary success, the inability of the writer to support himself and his family from the proceeds of the sale of his novels. Take, for example, Thomas Savage.

Here are his credentials: seventy-five years old, and still going strong, with his thirteenth novel, *The Corner of Rife and Pacific*, published last year by Morrow and following the other twelve into the maw of oblivion or onto the shelves of the guestroom. He is America's best kept literary secret. His most powerful novel, *The Power of the Dog*, set in his native Montana, published originally in 1967 by Little, Brown, has been hailed as the finest novel of the American west. But like most of his other novels, it barely earned back the publisher's advance. Not one of his thirteen novels has sold more than 10,000 copies. For the past quarter of a century, he has made scarcely enough to live on, even in Maine or Washington State, where he has worked to make his home away from Montana, with his wife, Elizabeth Savage (who died last year), herself a guestroom novelist.

For want of any classification, Thomas Savage may be compared in his depiction of the American West with A. B. Guthrie and Wright Morris, both guestroomers, Guthrie relegated there after years of success and popularity (he was my favorite novelist in high school), and Wright Morris perhaps having at last escaped the guestroom by virtue of his growing reputation.

Savage's *The Power of the Dog* is a fine story of two brothers on a ranch in Montana, one of them good, the other bad, one of them patient and reserved and decent, the other brutal and clever and destructive, one of them married to a good widow whom the other one, the mean one, drives inexorably into desperate drinking and to the brink of madness.

Naturally such a situation is bound to end in violence, and this one does, as many of Savage's books do. His name, Savage, is almost an adjective for his climaxes, which are ferocious and merciless, but his view of mankind is compassionate and civilized and highly intelligent.

He is most concerned with family relationships, the conflicts of siblings within the family unit as their identity, and it has been his misfortune to be reviewed in the *New York Times* by such as Eliot Fremont-Smith, who accused him of "sentimental grandiloquence," or, worse, the feminist poet Katha Pollitt, who said that anyone who, "in this day and age," believes in the importance of the family is not worthy of being taken seriously in the pages of the *New York Times Book Review.*

Such put-downs, perhaps, have kept Savage from the audience he deserves and consigned his books to the guestroom while such novelists who expropriate Savage's Montana as Thomas McGuane and Richard Ford become the darling of the literary establishment.

Is it surprising in the face of such neglect and scorn that the artist's own life would become increasingly tragic? Probably no novel that Thomas Savage could ever write would match the misfortunes and suffering of the story of his own life, which is almost too painful to tell. For a man who loves the idea of family to the point of obsession, Savage grew up in a terrible family: an alcoholic mother who died young, a father right out of *Death of a Salesman* who married four times and bequeathed his fourth bride to Tom's care when nobody else wanted her, when Tom and his own wife were struggling to make ends meet, as year after year his novels came out to be noticed, if at all, in the *New York Times Book Review*'s catch-all columns called "Briefly Noted" or "In Short," or, if the reviewer was thoughtful and sympathetic, the reviewer would wonder why nobody reads Savage and would conclude that the novel in question "might well win Savage the popularity he has long deserved," although the novel in question would likely follow its predecessors into obscurity and the guestroom.

Tom and Elizabeth Savage have faced tragedy in their life, of a kind that put them in the company of Job. And if anyone could make Tom Savage's life into a novel, it would not be himself but James Purdy, who is almost that contradiction in terms, a "famous" guestroom novelist.

At least Purdy is the one of those I'm mentioning whom, most likely, you've heard of before, or even read. The story of his struggle to become a writer is well known: like many novelists, he began his career by writing a number of short stories, which were rejected by every magazine to which he sent them. In 1956, he published his first two books, a novel and a collection of stories, at his own expense with a subsidy publisher, the last resort of the writer exhausting his search for approval, praise, honor, love. Nobody buys self-published novels, so he sent free copies to all of the prominent literary figures he could think of, who, of course, dumped the books into their guestrooms and forgot them . . . except for a few compassionate readers, including Dame Edith Sitwell, the English writer, who wrote back to Purdy with the first glimpse of approval and praise: the short stories, she said, were "superb, nothing short of masterpieces," while the novel was "a masterpiece from every point of view."

Encouraged, and with Sitwell's help, Purdy found a British publisher, Gollancz, who launched his literary career, just as, years earlier, the American poet Robert Frost had first published in England, and just as American novelist Janet Burroway, mentioned earlier, would publish her first three books in England before they were accepted in America.

In 1959, Farrar Straus published in America Purdy's novel *Malcolm*, which Edward Albee later converted successfully into a play, and there followed such novels as *The Nephew*, *Cabot Wright Begins*, and *Eustace Chisholm and the Works*.

In his long career, he has moved around to eight different publishers in this country: Farrar Straus, New Directions, Black Sparrow, Doubleday, Arbor House, and Viking. His books have been translated into twenty-two languages, and in 1975, the Modern Language Association of America at its annual convention devoted an entire seminar to his work.

And yet he remains essentially a guestroom novelist, never a best-seller, never popular, and never accepted by the critical establishment. Admiration for Purdy's unique manner, a flat ironic prose which often relates violent or horrifying events, has generally been greater in Europe, particularly in England, France, and Italy. As Purdy himself has observed, in America, "there are no serious book reviews," and he has never been accepted into "anaesthetic, hypocritical, preppy and stagnant New York literary establishment," an elusive, perhaps chimerical, but very real and very powerful fraternity of tastemakers.

Purdy is a writer's writer, and he has been much admired by his fellows, including Marianne Moore, Paul Bowles, William Carlos Williams, Angus Wilson, Langston Hughes, and Gore Vidal. Efforts to classify Purdy, to pigeonhole him, with such divergent labels as naturalist, realist, black humorist, and satirist, have compared him with Joseph Conrad, Graham Greene, William Golding, D. H. Lawrence, Carson McCullers, Alain Robbe-Grillet, and, of course, William Faulkner.

Recently, I asked Purdy which of his two dozen books of fiction he would nominate as the most likely candidate for a guestroom, and he suggested his 1974 novel, *The House of the Solitary Maggot*, pointing out that "the *New York Times* refused to review it despite frantic appeals from its publisher, Doubleday." That fact alone makes it eligible for the guestroom.

Why did the *New York Times* refuse to review it? Do they think of him as some of his detractors do, as petulant, childish, bitter, unable to grow out of the traumatic experiences of his early life? I will not presume to offer any understanding of the arcane methods of selection and rejection used by that august newspaper, other than to note, in passing, the frequency with which the guestroom novelists in this study have railed against it.

The House of the Solitary Maggot—the title comes from the townspeople's deliberate mispronunciation of the word "magnate" for the town's rich man—is actually the second volume in a trilogy called *Sleepers in Moon-Crowned Valleys*, although it has no direct connection to the other volumes, all of which examine the Midwestern American past, of Purdy's native Ohio. Critics noted that it has a more positive view of life than his earlier work, or at least its prose transcends the tragedy and squalor of the story. Irving Malin of the *New Republic* writes that Prince's Crossing, the fading hamlet which is its setting, is "a ghostland . . . filled with people unable to accept the facts of daily life, obsessed with bright visions of glory, fame and love. They are sleepwalkers."

The principal sleepwalkers are the narrator himself, Eneas Harmond, a hermit who has a plaque over his house reading "DO NOT DISTURB!"—the opening words of the novel and a key to its contents, and Nora Bythewaite, called Lady Bythewaite because she was born in England, who speaks into her tape recorder the history of her American family and the decline of the village of Prince's Crossing. Nora Bythewaite's three sons were fathered by a Mr. Skegg, the local magnate, or "maggot" whose house furnishes the title, who is irresponsible toward his offspring and toward Nora, and contributes to their ruin.

It is a more conventional story than most of Purdy's, and yet its patterns are distinctively and characteristically Purdian, as if its sleepwalkers are undergoing nightmares. Purdy has explained that the story contains "pieced-together, often broken fragments of my ancestors' lives," and that it is based upon "a chronicle of narratives I had heard from my grandmother and my great-grandmother. I had listened as a child to these women's endless recollections of small towns, and villages, and sinister cities."

William Peden has called Purdy "the prose-poet of the grotesque and the alienated" and has attempted to describe the sleepwalking experience in Purdy's work: "He leads us into a world in which customary values are reversed, where the familiar suddenly becomes terrifying, as though one walking through a well-known terrain were to find himself at the edge of a void alive with sights and sounds only partly recognizable." Others have commented on Purdy's uncanny knack for taking ordinary people and situations and transforming them into surreal aberrations, analogous for the reader to moving from picture to different picture in a shadowy museum.

Contemporary Authors, the register, historian, and bibliographer of every current writer regardless of stature, concluded its interview with Purdy by asking him, "What would you say to a young person who wants to write?"

And Purdy answered:

. . . all he can hope for is to be able to write the kind of book he would like to write. If you can do that, you shouldn't expect anything more. You shouldn't hope for fame or popularity or riches . . . There's a big difference between a book finding its audience and a book finding the public. The public only knows what it's told. The public will buy anything if it's told to.

The very best example of the guestroom novelist who has found his audience without finding the public is Richard Stern. Even more than Purdy, he is a writer's writer. His audience, small though it is, is filled with admiration. He has been compared to fellow Chicagoan Saul Bellow, who is one of his devout admirers, as well as a personal friend. He has been compared to Bernard Malamud, to John Cheever, to Henry James. Perhaps in his great love for words, for the sound of the language as well as its meaning, he is like Nabokov, and all that has kept Richard Stern from becoming rich and famous and widely read is his failure thus far to write his own version of *Lolita* . . . but perhaps he is working on it.

If his first novel, *Golk*, had been given a better name, perhaps *The World According to Golk*, or, because its hero is one reclusive mild-mannered television staffer named Hondorp, *The World According to Hondorp*, perhaps his subsequent novels, all nine of them, would have reached the bestseller lists, which none of them did, not even *Other Men's Daughters*, a book club selection and his most "accessible" novel.

He has had eleven different publishers, never being asked to remain with any one of them for more than two books. *Contemporary Authors* has conjectured that there are two reasons for his low profile in the world of letters: he prefers a profound psychological exploration of his characters, penetrating into what St. Augustine calls "the abysses of human consciousness," and he has decided to remain in Chicago, where he has been a professor of literature for thirty-four years at the University of Chicago, instead of the literary center of New York, because Chicago permits him to spend more time writing and less time "playing 'writer,'" as he would have to do for the establishment.

In 1986, however, he was given the Award of Merit by the American Academy and Institute of Arts and Letters, which makes him the most highly honored of these guestroom novelists, although that was the same year that his novel *A Father's Words* was published without creating much of a stir or running up any respectable sales.

A Father's Words comes close to being what might be called "typical" Stern novel, if there's any such thing: a story of a classic conflict between father and son, told in the father's words with pain and befuddlement and rancor and dismay and also a great paternal love and loyalty and forgiveness. Cy Riemer is a middle-aged Chicagoan trying to remain young, publishing a monthly newsletter in science for a limited audience and a limited income. His four grown children are still his concern, particularly Jack, the oldest, a misfit, a failure: "His life's a rebuke to mine," laments the father.

Father-son conflicts are usually told from the son's point of view, but the angle that Stern chooses allows him to explore the unique role of relationship that modern society has thrust upon any father, of being not simply a parent but a friend, a competitor, a sibling, a teacher, an alter ego.

Like most of Stern's books, it was much larger and more rambling in its original form, but he worked hard to pare it down to a mere 189 pages of crisp essentials, and the reader senses in it Stern's love for poetry and his constant reading of it. He was a good friend of Robert Lowell, and in his capacity as teacher at Chicago, he has taught a number of distinguished poets, including David Ray and George Starbuck. He has also worked as a kind of one-man creative writing faculty there, been the teacher of some good novelists who have come to occupy guestrooms of their own. The guestroom begets the guestroom, although Robert Coover's reputation has risen above it, despite such experimental bombs as *The Public Burning*, which may be found serving as doorstop or window prop in many a guestroom. Another Stern pupil, Douglas Unger, seems on his way to escape from the almost automatic consignment to the guestroom that the label "provincial" would bestow upon such fine country novels as *Leaving the Land*.

Two other pupils of Stern are actually on our list of guestroom novelists, although Thomas Rogers's recently completed sequel to *At the Shores* may rescue him from the obscurity in which he has languished since the publication, in 1972 (that good year for guestroom novels), of *The Confessions of a Child of the Century by Samuel Heather*. Rogers's first novel, *The Pursuit of Happiness*, was nominated in 1968 for a National Book Award and made into a movie, but his second, *The Confessions of a Child of the Century*, suffered the fate of many a second novel and was called "an honorable failure" and did not do well. Its protagonist is a somewhat unlikeable and callow young man who describes his own story as a "comical historical pastoral" and characterizes his own style of narration as "both high and low, banal and eloquent, witty and sloppy" as it traces his picaresque adventures from Kansas City to Boston to China by way of Korea, and the father-son struggle is highly reminiscent of Richard Stern. In the novel's self-referential climax, Samuel Heather attempts to give himself back to the real author but is rejected. For once, the *New York Times Book Review*, on page four (the closest to the front page that any of these novels achieved), praised the book: Jonathan Yardley called Rogers a major writer and said *The Confessions* "is fiction of the great depth and distinction, comedy in the classic sense, the tale of a happy human triumph over the varieties of 20th-century adversity."

Austin Wright was another student of Richard Stern, who told me that he'd personally want to see *Camden's Eyes* on the guestroom list. Stern, Rogers, and Wright are each children of the twenties, and each professors of English, and Wright, at fifty-eight, is the oldest. At the age of forty-seven, Wright published *Camden's Eyes*, which, as its title tells us, is told from the point of view of William Camden as he confronts the fact of his wife's adultery, and his eyes are able to fracture his world into prismatic facets of experience that are as intriguing as a modern painting. Each of Wright's novels is marked by an obsession to get behind the eyes of his characters and probe their interior voices and consciousness, but *Camden's Eyes* is his only tour de force, unmatched by his later novels. The *New York Times*'s Christopher Lehmann-Haupt said of it that "one might even go so far as to say that Mr. Wright has gone James Joyce one better, and diversified the interior monologue."

Richard Stern said of himself, "I'm almost well-known for not-being-well-known." Stern's notorious lack of notoriety may owe a small part to his name, not a distinctive name like "Saul Bellow" or "Bernard Malamud," and, in his case, confused with other writers. This is not the Richard Stern who wrote *Behavourial Techniques: A Therapist's Manual*, nor the Richard Stern who wrote *Semiconductor Chip Protection*, nor the Richard Stern who was president of the Mystery Writers of America and wrote two dozen thrillers, including the one on which the movie *The Towering Inferno* was based.

But at least Stern has some advantage over the Smiths, the Taylors, and the Williamses, many of whom are destined for the guestroom through no fault of their own, an unmemorable name. *Contemporary Authors* lists sixteen different writers with the name John Williams, and of these, five are published novelists. One of them, John A. Williams, is an excellent black writer, who wrote *The Man Who Cried I Am* and *!Click Song* (but a Mississippian, not the West Virginia John A. Williams who wrote several books about West Virginia).

Another, John Edward Williams, who prefers to be identified simply but confusingly as John Williams, won the National Book Award for the one 1972 novel destined for the guestroom but escaping from it by virtue of the award, *Augustus*, based upon the life of that noble Roman. In his long career, the sixty-seven-year-old John Williams has not been prolific, distracted by his mission to bring literary attention to the Rocky Mountains, where for years he was a professor at the University of Denver, and, like Richard Stern, a teacher of other novelists and poets.

Our John Williams has published only four novels of his own, the first two groping and a bit clumsy, the second two very mature and accomplished, of which the best is not *Augustus*, on the life of Caesar, but *Stoner*, on the life of an unremarkable English professor at a Midwestern University whose only traits in common with the author are a certain quiet reserve, a passionate love for words, and a view of the university as a refuge and fortress against the world's weakness.

Stoner is told in a surpassingly dispassionate prose, which is Williams's trademark, a tone that is not ironic or even wry but quietly understated, and not self-conscious except in calling unmistakable attention to its craftsmanship. John Williams is possibly our most polished artisan of the English language at its leanest and most effective without being minimalist: he can convey more through indirection than most writers can do with infinite embellishment.

And the simplicity of the prose of *Stoner* is as deceptive as the simplicity of its story, which seems not the stuff of which great novels are made, but which holds the reader from first page to last with the compassion and humanity of its telling.

We can only note in passing several other Williamses who deserve more attention than their common names afford them: the Thomas Williams who has written nine novels including the *The Hair of Harold Roux*, which won a National Book Award two years after John Williams's *Augustus*; the Wirt Williams who has written seven novels, three of them nominated for Pulitzer prizes; the Joan Williams who was Faulkner's friend and wrote *The Wintering* and *The Morning and the Evening*; and the Joy Williams who wrote *The Changeling* and many brilliant short stories.

John Williams's wonderful sympathy for the little life of Stoner could have been lost to us entirely, collecting dust on guestroom shelves, out of print along with his other volumes, including two excellent books of poetry, had he not been rediscovered recently by the University of Arkansas Press, which is bringing out new editions of his work in its Reprint Series.

University presses everywhere are in the front line of restoring and preserving neglected reputations, of bringing more and more worthy writers out of the guestroom and back into the classroom, the library, the living room.

Another easy-to-forget name is Taylor, and our best guestroom writer of short stories, as opposed to novels, which he hasn't had much luck with, is Peter Taylor. Then there is Henry Taylor, David Taylor, and the late brilliant British novelist Elizabeth Taylor, who had the misfortune of confusion with the movie star. *Contemporary Authors* lists seven writers with the name of Robert Taylor, all of whom are confusable with the two movie stars of the same name. One of them, Robert Lewis Taylor, is a guestroomer who wrote the delightful novel *The Travels of Jaimie McPheeters*. So it is little wonder that when a novelist with a name like Robert Taylor Jr. sees his first two books become lost in the guestroom, he will alter his name, inserting his middle name, Love, and becoming Robert Love Taylor, although the change did not have much apparent effect on the reception given his latest novel, *The Lost Sister*, which Algonquin published last fall.

You will love this Robert Taylor: *The Lost Sister* is set in Oklahoma during the twenties and thirties, and like Taylor's earlier novels and short stories, it is based on the history of his own family of Sooners. The title character is a dreamer named Cora Mae, who died at the age of nineteen in 1934, six years before the author was born. Like Williams's *Stoner*, the simplicity of the story is deceptive, running through ordinary lives during the years the Oklahoma oil boom dissolved into the Dust Bowl, but giving the eager reader some unforgettable portraits of people who are at once familiar to us because of the way they behave in love, marriage, and death and fascinating to us because of Taylor's ear for their nuances and his eye for their gestures.

Taylor, not yet fifty, the youngest of our guestroomers, will become famous if Algonquin, his publisher, has its way. This new publishing house, based not in any literary center but in Chapel Hill, North Carolina, has already established the reputations of several writers of quality who might have fallen short of popularity if someone less zealous than Algonquin had published them. Such bright new talents as Kaye Gibbons, Clyde Edgerton, and Larry Brown are becoming widely known and read, and if Jill McCorkle's splendid novels ever wind up in anyone's guestroom it will be only because the host or hostess has a high regard for the guests. And this spring, Algonquin will introduce two more brilliant first novelists, Dori Sanders and Jaimy Gordon, and publish new work by two established but not widely known novelists, Kelly Cherry and Terry Pringle.

But other writers Algonquin has tried to promote have for inexplicable reasons not caught on. The very first fiction title that Algonquin published, in 1983, was Leon Driskell's *Passing Through*, which will remind you of Flannery O'Connor and does for Kentucky what she did for Georgia. But you have probably never heard of Leon Driskell, unless you follow the annual anthologies of best short stories, whose editor, Shannon Ravenel, became Driskell's editor at Algonquin and says of *Passing Through*, "The book remains my favorite of all those I've edited in over thirty years I've worked in publishing." For a fledgling publisher's first title, the book did okay, but by no means received the wide readership it deserves.

But at least *Passing Through* garnered some respectable reviews and attracted serious critical attention, a happy fate denied to another brilliant novel Shannon Ravenel edited, Jim Peyton's *Zions Cause*, which the *New York Times Book Review* dismissed in its "In Short" catch-all columns with the put-down, "These Bible-quoters and churchgoers are afflicted with weak consciences and strong wills—and too often predictably so. . . . The author stumbles into a swamp of clichés." The *New Yorker* magazine also consigned its tiny review to the "Briefly Noted" column, but said of it:

A wonderful first novel, composed of twelve almost independent episodes, set in Zions Cause, the narrator's old Kentucky home, and then in New Zion, two miles away, after the T.V.A. covers Zions Cause with a lake. . . . Even in 1950, people in New Zion mean Zions Cause when they talk about "here," and no one seems to notice that Big Jack's Blacksmith shop was become a gas station. Jim Peyton's vision is akin to Buster Keaton's: blessed with ingenious clowning and erratic locomotion, and riddled with minor miracles you want to witness again and again.

If this is the first novel by a sixty-year-old that whets our appetite for more books by Jim Peyton, we may go hungry: Shannon Ravenel wrote to me recently, "Just after writing you about *Zions Cause* I got word that Jim Peyton has gone blind in one eye and is losing his sight in the other. *Zions Cause* will likely be his only book for sure, now. Well, it's like *To Kill a Mockingbird*, a life's worth of wisdom and talent."

What editors at Algonquin like Shanon Ravenel, Louis Rubin, and Bettye Dew are attempting to do for their discoveries, promoting writers of promise who might otherwise not find a publisher, Martin Shepard is doing for neglected and forgotten writers with his even smaller publishing house, aptly called Second Chance Press. He is giving American readers

a chance to rediscover in new editions such overlooked writers as Richard
Lortz, Donald Wetzel, William Herrick . . . and Berry Fleming.

Martin Shepard is a former physician and psychiatrist (he wrote a book
that remains one of Second Chance Press's perennial bestsellers called
Memoirs of a Defrocked Psychoanalyst) who, like James Purdy, got into
publishing to print his own books. But soon, he found himself reprinting other neglected books, and with the help of his wife, Judith, a poet,
he founded in a farmhouse on Long Island both Second Chance Press
and the also aptly named Permanent Press, for publishing original works
permanently. "Once we publish or republish," Shepard told me, "we keep
these titles in print and will do so much until we pass from the scene
(hopefully not too soon)."

After Second Chance Press had been in business just a few years, Berry
Fleming heard about them and sent them a copy of his novel *Siesta*, which
Harcourt had published in 1935, and Martin Shepard was so impressed
with it, he phoned Fleming to ask if he had any other novels, and, yes, of
course, Fleming had many other novels. After reprinting new hardcover
editions of *Siesta* and *Colonel Effingham's Raid* in 1987, Second Chance
Press began to reissue Fleming at the rate of four books a year through
1988, 1989 and 1990, and it still hasn't reprinted all of his novels.

The second chance offered by Second Chance Press is a slim chance,
with only a thousand or two thousand copies sold of each of the Fleming
novels, but that is much better than Fleming (or any writer) could hope
for on his own. For several years before Second Chance Press began to
republish him, Fleming was operating his own little publishing house in
Augusta, Georgia, called Cotton Lane Press, in order to print four new
novels that he wrote during the eighties. But not one of these sold more
than a hundred copies. So the relatively small printings of Second Chance
Press were truly a major, if terminal, renaissance for Fleming.

Of all of his nineteen books, *The Make Believers* is the favorite of the
author and of his new publisher, Martin Shepard, who calls it "a wonderful example of his most serious fiction." Because it was originally published by the small Louisiana house Pelican, it was largely ignored in 1972.
Shepard's reprinting of it has attracted a number of raves from reviewers
who have been impressed by its craftsmanship, the texture of its language,
and its epic scope: its 400 closely written pages cover almost fifty years in
the lives of two families in Fleming's mythical Fredericksville, his equivalent to Faulkner's Jefferson (and just as Jefferson was closely modeled on

Oxford, Mississippi, Fredericksville is clearly Fleming's hometown of Augusta, Georgia).

Fleming describes Fredericksville as "a small Southern town in which you had friends and one love, and if you chose an extra love you were likely to lose more in friendships than you gained in love."

The two families in *The Make Believers* have been compared to Faulkner's Compsons and Sartorises but are more versatile in their occupations: one of the family members is a congressman, one is a painter, and one is a psychotherapist, which you'll never find in Faulkner. Fleming's shrink doesn't offer pat theories to behavior but provides an important clue in the solving of a murder, the least of the conventional trappings of the Southern Gothic which appear here: a lynching, suicide, adultery, bastardy, and Southern justice or injustice.

In many ways, it is the kind of old-fashioned but intelligent novel that you can spend a couple of weeks losing yourself in, inhabiting its pages and becoming intimate friends with its characters. Not many novels are written like that anymore.

But in any public library or university library, in the fiction section of the *F*s, you'll find little or nothing of Barry Fleming, and not one critical examination of his work, nor any biography. Nearby, you'll find whole shelves given over to the works of William Faulkner, and the innumerable critical studies and biographies of Faulkner that keep on coming out and out.

When he died in the hospital last September, Fleming had just finished one of his last acts: selling a couple of copies of his Second Chance novels to the nurses in the hospital. The *New York Times* gave him in death what the newspaper had denied him in life: a notice.

Berry Fleming's personal library contained the writers he liked to read: the complete works of Henry James, the essays of Paul Valéry, the poetry criticism of Helen Vendler, and the works of Claude Simon.

He stored the novels of Faulkner in his guestroom.

A Garland of Guestroom Novels

Burroway, Janet. *Raw Silk*. Little, Brown, 1977. Bantam, 1986. Out of print.
Driskell, Leon *Passing Through*. Algonquin, 1987.
Fleming, Berry. *The Make Believers*. Gretna, Louisiana: Pelican Publishers, 1972. Second Chance Press, 1988.

Newlove, Donald. *Sweet Adversity.* Avon, 1978, paper, combining revisions of
Leo and Theodore (Dutton, 1972) and *The Drunks* (Dutton, 1974).
Peyton, Jim. *Zions Cause.* Algonquin, 1983.
Purdy, James. *The House of the Solitary Maggot.* Doubleday, 1974. Out of print.
Rogers, Thomas. *Confessions of a Child of the Century by Samuel Heather.* Simon
& Schuster, 1972. Ultramarine Publishers, 1972.
Savage, Thomas. *The Power of the Dog.* Little, Brown, 1967. Van Vactor &
Goodheart, 1983.
Stern, Richard. *A Father's Words.* Arbor House, 1986. Univ. of Chicago, Phoenix
Books, 1990.
Taylor, Robert Love. *The Lost Sister.* Algonquin, 1989.
Theroux, Alexander. *Darconville's Cat.* Doubleday, 1981. Out of print.
Williams, John. *Stoner.* Viking, 1965. University of Arkansas Press, 1988, paper.
Wright, Austin. *Camden's Eyes.* Doubleday, 1969. Out of print.

—————

January 12, 2001

Ed Gray
Arkansas Democrat Gazette
Capitol at Scott
Little Rock, AR 72203

Dear Ed:
The instant your package of book jackets arrives in our mailbox, I'll mail this
envelope, perhaps even today.
    It contains two separate but related articles:
    Tom Bissell's "Unflowered Aloes: Why literary success is a product of chance,
not destiny." I had just discovered the essay shortly before he accepted *Falling
Off the Mountain* at Holt, so when his email came notifying me of acceptance,
I used as subject line for my reply: "An aloe begins to bloom."
    In 1990, I was invited to give a lecture at Texas Christian University and did
extensive research and preparation for my talk, "The Guestroom Novelist in
America," which later I typed up and my agent tried to peddle to the *New York
Times Book Review, Atlantic Monthly,* etc., without any luck, probably because
the author is himself the epitome of the guestroom novelist. It has never been
published. It ought to introduce you to a lot of the other guys like myself who
are worthy but unknown.
    We're sitting on the pins and needles watching for the postman to bring
those jackets.

                                                              Best,

Let Us Become Arkansawyers

—1983—

STATE-OF-THE-ART" sewage plants? "State-of-the-art" nuclear warheads?

The state-of-the-language arts is collapsing all around us, perhaps almost in inverse ratio to the advance of technology. In the schools, children with very high scores in science usually have very low scores in the "language arts."

Vice versa used to be true also, but not any more, when from kindergarten on, today's kids are instilled with the determination that only science can make them employable and therefore useful and meaningful.

Someone should develop and write a state-of-the-art Primer of the Arts, a manual for businessmen, technologists, entertainers, craftsmen, journalists, and all other non-Art working folks, which would tell them where to get off. It would contain such basic truths as: Art despises money. Art cannot be used. Art works for no one. Art is its own reward. Art is long, life is brief.

Addiction to Diction

The art I am most concerned with—although I dearly adore the "visual" arts of painting, sculpture, and architecture—is the art of verbal expression. I am addicted to diction. In the schools, "language arts" is an umbrella term sheltering grammar, spelling, vocabulary, and such horrors as "parts of speech." The only "parts of speech" with which the artist of words should be concerned are the sounds and images the speech makes: the tones, the rhythms, the lilt and timbre and phrasing, the texture and tension and meaning of the spoken and written utterance.

The word-artist becomes hypersensitive to such shams and abuses as "doorbuster," which appeared in a *Gazette* advertisement for a store which conceitedly envisioned hordes of shopping ladies stampeding through its doors at opening time. "Co-hit" for the second half of a double feature is equally atrocious.

The motive behind such perversions of language is always commerce, i.e., greed. The only motive for "state-of-the-art" is a commercial one, to lull the public into believing that this is the best of all possible vacuum cleaners or missiles or sewage plants.

There are two other culprits in the state-of-the-nonlanguage-art game: women and academics. Richard Allin of "Our Town" in the *Gazette* has noticed and lamented the use of "chairperson" to replace "chairman" in deference to the ladies. This is getting to be old hat, but Arkansas has always lagged about five years behind New England in such fads.

In Vermont recently, I saw, at two different restaurants, I swear, references on the menu to the "waitperson," as in, "Ask your waitperson to describe the contents of our salad bar." Get ready, Arkansawyers, for an invasion of waitpersons around 1988.

Just the other day, I was invited to participate in a conference on "Multidisciplinary Approaches to the Study of Arkansas Traditional Culture," wherein I would be given a modest honorarium for making input in the form of a presentation in my area of expertise. I could only decline, rather rudely, commenting that "multidisciplinary," which I can't even pronounce, sounds like it refers to mixed-media bondage and flagellation, and I am no masochist.

Neither am I a practitioner of "input" in any form, and I cringe at the thought of making a "presentation" of my expertise or any other part of me.

Arkansas's cultural heritage, I felt constrained to explain, had nothing to do with these things. It was robust and of the earth; it admitted of no nonsense and was rightly suspicious of the academy in all of its manifestations. Conferences were limited to all-night fox or coon hunts, and all day singin' and eatin' on the ground.

Those conferees of yore, to a man, to a woman and child, called themselves "Arkansawyers." We disgrace our heritage by our well-meaning but misguided malapropism, "Arkansan," suggesting that we are lost Kansans, artificial Kansans, substitute Kansans. Hell, we can't even pronounce "Arkansan." Does it rhyme with "Tarkenson" or "Benson"? Dammit, the state of the Jayhawkers wasn't even admitted to the Union until the Civil War, a quarter-century after the state of the Arkansawyers.

The same chamber-of-commerce boosterism that once upon a time malled us with "plazas" and later "metrocentre malls" wants us to forget our heritage, not honor it, not remember the rough, primitive toil that felled timber and sawed logs to make a state of Arkansawyers.

Love of leisure and the good life, of state-of-the-art creature comforts that make us as cultivated as any Californian, to say the least, wants us to forget the hard labor implied in "Arkansawyer." Why, don't you know? Handsaws went out with the coal-oil lamp.

No, they didn't, buddy. The honest, craftsmanlike carpenter even today knows that he can't build a state-of-the-art outhouse without a good handsaw. And likely you'll find that he and other members of the local United Brotherhood of Carpenters and Joiners are proud to call themselves Arkansawyers.

John Gould Fletcher, our most celebrated poet, called us Arkansawyers in everything he wrote. Our greatest all-time writer, Vance Randolph, always made a point of calling us Arkansawyers. Both of those fine Arkansawyers are dead, but there are still good writers—Ernie Deane, Bob Lancaster, Don Harington, several more—who know we are Arkansawyers and insist we are Arkansawyers and will keep on calling us Arkansawyers until all of the rest of you folks get wise and do likewise.

"Arkansawyer" is going to be tough on headline writers. It's going to irritate bureaucrats, bank presidents, superintendents of schools, and a great number of Texans who will start wondering if they should call themselves Texawyers.

In the Dictionary

But the time of the universally designated Arkansawyer is coming. It's already here in all of our dictionaries: ARKANSAWYER, *n. A native of Arkansas.* Do we need an Act of Legislature to make it official?

In the "real" folklore of Arkansawyers, there is the magical mythical moment when state Senator Jones (or Representative Cassius M. Johnson, or whoever) delivered the ringing oration on the subject. "Change the name of Arkansas? Hellfire NO!"

If "forum" means "any public meeting place for open discussion," then I would like to use the *Gazette*'s Forum to stand up and shake my fist and yell, "Change the name of Arkansas? Hellfire YES! I'm an Arkansawyer!"

Searching for "Cities" That Didn't Make It

—1983—

OST CITIES OF ARKANSAS. It sounds as if I'm digging for Troy, or Machu Picchu, or Chichen Itza. And indeed, there are times when the search for a shred of information about Buffalo City or Mound City is so frustrating that I'd rather be wearing a pith helmet in the hot sun, up to my elbows in ancient bones and shards.

I don't wear a pith helmet, and I spend a lot of time in the air-conditioned comfort of Special Collections at the University of Arkansas Library. When it comes to fieldwork, I have to depend upon the excellent hearing and good tape recorder of my colleague Kim, who spends hours talking with octogenarians and nonagenarians (and thus far one centenarian).

What are we looking for? As one octogenarian in ex–Marble City (now Dogpatch) said to Kim at the conclusion of her interview, "I'm really glad you're doing this. It's really nice that someone is interested."

We aren't a *Foxfire* team searching for lost folkways, although the ones we find are incidentally interesting, incidental to the life of the Arkansawyers who founded and settled communities in ideal locations and named them this "City" or that "City," and hoped, beyond all expectation and against all odds, that their little towns would become flourishing metropolises in time, given a chance and good weather.

The *Oxford English Dictionary* comments that "city" in "the newer states of the American West" is "often given in anticipation." Anticipation is the key word, or rather one of them, and the other key word is dignity. The word "city," derived from the French *cite* from the Latin *civitas*, was widely used in England as well as in America with considerable laxity as little more than a synonym for "town," because there is a traditional feeling of dignity about it — inherent nobility and worth and the anticipation of honor.

Traveling in Texas as long ago as 1843, the British novelist Frederick Maryat complained that "every individual possessing three hundred acres of land calls his lot a city."

Arkansawyers have never been as vainglorious and overoptimistic as Texans, but around 1843, quite a few of them were sprinkling "cities" in every corner of the map of the new state of Arkansas. There is no telling how many. At last count, we have located forty-one of them, but just when I think I've found them all, another one pops up in some remote area. All of the states west of the Mississippi have miniature municipalities which once aspired to the grandness of cityhood. Some of them achieved it: Kansas City, Oklahoma City, even Iowa City.

Arkansas City didn't make it. Lord knows, it tried. Once, it had floating operas and Chinese laundries, and ladies and laughter. It had a past so colorful that Judy Bixler, the present mayor's wife, has warned us before our researches have begun: "Arkansas City wasn't historical; it was hysterical."

Is Arkansas City "lost"? Yes, if you consider that it has been abandoned not only by most of its population but also by Old Man River himself; the Mississippi has up and gone a mile east, leaving the town forlorn behind its unneeded levee.

Some of the cities are lost because they almost qualify as ghost towns: Sulphur City, Cherokee City, Mound City. Some have a few good people still around but never were on the road to anywhere, let alone cityhood: Cave City, Lake City, Garland City, Webb City.

Some of them like Bear City once had a city-like census that shrank to almost nothing. Of Bear City's 12,000 people in 1887, there are only one one-thousandth remaining today.

None of these places were named "city" as a joke. There is something mock heroic about all of them, but not in the sense of mockery, only in the way each of them reflects the puny individual's yearning for fulfillment and dignity.

The Arkansas Endowment for the Humanities has generously funded the early stages of our research, which will culminate in a book exploring in depth twelve of these cities.

I am primarily a novelist, but several of my novels have been concerned with ghost towns, principally my own mythical Stay More of Newton

County, which never actually aspired to cityhood but grew to considerable size at the turn of the century before the boom burst and the dreams died. I see the ghost town, or in this case, the ghost city, as a metaphor for the lost places in the human heart.

The title *No Need of the Sun* comes from the beautiful line toward the end of Revelation: "And the city had no need of the sun, either of the moon, to shine in it, for the glory of God did lighten it . . . " The city that John the Divine had in mind, or in heart, was the celestial City of God, but all cities, however tiny, are His handiwork and need no more sunlight to keep them shining.

Songs of Sunlight and Water

—1989—

IKE THOREAU, WHO TRAVELED a good deal in Concord, William McNamara travels widely in his backyard: Cave Mountain, Edgmon Creek, the headwaters of the Buffalo River. Here, in the storied fastnesses of Newton County, he lives, hikes, explores, sketches, and lays down watercolor in gorgeous pictures that capture the inner spirit of the Ozarks.

View from the Mountain, a major show of forty of McNamara's paintings, is hanging at the Arkansas Arts Center in Little Rock until July 23. Gallery visitors this month will share what has been a well-kept secret in the art world: Arkansas has one of the most original, the most dazzling, and the most satisfying of contemporary American artists.

Call him a realist. Don't call him a Photorealist—a label he isn't happy with, bestowed as it is on a wide range of recent painters who imitate "reality"—although at first glance, and from a distance, McNamara's pictures seem to be blown-up color photographs.

Call him an Arkansawyer. He came with the wave of Ozark in-migrants rushing back to the land in the mid-seventies; but, unlike the majority of them, he stayed until he found his niche. And unlike the vast majority of artists who must live in a college town and teach for their subsistence, McNamara has managed to fend for himself in the wilderness. This has been often very difficult and unprosperous—until recently, when his pictures have begun to command respectable prices and find their way into some prominent collections.

Today, he and his family (wife Milancy and three sons) enjoy a measure of security in their steadily expanding tar-paper mansion at the end of a road atop Cave Mountain (the post office address is Ponca, but that hamlet is twelve miles off). With the security has come a sense of confidence, fulfillment, and—his favorite word—energy, which has resulted in the recent creation of his very best work. The McNamara paintings of this past year, including those illustrated here, are his masterpieces.

By anyone's standards, they are masterpieces. No photograph or reproduction can do justice to a McNamara painting; looking at one not in the original, not in person, is like listening to a phonograph record instead of a live performance, or like watching a video instead of a big-screen movie—or maybe even like watching a movie instead of reading the novel on which it is based.

You have to see one. You have to stand up close to one and marvel at these contradictions: it is only watercolor, and yet it could be oil or tempera or acrylic; it is only a piece of paper, and yet it could be a huge canvas; it seems to be infinitely detailed, and yet, if you get too close, you become lost in a wild maze of expressive calligraphy.

And what appears to be only a near glimpse of a woodland scene turns out to be an exploration of several levels of "reality" (which, Nabokov insisted, must always have quotation marks around it).

Take, for example, the picture called *Sunlight Dialogues*, arguably not just the best-in-show, but one of the major statements in the career of this or any artist. Except for its size, forty-one by twenty-nine inches, it doesn't appear to stand out from its neighbors in the show. There is no human figure, no babbling brook or plunging waterfall, no real depth of space, just a close-up of a quiet, still, ferny woodland pool: a lichen-covered rock, some dead leaves, and a white moth floating on the surface of the water, some reflections in the water.

The title, an allusion to a John Gardner novel, was suggested to the artist by Milancy, who'd read the book. McNamara doesn't like allusive titles; he would have preferred calling it simply *The White Moth*, because that insect provided the starting point for the conception of the picture. But Milancy McNamara's suggestion reveals itself: this picture is not so much "about" a woodland pool or water or a white moth, but about the conversation going on between those things and the sunlight. The sunlight is hidden and everywhere, transcendent and bewitching, revealing the humble forms of nature as no artist, no eye, has seen them before.

Townsend Wolfe, director of the Arkansas Arts Center, calls this painting "magic." Of all McNamara's explorations of water, his favorite element, it is the most stunning. "He loves all of water's forms," Milancy says, "the running and the still, the frozen and the free, what is on it, what is through it, what is reflected in it."

For a man in love with water, it is appropriate that his chosen medium is watercolor. But he scarcely ever uses the medium in the traditional fluid manner of broad washes and runny edges; his strokes are crisp and clean and almost dry. And he often layers them, which seems to contradict the transparent *alla prima* manner of watercolor. His use of watercolor resembles Andrew Wyeth's use of egg tempera, but McNamara prefers watercolor to tempera because it's not as fragile and messy.

Doesn't he use photography? "Sure, I used a photo for *Sunlight Dialogues*," McNamara says. "A photograph helps speed up the process. It's like a drawing study, a guide. The main thing wrong with photographs is that you have to work directly from life to feel the energy."

That word again. Bill McNamara (his wife and close friends call him Billy) does not strike one as an energetic man. This is another contradiction: his relaxed, easy, somewhat shy manner, his casual appearance (he looks like Hemingway on permanent vacation), his erratic work habits and lackadaisical schedule—all fail to indicate the obsessed dedication he brings to his work, and the long hours he devotes to each painting.

For McNamara, though, painting is all mixed up with living. He can paint with one of his sons around, even in his lap. He has a cluttered "studio" but rarely uses it, instead painting anywhere he can sit: the kitchen, the porch, the yard, or, his favorite place, way off in the woods.

⚡⚡⚡

William McNamara was born on the third of September, 1946, in flatland Louisiana, in the country not far from Shreveport. His mother was an artist of sorts, a photo-retoucher, and he remembers at the age of three seeing one of her amateur paintings: a tree in an ice storm. His mother was serious enough about art to sign up for an expensive correspondence course, the home-study lessons of the realist brothers Moses and Raphael Soyer. She didn't feel like finishing it, though, so Billy, at the age of twelve, took over and did her lessons for her, receiving praise from the Soyers, who thought they were still working with Mrs. McNamara.

McNamara didn't take art in high school. He won a math scholarship to Shreveport's Centenary College, where he came under the spell of artist Willard Cooper and changed his major. After graduation, he was influenced by a friend to travel to New Mexico Highlands University for his graduate degree. There, in an adobe house at seven thousand feet, he had his first experience with the discovery of "energy."

His master's degree got him a job back home at Centenary College, where he taught drawing and composition for five years. He liked—and misses—teaching, but he was restless. In the fall of 1972, he and Milancy, whom he'd met when both were nineteen (they were born just one day apart), ran away to Europe, took an apartment in Madrid within walking distance of the Prado, and began to haunt the museums.

In Vienna, he tried to get into the Albertina to see Dürer's wonderful watercolor *The Great Piece of Turf,* but that room of the museum was closed off, and he had to "communicate" that he needed badly to see it before they let him in. That Dürer, one of the great masterpieces in the medium that McNamara would come to call his own, would have a profound effect on his view of nature up close.

"That trip to Europe," McNamara says, "made me want to come back to America and find a place to be." Earlier, in 1970, he had bought a pickup truck with a camper and taken off for the western states, just traveling to see as much as possible. In his statement for *View from the Mountain,* he relates: "In 1970 I spent nine hours beside a river in Idaho, working on a watercolor of rocks at the water's edge. It was the first time I had put such concentrated effort into a painting, and it was the first time I had used watercolor with no formula. It was a pivotal point that set me in the direction I still follow."

The year after the trip to Europe, Bill and Milancy discovered the Boston Mountains of Arkansas. His mother's family had come from the Ouachitas; he had tried looking for a piece of land there, and also in New Mexico. One Easter Sunday, he and Milancy came driving into Jasper, Newton County's tiny seat, and they fell in love with the place. A real-estate agent showed them on a topographical map a forty-acre parcel atop Cave Mountain, then took them there. Wild irises were in bloom, and a hawk, like an omen, was soaring overhead. They decided very quickly that they had found their home.

⚡⚡⚡

The visitor to *View from the Mountain* looking for signs of human habitation will find only the faintest suggestion of a house roof in the far distance of *Winter Sunset,* conspicuous by its geometric regularity in a world of natural irregularity. The world that McNamara paints would seem to be uninhabited and uncultivated by humankind, except for the occasional female nude, who most often seems a part of the landscape, if not a symbol of it.

"I have a great affinity for trees," McNamara says. "Natural patterns are more appealing to me." The angular patterns of the cityscape, metal and glass, the stuff of the art of such celebrity Photorealists as Richard Estes and Robert Cottingham, leave McNamara cold. "In a city," he says, "I don't know what to paint."

He is a constant hiker, sometimes taking a backpack along with him and penetrating into the deepest corners of Newton County and the Ozarks. Certain places, when he finds them, make the hair on his neck rise—benevolent places, places that instantly emanate a feeling of, if you'll forgive that word again, energy. "Energies," McNamara corrects it to the plural. "Whenever I find those energies coming from the place itself, I know I have to paint it."

Waterfall in Bower Hollow is one such place. The waterfall isn't as spectacular as that of Hemmed-In Holler, isn't nearly as high or as well-known, isn't as "picturesque" as several other Arkansas waterfalls, but McNamara was so drawn to it that he spent a total of four months painting the scene, an unusual length of time to stick with one watercolor. It is a big picture, sixty inches tall. The viewer is tempted to move in close, and, getting near the paper, discovers with a shock what McNamara's style is really like. He isn't Photorealistic at all! The dancing rhythm of his brush strokes is more like the "action" painting of Abstract Expressionism.

Up close, the viewer can spend many long minutes moving from one small area of *Waterfall in Bower Hollow* to another. It is almost like listening to music: the tempo changes, the instruments change, surprises in timbre occur, subtle transitions of passage seize a melodic line and develop it.

Maybe, it has been suggested, those infinite traceries of natural patterns, that complicated embroidery of tree-twig and rock-strata and water-cascade, are some kind of language, trying to tell us something. "I can't put into words," McNamara says, "but I understand it. Until I have painted a tree, I don't *know* it, I don't know what it's trying to say to me. When my brush begins to dance, it's almost as if I'm making up my own new alphabet as I go along."

⚡⚡⚡

All of the nudes in *View from the Mountain* are Milancy McNamara. Her appearance in *Shadowed Figure* brings to mind Renoir's *Nude in Sunlight*, similarly dappled, but the differences are instructive. Not that the Renoir is more luscious, nor that his sunlight is warmer, but, like the

Impressionists in general, Renoir seems to have thrown his eyes out of focus to see not the woman but the *idea* of her ripe femininity. It would be too easy to say that Renoir is more romantic, McNamara more objective.

But as an admiring critic said of Monet, the Impressionist whom McNamara most resembles, "He was only an eye, but what an eye!" McNamara has been known to preach that the eye is a muscle that has to be developed. He has certain tricks of using that muscle, such as deliberately crossing his eyes to "look" at the subject out of focus or to gauge its patterns and "to separate my awareness from my focus," a technique he used to impart to his students.

"I'd love to know what the Impressionists would have thought of my work," he says wistfully. *Shadowed Figure* might have impressed them, but it would have delighted Thomas Eakins, the dean of American realism, who was partial toward the back side of the female nude, believing it to be more interesting than the front. Like Eakins's nudes, McNamara's are usually shown from the back; hardly ever is the face visible—not because of Milancy's modesty, but because the female becomes more universal if she has no specific personality.

Dappled with the shadows of tree branches, the nude in *Shadowed Figure* becomes a kind of Daphne, the mythical beauty transformed into a tree by the touch of Apollo. McNamara's touch turns the woman into a tree here, and elsewhere, he turns her into a formation of boulders or a metaphor of the silhouette of Ozark mountains.

In such suggestions and metaphors lies McNamara's inventiveness, even his genius. To the charge that McNamara only imitates nature—only strives for surface verisimilitude, albeit of the highest order—one has to respond with the knowledge that he spent years as an "abstract" artist before converting to realism. He still has tremendous admiration for Picasso, whose many styles he often copied in his formative years as a painter. "Making abstract pictures taught me design and composition," he says, "which you can't learn just by looking at something." In fact, he still occasionally makes an abstraction, but these don't find their way to the galleries for public sale.

Several galleries in Arkansas offer McNamara to the public, at least in the form of reproductions. Milancy is also the "business manager" for her husband. During their lean years, she began to hit the road, persuading art galleries and frame shops to carry reproductions of the more popular "scenes" McNamara had painted. (He is careful to distinguish "reproductions" from "prints," which they are not.) Now, such places as

The Sketch Box in Little Rock, Fayetteville's Frame Place, and especially Susan Morrison's gallery in Eureka Springs and The Gallery in Harrison are a steady source of supplementary income for the McNamaras.

The next step in this success story ought to be the acquisition of an apprentice. Most of the major Photorealists, Super-Realists, and such Neo-Surrealists as Fayetteville's Donald Roller Wilson have one or more apprentices, or "studio assistants" as they are called—young men and women who volunteer to help with the hard physical execution of the paintings in return for exposure to the master's teaching and methods. McNamara doesn't have an apprentice, but he confesses he would be receptive if one came knocking at the door.

If the apprentice doesn't show up, will one of McNamara's boys grow up to become his father's disciple? Whenever McNamara wears out a brush, three or four times a year, he gives it to one of his kids. Already, John Michael McNamara, a third-grader, has a painting that showed recently at the Arkansas Arts Center in a statewide show of children's art. If John doesn't turn into Jamie Wyeth, then perhaps it will be Christopher, who is only four and who attends nearby Headwaters School, one of whose teachers is the "Kate" who appears in McNamara's portraits in the show.

It is a happy and busy household, the boys' only complaint being that they don't have any friends on the same road. Bill and Milancy are private people who relish their isolation and know what to do with it, although they confess to missing the resources of a university library and such things as plays and live music.

For Bill McNamara, though, the live performance he most enjoys is the ongoing extravaganza of the natural world. The water talks to him, and so do the rocks. The trees sing to him, and so does the sky. He listens while he watches, but it is the watching that matters most: the eye that takes it all in and puts it all down, in watercolor on rough paper, for all of us to know.

Arkansas's One and Only Hero

—1997—

ALBERT PIKE WAS the only hero Arkansas ever had.
"Hero" has to be understood not in the modern sense of
valiant and self-sacrificing, which Pike was not, but in the classic sense: celebrated for bold exploits and favored by the gods. Mythic.
Legendary. Larger-than-life. Bill Clinton is much more famous and
mighty, but his life story lacks the color of Pike's.

Today, Pike is remembered only in Masonic lodges all over the country which were named after him. In his hometown, Little Rock, there
is the huge neoclassic Scottish Rite Temple on Scott Street, and nearby
the remains of the once-grand Albert Pike Hotel, which had the finest
lobby and the finest dining room in the state, and, of course, his gorgeous
antebellum mansion at Seventh and Rock, converted into a museum of
decorative arts.

But not an awful lot of places and things have been named after him.
Neither Arch Street Pike nor Twelfth Street Pike get their names from
him. Many towns do have a Pike Street, and North Little Rock has its Pike
Avenue, which led to Camp Pike, as the army base was known for years
before changing into Camp Robinson. Hot Springs has its Albert Pike
Avenue, home of McClard's Bar-B-Q, Cook's Ice Cream, and the Lake
Hamilton Resort.

Elsewhere in Arkansas, there is the Albert Pike Recreation Area in a
remote corner of the Ouachitas, and the Albert Pike log-cabin school-
house at Van Buren. Few public schools have been named after Pike, who
began teaching school at the age of sixteen in Massachusetts. Pike County
and its lost town, Pike City, were named not for Albert but for his cousin
Zebulon Montgomery Pike, after whom Pikes Peak was named.

Most Arkansawyers have heard of Albert Pike. Few know just who he was, and, as the review of the new biography of him makes clear, few general readers would want to wade through a 600-page book about him.[1] At a time when even Roy Reed's magnificent biography of Orval Faubus is having trouble with the name recognition that younger generations withhold from such an old codger, there are not going to be lines of people at the bookstores which carry the Pike book.

In his own lifetime, Pike, who, like most great men, was quick to bear a grudge and slow to let it pass, often bemoaned what was happening to his reputation. Unlike most great men, he often sulked and sought retaliation. After the battle of Pea Ridge, the South accused him, a Confederate general in charge of reluctant Indian troops, of responsibility for the South's defeat, while the North accused him of allowing his Indian troops to scalp the dead and wounded Union soldiers. He spent years seeking vindication.

Literary critics have easily dismissed his poetry, Byronic though it was, and bad though much of it was. The simple truth was that Pike may have possessed the talent to become an American Byron, but was too busy with all his other undertakings to devote himself to poetry.

He grew up with the state of Arkansas, having become an Arkansawyer in 1832 when it was still a wild territory. After a hectic adventure on a trip to Santa Fe that reads like Wild West fiction (and inspired my own second novel, not published), Pike taught school in the Ozark wilderness before moving to Little Rock to become a successful if highly controversial newspaper editor.

He not only observed and commented upon but actively participated in most of the political activities of early Arkansas during its transition from territory to statehood. This was the gallant era of duels, and Pike himself fought one, challenging a man who had impugned his honor. He smoked a cigar during the combat, which, after both parties missed each other twice, was stopped inconclusively.

Physically he was a giant of a man and had enough quirks, habits, and eccentricities to charm a novelist or give gainful employment to a political cartoonist. If only John Deering had been alive in those days! As a teenage frontiersman, Pike began cultivating a Buffalo Bill demeanor that segued into the permanent image of Pike that looks out at us from many photographs, from Charles Elliot Loring's painting, and from a full-length monumental statue in Washington, D.C.: long dark flowing hair, full beard and mustachios not quite concealing a sensuous mouth, long and strong nose, highbrow forehead, and piercing but romantic dark eyes.

When he was an old man living in Washington as the Supreme Grand Commander of the Ancient and Accepted Scottish Rite of Freemasonry, he fell in love with a remarkable girl of nineteen, Vinnie Ream, a sculptress (rare in American art), and he maintained a relationship with her for the rest of his life that was supposedly "pure" but unquestionably intense.

The best sources of his biography come from his *Essays to Vinnie*, five volumes of fine-ruled paper, each lettered on the front cover, "Vinnie. Pegni d'affetto"—peg of my heart. But she married a much younger man, and he had to add jealousy to the afflictions of old age—neuralgia, gout, dyspepsia, rheumatism, lumbago—that beset his last years, which he lived as a recluse in the Masonic House of the Temple, where he died in 1891.

His masterpiece, to which not even the Masons themselves give much notice any more, was called "Morals and Dogma of The Ancient and Accepted Scottish Rite of Freemasonry"—a formidable mouthful for what is some of the best poetic philosophy ever thought and penned. This volume of a thousand-plus pages was printed so often as a Masonic manual that you can still find it cheap in second-hand bookstores, with a warning on the title page: "ESOTERIC BOOK, FOR SCOTTISH RITE USE ONLY; TO BE RETURNED UPON WITHDRAWAL OR DEATH OF RECIPIENT."

The book, in the process of raising the mason from apprentice through thirty-two degrees culminating in "Master of the Royal Secret," contains a lot of Masonic mumbo-jumbo, but it also contains splendid wisdom, some of the finest philosophy ever written by an American . . . and ever ignored by the public and intelligentsia alike.

But computer-users are probably familiar with "The Wisdom of the Ages," a shareware resource of thousands of quotations from all the world's great thinkers and writers. There are more from Albert Pike than any other person. A sample: "Faith begins where Reason sinks exhausted."

Pike's reason was exhausted after the debacle of Pea Ridge, when he went into seclusion at a remote hideaway in the Ouachita Mountains called Greasy Cove . . . not to be confused with Faubus's Greasy Creek. "The attachment to solitude is the surest preservative from the ills of life," Pike wrote.

At Greasy Cove, Pike brooded and wrote the "Morals and Dogma," and there I attempted to find him in the novel I wrote about him, which I discuss elsewhere on this page.

My favorite passage from "Morals and Dogma":

Action is greater than writing. A good man is a nobler object of contemplation than a great author. There are but two things worth living for: to do what is worthy of being written; and to write what is worthy of being read; and the greater of these is *the doing*.

On the History of the Porter Prize

—2004—

WE USED TO SAY "Thank God for Mississippi," because that state kept Arkansas from being last in practically every category . . . except literature. Mississippi has produced so many great writers that, to use an Ozarks expression, "their feet are stickin out the winders," and that overcrowding forced one of their best ones, Jack Butler, to emigrate to Arkansas.

As a student at the University of Arkansas, Jack Butler came under the care of a legendary English teacher named Ben Drew Kimpel. A native of Fort Smith, Ben Kimpel wrote his PhD dissertation on Herman Melville at the University of North Carolina, another state where the writers' feet are stickin out the winders . . . in fact, at last count North Carolina has more writers than politicians.

Young Kimpel returned home to teach at the University in 1952, and the following year he was my freshman English teacher and I got to watch the qualities that were to make him into a legend: his deep belief in the written word and his selfless devotion to students who wanted to master it.

By the time Jack Butler finished graduate school, Ben Kimpel was chairman of the department and already the most sought-after teacher on campus. Not long before Kimpel died in 1983 (his funeral was on Shakespeare's birthday), Jack approached him with the idea of starting an annual award to honor Arkansawyers with great talent and promise as writers. Jack wanted to call it the Kimpel Prize, but Ben, while he thought it would be a great idea, was too modest to allow the prize to be named after himself. So he suggested naming it after his mother, Gladys Porter.

Not long after that, when Jack had moved to Little Rock to work as a statistical analyst for the Public Service Commission (novelists have a hard time earning a living if they're not John Grisham) but was teaching a creative writing course for Words, the literary organization, one of his students was Phillip McMath, a young lawyer.

Butler and McMath discovered they had in common not only that they were both working on their first novels, Butler's *Jujitsu for Christ* and McMath's *Native Ground* (both published by August House of Little Rock) but also that Ben Kimpel, their former teacher at the University, had helped both of them with their novels.

Jack told Phil about his idea for a literary prize to honor Kimpel. The two men drank forty beers together (not all the same night) and they grew nostalgic about what a great teacher Kimpel had been. They also discussed the state of Arkansas letters and how important it was to encourage writers and help them with a monetary gift. Phil said, "What the hell, let's just do it, hey? We'll just do it. Right?"

And they did. Neither of them knew anything about getting an award started, but Phil could handle the legwork of getting the Porter Prize incorporated. A Little Rock patron of the arts, Bill Pumphrey, a friend of Jack's, offered the use of his house for the first award in 1985, which went to Leon Stokesbury.

Bill Pumphrey and Fred Darragh were guardian angels for the early years of the award, and the third year the award was held at Fred Darragh's grand house, with actress Mary Steenburgen attending to present the prize to me. It was, next to my wedding, the biggest event of my life.

Subsequent annual ceremonies were held at the Museum of Natural History and then at the present location, the Central Arkansas Library. When Jack forsook Arkansas in 1993 for New Mexico and deprived us of one of our greatest writers, Phillip McMath took over the year-to-year management of the award, soliciting the winners to vote each year for their successors. Thus the Porter is self-perpetuating and now, as of tonight, is on the verge of enormous expansion. Our feet will be stickin out the winders.

Ironically, the two men who founded the prize were both highly deserving of being honored by the prize themselves . . . but of course they weren't eligible. I suggest to my fellow honorees that we award both of them an honorary Porter Prize.

Comfort Me with
Chicken and Dumplings

—2005—

ET ME SEE YOUR HANDS. How many of you would say your favorite food is chicken and dumplings? You're in good company. The
cook at Graceland reported that Elvis loved the dish more than
any other. Try Googling the internet to see those thousands of lists of
favorites, and under "favorite food," you'll find chicken and dumplings
more than any other single dish.

Would a condemned man choose it as his last meal? In my novel *The
Choiring of the Trees*, Nail Chism, an Ozarks mountaineer wrongly convicted of rape, escapes the electric chair not once but three times, and
each time he has requested as his final feed a platter of chicken of dumplings. After his last escape, not just from the chair but from the prison,
hiding out in the woods east of Stay More, the young woman bringing
him his meals collects from the friendly neighbors twenty-five bowls of
chicken and dumplings. He never tires of them.

I've told my mother-in-law, who makes the best I've eaten, that I could
eat her chicken and dumplings for breakfast, although I never have . . .
yet. Somehow they wouldn't go well with coffee. They do go well with
Chardonnay or Pinot Grigio, champagne or Dr. Pepper, milk or beer, or,
the drink they complement best, iced tea.

Whenever my wife Kim and I visit her hometown, Beebe, Arkansas,
her mother, Jacque Gunn, always makes up a big pot of chicken and
dumplings, serves it once, and gives me all the leftovers to take home,
where I can have another meal or two or three from them. It was needless
of me to ask her for the recipe, because she'll never let me run out long
enough to want to make my own.

But she reported that she got the recipe many years ago from a black woman named Hettie working at the old Franke's Cafeteria in downtown Little Rock, a fabled culinary establishment. Hettie noticed that Jacque brought her daughters there often, and the girls always had chicken and dumplings, so Hettie observed that in view of their fondness for the dish, Jacque ought to make it for them. And Hettie gave Jacque the recipe, which she used at home thereafter.

The recipe called for thin strips of dumplings, sometimes called "flat" or, in the mountains, "slick" dumplings. There are two rival camps of dumpling-fixers, just as there is a dichotomy in everything: red states and blue states, Christians and Jews, artists and scientists, males and females. The other camp, to which I belonged for many years before being converted by my mother-in-law, makes dumplings that are thick or blobbish or fluffy.

Long ago, when I was raising my own daughters in New England, I made chicken and dumplings at least once a month for Sunday night supper, and used a recipe that called for tablespooning the batter directly a blob at a time into the boiling stew. My daughters loved it . . . but I can only assume that when they moved out into the world they discovered the superiority of strip dumplings.

It's sort of like the distinction between a stack of nice fluffy pancakes and Swedish pancakes, which get their appeal from their thinness. The eating of food calls into play four senses: vision, taste, smell, and touch. It is the touch of various foods as they come into contact with the lips, and then the teeth, and then the tongue, and then the throat that accounts for the fact that Italians have so many different shapes and sizes of pasta, and the fact that flat dumplings seem to slide right down the throat, which fact, in turn, accounts for the fact that so many eaters of chicken and dumplings must always go for second helpings . . . or third. It is the most second-helpinged of all foods.

It is also, in its origins, the most international of dishes, variations of which were imported to this country from all the countries of the world. Despite the charming southern insistence that chicken and dumplings are a distinctly southern dish unknown to Yankees, there are probably as many people in the north who love Sunday night suppers of chicken and dumplings. One of the best recipes I've seen for the dish is in the classic *L. L. Bean Book of New England Cookery*, which makes it sound like something that Vermonters and New Hampshirites all were raised on . . . except that it calls for adding various seasonings to the dumpling dough: parsley, dill, marjoram, and savory (and also preaches the blob method).

This brings up a second dichotomy of dumpling-fixers: the purists like my mother-in-law who don't add anything to the dumpling dough (except salt and baking soda), and those who like to spice up the dough. Jack Butler, the great novelist and poet, gives in his cooking manual *Jack's Skillet* a fine recipe that calls for dill in the dumplings, but I haven't tried it, and I think I'll save the dill for fish and pickles. Of course, the dumplings will absorb the flavors of whatever herbs or spices you put in the broth.

But whether you like 'em in strips or blobs, seasoned or plain, served in bowls or on plates, or even from a can of Campbell's Soup "Chicken 'N Dumplings," you know why it's your favorite food: it feels good, it tastes delectable, it calls up an assortment of good memories, it makes the day seem prettier, and it comforts you like no other food can.

Accepting the
Oxford American Award

—2006—

[Thank you, my dear friend Arch.][1]

THE FIRST NEWS of this event appeared last week in the *Democrat-Gazette* on the obituary page. My wife is grateful for the cards of sympathy she received. Philip Martin corrected that misconception with a splendid article in yesterday's newspaper.

But really, to call an award "Lifetime" makes it sound as if they've already pulled the green quilt over me. And all of those wonderful tributes from my fellow writers are in the nature of a memorial service.

Who wouldn't enjoy the privilege of attending one's own memorial service?

I couldn't have chosen a better group of eulogists myself: Miller Williams, the finest poet; Molly Giles, the sharpest short-story writer; Kevin Brockmeier, the best younger writer of fiction; and Jack Butler, who is simply the best, period.

I might be forgiven for nicknaming this sculpture "Phoenix," with double meaning: myself alive again after being ashes, and the *Oxford American*, alive again after being ashes. The publication bills itself as "the Southern Magazine of Good Writing," I think of myself as "a Southern author of Good Writing," but in both cases, although the quality of the writing is paramount, it is the entertaining content which matters most. The *Oxford American* deserves a Lifetime Award for Journalism.

And I thank all of my friends there, who are here, for allowing me to violate the rule, "Persons associated with the company are not permitted to enter the contest." Because I *am* associated with the company. I have written for the *Oxford American* several times, and I expect to go on writing for it many more times. The only difference that this award should make is that I ought to get better paid for my stuff.

Much more important to me than the award is the possibility that it might increase the population of Stay More, that mythical, magical little town that is the setting for all my work. You can't physically go there; it isn't on any map, except the map of your own mind, which you are allowed to redraw as you like. There's truth in the idea that Stay More is hard to find but even harder to leave . . . which is the real meaning of its name. If somehow I can get you there, you won't ever want to leave.

I can't leave this platform without expressing my profound thanks to the one person who is most responsible for it all—my wife, Kim.

Thank you. And thank you all for being here to share this occasion. It's wonderful to see you all.

First Dates, Blind Dates, Fan Dates, Last Dates

—2009—

ORROWING MY MOTHER'S CAR, I set off down Cantrell Road
to have my first date with you. All I knew about you was that
you had, a few months previously, written to me the only fan
letter I had ever received from my native state. And that your voice on the
telephone was sweet. You had told me how to find Cajun's Wharf, but here
I was, trying to make a left off Cantrell, waiting and waiting for a stalled
freight train to move on.

I confess that I used up a good bit of that wait trying to imagine what
you would look like. Tall enough to fit me, I hoped. Properly adoring
without being fawning. Possibly blond. Possibly independently wealthy.
A plantation owner's daughter. You had to be a college graduate, because
your fan letter had been so intelligent.

You had caught nuances and permutations in *Some Other Place. The
Right Place.* which had escaped everybody else, including all the reviewers. You were such a novelist's dream that I wondered seriously if you
were just a product of my solipsism, a central theme in the novel. My
mental image of you certainly was too close a match for the novel's heroine, Diana, although her daddy owned not a plantation but an insurance
company.

I began to wonder if the stalled freight train blocking my way was trying to tell me that you weren't really there at all. After a while I began to
consider the possibility of abandoning the car and trying to hoof it the
rest of the way, if I could get under or over that damned string of boxcars.
If you had already arrived, and you really existed in flesh and blood, you

were probably getting impatient for me to show up. Quite possibly you were thinking that I may have been a product of *your* solipsism.

You were not my first blind date. As a teenager, a pal of mine who was a student at the Arkansas School for the Blind persuaded me to take him and his date, with another date for me, to the drive-in movies, where they necked in the back seat while I tried to get up my nerve to neck in the front seat. She was very pretty but her eyes were blank.

Your eyes, when finally that freight was pulled or shoved on down the track, turned out to be so sparkling blue that I scarcely noticed your green-and-fuchsia floral midcalf-length dress, your height, your blonde hair, and the copies of my books you had under your arm. Derek told us he was our "Cajun" for the evening, and he served a bottle of B & G Vouvray, which we consumed entirely. How do I remember these things? Because you kept souvenirs which are still in our files.

That dress is wrapped in plastic in our attic, and your hair is still blond, thirty years later. And if there is such a thing as solipsism, it is mighty convincing.

II

REVIEWS

⚡⚡⚡

✦✦✦

IN AN INTERVIEW that Donald Harington did to accompany one of the dozens of reviews that he supplied to the *Arkansas Democrat-Gazette* during the 1990s and 2000s, his fellow Arkansawyer Miller Williams answered a question about his new novel with words that could not have been dearer to Harington's heart: "Every piece of fiction is to some extent autobiographical—a kind of confession—but it doesn't have to be a diary. As Picasso said about all creative work, it lies its way to the truth."

Except, of course, that Harington wouldn't have limited the inevitably autobiographical nature of writing to fiction. As these reviews show, it's not just Harington's novels that can be read profitably as the author's de facto autobiography. Harington just as naturally embedded into his reviews a complicated, often cantankerous image of himself as the worldly scholar, the underappreciated novelist, the stern public intellectual, and the incorrigible lover of literature, art, architecture, folk speech, material culture, and Arkansas as a bracing setting for expansive American possibilities. In fact, it's possible that Harington puts his wide array of learning on even fuller display in these reviews than in the essays and articles above. While he did have to confine himself in these short critiques to the two- or three-sentence mini-paragraphs required for narrow-columned newspaper publication, these restrictions never obscured his strong opinions or his unmistakable competitiveness. Duane Michals may dazzle Harington with his photographs (see p. 66 below), but more importantly, Michals's audacious art pricks the pride of the older but equally audacious artist who was reviewing his book. The appreciative, admiring Harington of "The Guestroom Novelist" certainly shows up in these reviews, but that generous figure is regularly shadowed by the frustrated novelist who counts up the number of volumes that the Library of America devoted to writers whose work (he clearly felt) did not deserve such literally beautiful treatment any more than did his Stay More novels.

53

The Library of America scorecard appears in Harington's review of
the prestigious publishing house's canonization of Nabokov, Harington's
great teacher and inspiration, who appears with telling frequency in
these reviews. At the time Harington published this review in the mid-
1990s, he was about the same age as Nabokov was when the older writer
left teaching altogether to live out his final decades in a luxury hotel in
Switzerland in comfort and financial ease, thanks to the massive success
of *Lolita* (1958). Harington's palpable desire to follow his mentor's example
grew more and more unmistakable in his novels of the '90s. After *The
Cockroaches of Stay More* was published in 1989 to impressive reviews
but comparatively weak sales (see p. 217 below), Harington embarked on
a series of genre-novel experiments to see if any of them would prove
popular enough to stick with: a prison novel (*The Choiring of the Trees*,
1991), a doctor novel (*Butterfly Weed*, 1996), a war novel (*When Angels
Rest*, 1998), and a political novel (*Thirteen Albatrosses, or Falling Off the
Mountain*, 2000). The one '90s novel that didn't fit the genre-experiment
mold was *Ekaterina* (1993), Harington's tour-de-force inversion of *Lolita*
and his most concentrated homage to Nabokov, in which the protagonist,
a ravishingly beautiful woman who has escaped from a former Soviet-bloc
country only to take a creative writing course taught by the novel's avatar
for Harington, ends up writing bestsellers that allow her to take over the
luxury suite of perhaps the most storied hotel in the Ozarks. But none of
the genre experiments (or *Ekaterina*'s Nabokov homage, for that matter)
worked as Harington hoped; by the time that *Butterfly Weed* appeared
in paperback, Harington's publisher, Harcourt Brace Jovanovich (HBJ),
was enclosing postcards in his books that offered readers a free Harington
novel just for mailing the card in. *Butterfly Weed* was the last Harington
novel that HBJ published, leaving him to search, ever more desperately,
for publishers of his subsequent novels.

While reading the reviews from this period, it helps to remember
Harington's contemporaneous (and increasingly protracted) struggles to
get his novels published. The brief bios he included with many of them
sometimes directly connected elements of the reviews to his novels, clear
pleas to readers to proceed to his books. But still more, it's the didactic
and prescriptive tones that most reveal the author's wish for greater readership of his work, a university professor trying somehow to teach his way
into his readers' hearts and thereby onto their bookshelves. His review of
two volumes dedicated to the controversial work of the painter Balthus,
for instance, doesn't just draw on his deep knowledge of the artist or his

historical and theoretical contexts; it also unhesitatingly justifies a viewer's potentially erotic response to Balthus's depictions of decidedly underage subjects—Harington (who, in one of his early novels, quotes an Ozarks definition of a virgin as a five-year-old girl who can run faster than her father and brothers) using a newspaper piece to make a philosophical plea for art's erotic license that would equally benefit his own unapologetically (and sometimes outrageously) erotic work.

Much of the Trojan horse work he does in these reviews is more subtle. In a review of three "coffee-table" art books devoted to the preservation of old houses, rustic furniture, and tools, Harington cleverly bridges any supposed gap between high art and the materials of folk culture, finding in the homespun and the home-fashioned as much evidence of the enduring (and endearing) work of the human imagination as in any of the reviews dedicated to the famous painters who supply our art museums' walls. He even works in a quotation that applies as much to his postmodern hillbilly contributions to the history of the novel as it does to the loving preservation of historic homes: "The challenge—and the obligation—is to live a contemporary lifestyle and yet sustain the historic presence and integrity of this structure so appropriately called the *house of the people*." And in his review of a book called *The Parthenon and Its Impact in Modern Times*, Harington doesn't just (rather shamelessly) quote himself from his "latest novel, *Butterfly Weed*," but also explains some of the obscure but delightful ironies embedded into mythologically inspired place-names in America, once again having his dumb hillbilly-joke cake and eating it like the learned scholar too, culminating with another double-edged statement, one that applies just as well to his books as to the one he was reviewing: "Whether for casual browsing or for extensive study, *The Parthenon* will satisfy the civilized mind."

Kim Harington once mentioned that she, too, had begun writing reviews because they provided a useful supplement to Harington's teaching income during the years when his novel sales continued to disappoint and it became harder and harder to find a publisher for his work. That additional (and most practical) motive complicates the appeal of these pieces all the more, the professor of art history trying to do the frustrated novelist a favor without sullying either of their reputations for discipline, rigor, or honesty. Keeping his envy at bay when he wrote of other, more successful novelists whose work he genuinely admired (like Nabokov or Peter Straub or Kevin Brockmeier or Daniell Woodrell) must have required even more restraint than the reviews dedicated to art or history or Arkansas subjects, but these reviews continually show Harington to be up to the task. Even so, sometimes, he clearly couldn't stop himself from foregrounding his frustration, as in the marvelous, despairing end of his review of *The Annotated Huckleberry Finn*:

> Not to have read *The Adventures of Huckleberry Finn* is sad. Not to purchase this brilliant annotation and use it and treasure it is excusable but mournful.

The Parthenon and Its Impact in Modern Times

By Panayotis Tournikiotis
(Melissa Publishing House, 1996)

EVERYONE BELIEVES the Parthenon is the finest building ever built. Even in its ruined condition, it continues to draw hordes of tourists who make long pilgrimages to see it. All books on art history give it a special place of honor, with more words of praise and explanation than can be found for any other single artwork in the history of mankind.

In fact, so many dozens of books and thousands of essays have already been published about the Parthenon that the arrival of this new volume, not affordable by the casual art lover, would seem superfluous if not extravagant.

What can this book do for you? Especially if you've already learned in school that the Parthenon is the most perfect embodiment of rational thought and man's urge to create order out of chaos, that it was the culmination of a vast public-works program started by Pericles at the height of his "Golden Age" in the fifth century BC, that it is the best possible culmination of the evolution of the Doric order of architecture, that, as I customarily point out to the amazement of my art history students, it has not one single straight line in it despite seeming to be the epitome of straight-lineness?

Whether you approach this fantastic structure from the angle of the historian, the art student, the sculptor, the architect, the politician, the mythologist, the town planner, the tourist, the philosopher, or simply the lover of beauty, *The Parthenon* can help you understand just what it is about the building that makes it so truly monumental.

⚡⚡⚡

Here are assembled eleven essays, each of them extensively and beautifully illustrated, written by architects, archaeologists, art historians, or simply thoughtful writers, and dealing with every conceivable aspect of the Parthenon, its conception, design, history, and influence . . . including its apparently paradoxical influence on "modern" architecture.

Architecture is, after all, the attempt to assert man's domination over nature. Whether it is a crude shack built in and of the forest or a towering skyscraper, any building is, first of all, man's way of gaining shelter against the chaos of the environment. Why does a small child erect out of sofa cushions a tiny habitation?

The Parthenon was simply (but with infinite complexity, as this book shows) the noblest, grandest, happiest manifestation of that basic urge. Inspired by the gods, perhaps (or at least by one wonderful goddess, Athena), the architects Ictinus and Callicrates collaborated under the direction of the sculptor Pheidias to plan and erect a temple which would not merely be a marble shed housing the cult statue of Athena but an abstract work of sculpture in itself: a constant reminder to the human eye of the ways to rise above the confusion and fury of life.

The Ozark town named after this building, an actual town south of Jasper in Newton County, which the old-timers still pronounce "Par-THEE-ny," was most likely named in ignorance of its meaning, as I've pointed out in my latest novel, *Butterfly Weed*, wherein "Vance Randolph" explains:

> All over America people were naming their new towns after Greek towns, and this Newton County feller thought he was doing the same, but he was mistaken. The name of the town was Athens. There was a hill in Athens called the Acropolis, meaning "high town," and he might have used that name . . . but he didn't. He used the name of the temple on top of that hill. For all he knew, he might as well have called the town "Innocence" or "Chastity" or "Maidentown" or "Virginville."

Parthenos means virgin in Greek and refers to the fact that Athena, goddess of wisdom, was virtually the only one of the ancient deities to retain her virtue. The namer of Parthenon, Arkansas, was not alone in being unaware of this fact: as *The Parthenon* points out, among the famous visitors to the building was the accidental tourist Sigmund Freud, who, detouring there en route to Corfu, could only remark: "So all this really *does* exist, just as we learnt in school!"

Characteristically, Freud would later analyze (to death) his own reasons for not having been more appreciative during that chance encounter (although he did not consider the ramifications of his shyness in the presence of a virgin). But his reaction is understandable: all of us try to protect ourselves against becoming overemotional in the presence of magnificence, fame, passion, absolute beauty . . . anything overwhelmingly grand.

After all, this human resistance was precisely what Ictinus must have been trying to overcome when he took such pains to design the structure with built-in distortions to compensate for the natural distortions of the human eye. The architect Manolis Korres discusses in this book (and illustrates with his own axonometric drawings) all of the ways that Ictinus designed each component of the building so that its measurements would be as mathematically perfect as the human mind could conceive.

Korres, whose love for the building suffuses every page, also is responsible for the lively essay on the history of the Parthenon down through the centuries to modern times, how the Parthenon was misused, misunderstood, abused, mutilated, and ultimately ruined. In our glorification of the building, we tend to forget that it has become famous only in relatively recent times; throughout the middle ages and even the Renaissance, it was not the "ideal" landmark that it has become to us.

One of the book's most fascinating aspects, treated in three separate chapters, considers the way modern Greeks themselves, as opposed to tourists and other outsiders, have viewed their supreme edifice: how Greek society has appreciated it, how the Greek people have participated in the recent extensive project to restore and reconstruct it, and, lastly, its impact upon the consciousness of modern Greek poets and thinkers.

Whether for casual browsing or for extensive study, *The Parthenon* will satisfy the civilized mind.

Balthus

By Claude Roy

(Bulfinch, 1996)

ART HISTORIANS don't know what to make of Balthus. It's bad enough that he goes by just one name (the full name, Count Balthasar Klossowski de Rola, is eminently forgettable). It's worse that he has been branded as "figurative."

It's inexcusable that he can't be pigeonholed (although some art historians have tried desperately but unsuccessfully to call him a Surrealist). But worst of all, it's suspicious that his favorite subject matter is the same thing that got Nabokov into trouble: pubescent girls.

Soon in these pages I'll be writing about the stunning new trio of Library of America volumes devoted to the best work of that towering literary giant, Vladimir Nabokov, who has been belatedly and posthumously getting the serious attention that was deflected by the notoriety of his *Lolita*, arguably the finest novel of the century but inarguably the most scandalous one (and now being made for a second time into a motion picture).

⚡⚡⚡

The presumption that Nabokov himself had a lust for twelve-year-old girls is like assuming that the editors of this newspaper are rapists because they print so many stories about rape and is just as ridiculously unfounded as the presumption that Balthus is a dirty old man who can't keep his hands off his comely little models.

"The fabled theme of the languid adolescent girl, which Balthus has treated repeatedly," writes his eldest son in his book on his father, "has nothing whatsoever to do with sexual obsession, except perhaps in the eye of the beholder."

Now the beholder's eyes must choose between two simultaneously published volumes, by the Bulfinch Press of Little, Brown, and by Abrams, both with the same title, *Balthus.* Indeed, the concurrent appearance of the two books is testimony to the renewed esteem in which this exceptional painter is being held by public and critic alike.

It is my difficult task to help the beholder choose between the two, and, perhaps into the bargain, relieve whatever guilty feelings the beholder may have: it's perfectly all right to be turned on by the provocative poses of these sultry young ladies.

Neither of the commentators on these picture books is a professional art historian. The eldest son, Stanislas, who contributes a scant five pages of text to Abrams's sumptuous coffee-tabler (or bedside-tabler), lives in Malibu, California, and has previously published only two books on alchemy. Claude Roy, who provides a much longer and more helpful text to Bulfinch's more comprehensive and scholarly volume, is a distinguished French novelist and a close friend of Balthus.

It might be argued that neither an eldest son nor a good friend is objective enough, detached enough, dispassionate enough, or critical enough, to say the right things about an artist. The eldest son makes a strong case for his father's contention that the best text is no text at all: Balthus has shunned reporters, discouraged photographers, and repeatedly affirmed his conviction that an artist's biography lends nothing to the understanding of his work. (By all accounts, this has nothing to do with his desire to hide his private entertainment of his pubescent models but simply the belief commonly held by many artists that the work of art should speak for itself without the distraction of extraneous commentary.)

If you buy an art book primarily to enjoy the pictures, then the Abrams *Balthus*, with minimal commentary by the son, not only is better in the quality of its reproductions but also will set you back twenty dollars less. But if you want your art book really to teach you something about the pictures you're looking at, to help you understand them better, to find things you might miss, then unquestionably, the Bulfinch job by novelist Roy is far the better of the two.

Consider, by comparison, how each of the two books treats the recent *Cat with a Mirror III* (1989–1994). The Abrams volume has it on the cover, as well as in four illustrations, including extreme close-ups (helpful) of the cat, the girl, and even the red-and-white quilt; and there is also, to show its development, the *Cat with a Mirror II* (1986–1989), with another close-up of the cat. The quality of the reproductions and the close-ups are superior to those in the Bulfinch.

But the Bulfinch volume has an entire chapter, "The Time-Charmer," devoted to the development of this motif, including the far more stunning *Cat with a Mirror I*, the first in the series (1977–1980), in which the girl is naked, with Claude Roy's text elucidating the transformations, and, perhaps best of all, a "documentary" snapshot photograph of the young model, who is shown looking at the aged Balthus out of the corner of her eyes with an impish grin that not only echoes that of the girl in the painting (version I), but is, as they say, worth the price of the book.

Also, the Abrams version does not show the naughty *The Guitar Lesson* (1934), because, as son Stanislas points out, "Despite my desire to include it in the present work, my father has refused to endorse its further dissemination." But the Bulfinch version has the painting in all its wicked glory, waiting for the eye of the beholder.

Balthus has another thing in common with Nabokov: both men moved to Switzerland for their "retirement." But Balthus is still alive, at eighty-eight, watching with an impish grin as his reputation, fueled by postmodernism's love of the image, takes off and soars.

The Library of America's Nabokov

Edited by Brian Boyd
(Library of America, 1996)

P ARADISE," John Updike calls the Library of America, the non-profit publishing program reprinting America's best literature in handsome, permanent volumes, ninety of them so far.

Updike's own novels will be included eventually, inevitably, and meanwhile, he can exclaim, "I'm thrilled that Nabokov, the writer that meant so much to my own literary formation, is entering the textual paradise of the Library of America."

Ditto from Harington. The simultaneous publication of these three volumes, each in gilt-stamped forest-green cloth and just the right size for the hand, is final confirmation of my long-held belief that Nabokov is the greatest American writer of this century, never mind his Russian background. His influence may be seen in every one of my novels, not just *Ekaterina*, which was written in homage to him.

Of the great American writers included in the Library of America collection, only two, Henry James with nine volumes and Mark Twain with five, have more volumes than Nabokov now does, while six others have the same number, three (Henry Adams, James Fenimore Cooper, Faulkner, Melville, O'Neill, and Francis Parkman).

That pantheon is distinguished company, and doubtless will further enhance the stature of the writer who was once famous only for his scandalous novel about an older man's infatuation with a twelve-year-old girl nicknamed Lolita.

Best of all, the Library of America editions are newly researched and edited, their texts correcting long-standing errors and incorporating Nabokov's penciled corrections in his own copies of the books, supplied to the Library's research staff by the author's son, Dmitri Nabokov. And with further editing and extensive annotations by Brian Boyd, Nabokov's brilliant and indefatigable biographer, the resulting texts are the most authoritative versions available and can replace the earlier editions in any Nabokov collector's library.

For example, my own copy of *Pale Fire*, which I consider Nabokov's best novel, is the 1963 Lancer paperback (fifty cents), which is yellowed, falling apart, and punctured from my own annotations, especially those questioning the typographical errors and such obscurities as "the complexities of Zemblan ingledom" (since my novels are overrun with Ingledews). Not only are all the mistakes corrected, but Brian Boyd explains that the latter word is from "*ingle*, 'catamite,'" which is handy but disturbing to know.

There are two ways to read Nabokov (both of them requiring the heeding of his own rule: anything worth reading is worth reading twice): it is quite possible to enjoy his clever plots and his masterful wordplay in English without knowing a single one of his esoteric or abstruse allusions; and it is possible to be infinitely rewarded by knowing, or taking the trouble to find out, just what he means . . . and means . . . and means.

In a tireless effort to annotate the eight novels in these volumes, Professor Boyd, a senior lecturer in English at the University of New Zealand, not only searched out the most recondite references and allusions in Latin, French, Russian, German and "Zemblan," but also solicited help with some puzzling words and expressions from members of NABOKV-L, the internet discussion group devoted to the master's work.

Lest there be howls of protest at the Library of America's omission of such great Nabokov novels as *Laughter in the Dark*, *The Defense*, and *Invitation to a Beheading*, it should be kept in mind that the three Library of America volumes must perforce be limited to only what Nabokov wrote *after* coming to America in 1940, or, rather, his beginning in 1938 his first novel in English (after nine in Russian), *The Real Life of Sebastian Knight*, that intriguing literary mystery about a famous novelist the same age as Nabokov, the first novel in this collection.

It is followed, in Volume One, by his political novel of a philosophy professor mired in the bureaucracy of a police state, *Bend Sinister*, and by Nabokov's third-person autobiography of his early years, *Speak, Memory*.

Volume One is the slenderest of the three, so, if the casual reader can afford only one of the three thirty-five-dollar volumes, Volume Two would be best: it contains, in addition to the comic masterpiece *Pnin* and the truly brilliant tour de force *Pale Fire*, which Mary McCarthy accurately called "one of the great works of art of this century," not only *Lolita* in all her glory but also the screenplay that Nabokov wrote of *Lolita* for director Stanley Kubrick. (Timely, if we're ever given the chance to compare it with the recently filmed — and still seeking a distributor — version which Stephen Schiff wrote for Adrian Lyne, starring Jeremy Irons as Humbert and the funny Dominique Swain in the title role.)

Volume Three (1969–1974) completes the set with *Ada or Ardor: A Family Chronicle*, the pastoral blockbuster Nabokov liked to think of as his greatest book but which, alas, has found few people willing to give it the requisite second reading; *Transparent Things*, a slight novella, and his last major novel, quasi-autobiographical, *Look at the Harlequins!*

Space permits only mention of all these novels, rather than an actual review of them. For the reader who already knows and loves this master's work, the set offers the satisfactions of permanence, elegance, and completeness. For the reader who has not yet discovered Nabokov, the set offers an excellent chance to watch in constant action the supreme expert of literary invention, deception, narrative, and unforgettable characterization.

If there is a shortcoming to the set, it is that none of Nabokov's short stories could be included. He is unsurpassed in his command of shorter fiction, and no collection of his work is complete without the brilliant stories he wrote in America. But after all, Knopf published last fall his collected stories in a 655-page edition, and the Library of America has had to exclude short stories from its compendia of even such great storytellers as Faulkner.

The Essential Duane Michals

By Marco Livingstone
(Bulfinch, 1997)

THE FIRST TIME I EVER SAW a "book" by Duane Michals, his fetching *Real Dreams: Photo Stories* (1976), I pictured him as a smart-ass young experimental photographer, the sort of punk who'd have "Duane" as a name.

Now I know he isn't young—he's been shooting off his camera and his mouth for forty years, but he is certainly experimental: no other photographer has performed such stunts in transforming photography from its depictive, documentary function into a highly introspective capacity for narrative sequence. And he is just about the most smart-ass artist alive.

Imagine Lewis Carroll and Walt Whitman collaborating to do the words for a book of images created by giving a camera to Balthus and Magritte and asking them to collaborate in making some storytelling pictures. The result would be Michals's one-man show: he does the words as well as the images.

Now all of his best work is collected into a definitive, glossy, expensive coffee-table adornment, a welcome souvenir for Michals fans and a stunning initiation for those who haven't yet sampled this master's bold forays into the reinterpretation of "reality."

Like Nabokov, Michals puts quotation marks around that word because, as he once remarked to Marco Livingstone, the curator and commentator for this collection, "Photographers deal with reality exquisitely. There's no other art form which reproduces reality with that kind of fidelity. But to me that is to say that appearances are the only thing which we consider to be real. What about dreams, what about fear, what about lust, what about all those intimidations which we perform on each other? These experiences, to me, constitute reality."

"Dreams, Fear, Lust, and Intimidations" might have made a good title for this volume, but *The Essential Duane Michals* was chosen, carrying the implication that there might be some non-essential Michals left out, and also the implication that Michals's work is necessary, indispensable, that art cannot live without him . . . which is *almost* true.

Unfortunately, there is a certain faddishness about Michals's work, of which he himself is well aware (and proud), and of which the coming-out of this book is a clear manifestation. Michals is essentially a magician. (The cover depicts him pulling a human head out of a magician's hat, pointing to it, wrapped around on the back side of the jacket.) Like the best of magicians, he depends upon the satisfying gasps of the audience at the clever, seemingly impossible stunts he performs.

And what stunts they are! I'll never forget my first view of *Things Are Queer*, a virtuoso sequence demolishing both time and scale: a photo of a conventional bathroom turns out to be a midget's john or else inhabited by a giant, and an even greater giant discovers that image in a book which he reads as he carries it away down a dark hall, our last view of him becoming a distant image which, we discover, is framed and hanging over the lavatory in that original little bathroom.

"It is like being taken on a tour of the universe," Livingstone says about this sequence, "only to be dropped off at the point of departure, none the wiser."

Michals is notorious for being the first to write words all over his pictures, and, from there, to move on into the realm of verbal text, written narrative. As a poet of images he is brilliant, but as a poet of words, he is distinctly second- or even third-rate. There is a certain studied naiveté to his narratives which is more often cloying than helpful.

While Magritte was still alive, Duane Michals paid a visit to his idol and received permission to photograph him, in his house and in his garden (double-exposed) in a series of images that capture beautifully both the essence of that greatest of Surrealists and Michals's abiding admiration for him. (One of the best in Michals's series of "Overpainted Photographs" is called *Ceci n'est pas une photo d'une pipe*, which is a parody of both Magritte's best-known painting and of Michals's own approach.)

Michals is often hilariously funny, a quality all too rare in "serious" art. My favorite is a single, *There Are Nine Mistakes in This Photograph. Can You Find Them?*, which is a take-off on the popular syndicated features of the funny papers. It is the penultimate picture in the book, leading up to his "last words":

A FAILED ATTEMPT TO PHOTOGRAPH REALITY. How foolish of me to believe that it would be that easy. I had confused the appearance of trees and automobiles, and people with reality itself, and believed that a photograph of these appearances to be a photograph of it. It is a melancholy truth that I could never be able to photograph it and can only fail. I am a reflection photographing other reflections within a reflection. To photograph reality is to photograph nothing.

Included among an assortment of commercial extracurricular activities, such as assignments for national magazines, there is an advertisement for GAP, a self-portrait of Duane Michals in denim jacket and jeans, and the blurb, "NARRATIVE. It's how you forge a context by linking what seems unrelated. Classic Gap, for individuals who reach conclusions on their own."

Michals is a master at linking what seems unrelated, at uncovering the incongruities of life, time, scale, and feeling. By failing in his attempt to photograph reality, he invented a whole new world, which is yours for just fifty dollars.

Three for Christmas

Caring for Your Historic House,
by Heritage Preservation and National Park Service
(Abrams, 1998)

Y OU MIGHT BE LIVING IN a historic house without knowing it. If somebody gives you this book for Christmas, it could inspire you to look upon those tedious odd jobs you've been doing as worthy maintenance.

This book will convince you that your house is historic if it's at least fifty years old, typical of its period or style, and has something significant in its setting, design, materials, workmanship, or history.

So many books and magazines have been published on the subject of *restoring* old houses without dealing with the question: now that you've fixed it up, how do you take care of it? Here is the ultimate guide to the subject of *preventive maintenance*: how to understand your dwelling from cellar to rafter, how to spot trouble, how to fix what goes wrong.

Twenty-two authors, each an expert in a particular area of restoration and preservation, offer advice and practical how-to in every task of daily, weekly, monthly, and yearly maintenance. Often, all that is required is vigilance, watching out for such things as water damage, but occasionally, the work to be done requires professional help, and this book tells you how to choose the best help available.

The list of authors reads like a Who's Who in historic preservation, and includes the editor of *Old-House Journal*, the head of Philadelphia's top plastering service, the principals of several restoration architecture firms, New York's leading paint-and-finish expert, and the country's top stonemason.

A handy index, from acrylic adhesives to zoning of interior systems, covers every conceivable task and problem in the upkeep of aged and aging dwellings, including roofs, masonry, exterior and interior woodwork, wallpapers and plaster, flooring, heating and cooling systems, lighting systems, and kitchens and bathrooms. There are chapters also on caring for the landscape, fire protection, and a very handy concluding chapter on legal matters: appraisals, insurance, preservation easements, and estate planning.

The preface is penned by the occupant and overseer of the most historic house in America—the White—and she observes, aptly, that "the challenge—and the obligation—is to live a contemporary lifestyle and yet sustain the historic presence and integrity of this structure so appropriately called the *house of the people.*"

Likewise, owning and keeping any historic old house should not sacrifice a contemporary lifestyle and its conveniences. *Caring for Your Historic House* will show you how to enjoy living in an old house without becoming old yourself.

Rustic Style, photographs and text
by Ralph Kylloe (Abrams, 1998)

Chances are, your historic house won't have any furniture of the delightful variety that fills *Rustic Style*, a charming fantasia of tree limbs, roots, bark, twigs, and even antlers.

This is the kind of furniture you expect to see in a hunting lodge, fishing camp, wilderness log cabin, or, occasionally, some backbrush inn or B and B. But more and more people are putting an occasional piece of rustic furniture, perhaps crafted in the Ozarks or sold in innovative design shops like Fayetteville's HomeWorks, into their bedrooms and kitchens or beside the living-room fireplace, especially if the latter is made of rustic stone.

Surprisingly, as this book points out and in case you've actually got some rustic furniture in your historic house, much good rustic furniture was made in the last century, and Americans have been enjoying both outdoor and indoor chairs for generations.

Author and photographer Ralph Kylloe, who runs a well-known rustic furniture gallery in the Adirondacks (where else?) and himself lives in a log-style house packed with authentic Adirondack-style furnishings, points out that rustic is not merely a style but a way of living. He traces the origins of it to our earliest ancestors, who lived by their wits and avoided lying on the damp earth or sitting on hard rocks by fashioning beds and chairs from saplings and limbs.

Thus the appeal of the furniture is to our primordial sense of living not only in nature but *with* nature. Paradoxically, as the book lavishly illustrates, some of the best examples of contemporary rustic furniture are not only very sophisticated in their construction and workmanship, but also, unfortunately, anything but rustic in their prices.

The book's appendix includes a resource list of today's top artists and dealers in rustic furniture and accessories, and all of these people make a very good living indeed from their wares.

Although the book distinguishes among regions of rustic furniture —the Adirondack, the Appalachian, the Southern, the Southwestern, and Rocky Mountain styles—there is nothing on, or from, the Ozarks or the Ouachitas, where mountain people have produced rustic furniture of their own for generations, and where dealers search out and find bargains.

Customarily, rustic furniture is accessorized by backgrounds of Navajo rugs, Pendleton blankets, fishing creels, snow shoes, Adirondack canoe paddles, and antler chandeliers.

Fanciful and sylvan as the style can be, it has two drawbacks worth considering: it doesn't look very comfortable and in some cases downright isn't; therefore, its appeal is primarily visual, or aesthetic, but here too it's a matter of personal taste. The same people who aren't comfortable out in the woods, perhaps because of nature's chaos or because you're surrounded everywhere by prickly, spiny, jabbing, brambly, barbed, thorny things, will not be snug and cozy in rooms full of rustic furniture.

Tools: Making Things Around the World,
by Hubert Comte (Abrams, 1998)

And finally, to adorn your rustic tree-stump table in your historic house, a different kind of coffee-table book: a big, beautiful, endlessly inviting compendium of tools. Everything you ever wanted to know about hammers, axes, knives, adzes, saws, drills: where they came from, how they evolved, which societies used them, and even what they will look like in the future.

The author, like this reviewer, is a teacher of art history, and thus has a fine appreciation for the *appearance* of tools. A tool might be thought of as a work of sculpture but one which evokes through its form its function and thereby is visually "loaded." A tool is ready to go. Its very existence suggests how man is separated from the other animals, not just through ingenuity but also through readiness.

Just as there are people who decorate their interiors with wall-hung tools that will never be used, the primary appeal of this book is decorative— not as a coffee-table adornment but as a picture-book filled with color photographs of every conceivable tool in history and also with color paintings, some by the old masters (Tintoretto, Brueghel, Hokusai, et al.), which depict a variety of tools being used.

There are some strange tools here you may never have seen in your friendly hardware store: sugarloaf cracker, bungstart, bretture, dibble, saunier, rainette, teasel, secateur, and smille. The most common of tools, the hammer, comes in forty-one different varieties. All told, there are more than three hundred hand tools shown and described and explained.

The only minor drawback is the same noted above in *Rustic Furniture*: none of the examples discussed comes from Arkansas, where a great many tools were devised by the frontier settlers to make their way in the new world. Not even the famous Arkansas whetstone, necessary to keep so many tools sharp, gets mentioned.

But that's a quibble. The real danger of giving this book to someone on Christmas is that you won't see them again for a long time: they'll disappear into its pages.

Home Grown Stories and Home Fried Lies

By Mitch Jayne

(Wildstone Media, 2000)

HERE IS A DELIGHTFUL new installment in the venerable but discontinued tradition of Ozark joke books, unlike any of its hoary predecessors in the civility and humanity of its author. Mitch Jayne is an old Missouri codger who once (1970) wrote the best novel, *Old Fish Hawk*, to come out of the Missouri Ozarks, and who was semifamous for a long time as the bass player for the Dillards, Andy Griffith's band.

Now with the abundant help of his wife and partner, Diana Jayne, a magnificent illustrator, he has put together what he subtitles *Words With The Bark On Them and Other Ozark Oddments*, which, in the tradition of all those old Ozark joke books, will probably be sold in gift shops, airports, truck stops, and tourist joints.

You may not be able to find it at your corner bookstore, but they can order it for you. Or you can simply order it from Amazon.com or one of the other online booksellers. It will provide hours of amusement, edification, visual delight, and a satisfaction of your nostalgia for the good old times, in the Ozarks or anywhere.

The tradition got started way back in 1903, when one Thomas W. Jackson got rich selling an awful paperback called *On a Slow Train Through Arkansas*, which, like Mitch Jayne's book, carried a long subtitle: *Funny Railroad Stories, Sayings of the Southern Darkies, All the Latest and Best Minstrel Jokes of the Day.* None of it had very much to do with Arkansas, except to capitalize upon the state's reputation, even then, as a butt of jokes.

The book sold so well that Jackson followed it up with a sequel, *Through Missouri on a Mule*, and others hopped on the bandwagon (or the snake oil wagon): Marion Hughes in 1904 published his *Three Years in Arkansas*, which received from Arkansawyers even more hostility than Jackson's book, which in turn made it difficult for a more respectable book like the 1905 *Opie Read in the Ozarks, Including Many of the Rich, Rare, Quaint, Eccentric and Superstitious Sayings of the Natives of Missouri and Arkansaw* . . . a subtitle which would do just as well for Mitch Jayne's *Home Grown Stories.*

Throughout the last century there was a steady national market for collections of rich, rare, quaint, eccentric, and superstitious sayings of the Ozarks, such as "Mirandy's" *Breezes from Persimmon Holler,* Cora Pinkley Call's *Trail Blazers of the Ozarks,* and "Doc" Roy Edwin Thomas's self-published "Dox Books" on a variety of subjects (although his last work, *Come Go with Me,* which I reviewed in these pages, was respectably published by Farrar, Straus and Giroux).

In the '60s and '70s, you could stop at any Stuckey's and pick up for a dollar a slim paperback like Zeek Zinderman's *Hill Latin: An Ozark Hillbilly Lingo Dictionary* or Lowell Davis's *The Ozark Hillman's Handbook.*

Even the great Vance Randolph, whose two-volume *Ozark Folklore: An Annotated Bibliography* meticulously listed and discussed all the dozens and dozens of such books, got into the game himself with the publication of such things as the Haldeman-Julius booklets, *Funny Stories About Hillbillies, Funny Stories from Arkansas, Wild Stories from the Ozarks,* etc.

But the national taste for the rich, rare, quaint Ozarks seemed to evaporate like the dew on a July morning's meadow, or like the old Ozark words and expressions themselves, which were swept away under the homogenizing effect of television, and the national determination to speak a common language in common accents coast to coast.

Thus, when a compendium as beautiful as Mitch Jayne's book arrives on the scene, the first such in many years, it provokes delicious pleasure in encountering again those rare and quaint but infinitely expressive old Ozark words, and that tradition of the Ozark storyteller who can make you laugh one minute and sob the next.

Jayne presents an omnium-gatherum of jests, reminiscences, whoppers, skits, rules, polemics, bawdy tales, precepts, and word lists, as antiquated as that meerschaum pipe he's smoking on the cover, and as sharp as that bear-claw necklace he's wearing, all of it handsomely and copiously illustrated in expressive realism by the drawings of his talented artist-wife Diana.

The art alone is worth the price of the book.

Which isn't to say that Mitch Jayne doesn't wield a way with words that is as keen and revelatory as his wife's pictures (if he doesn't have her energy, it's maybe because he's twenty-two years older than she). He's a raconteur in the best French meaning of the word—giving an account or reckoning—and also in the best Ozark tradition of storyteller. Reading him reminded me constantly of the old men sitting on the store porch at Drakes Creek (Stay More), swapping tall tales and trying to outdo each other not with their whittling but with their yarn-spinning.

He may be the last of his breed. He's so good at what he does that we're inclined to forgive him his manifestation of the common rivalry and feuding that existed between Arkansas Ozarkers and Missouri Ozarkers (the former called the latter "pukes"), who held in agreement only one thing: that Missoura is not pronounced "Missouree" the way the Yankees say it.

Jayne pokes frequent fun at us Arkansawyers, admitting that "Missourians have always saved up their best jokes for Arkansas." "Remember this is educational material," he writes at the end of his introduction, "and after use should be disposed of in a safe and appropriate manner, i.e., give it to somebody from Arkansas." There's a chapter on "The War Between the States" that contains jibes (Question: Why is an Arkansas divorce like a tornado? Answer: In either one, somebody's bound to lose a trailer) and even the hilarious "State of Arkansas Residency Application" that has check-boxes to end all check-boxes.

But a chapter devoted to jests at Arkansas can end with words as eloquent as these:

> The mountain people, always living from season to season, have forevermore wondered about these people who find time to become worry-specialists; like people who handle rattlesnakes for religious reasons, Jehovah's Witnesses, people against wearing hides or fur, vegetarians, astrologers, end-of-the-world prognosticators, non-smokers who suppose that cigarettes are more toxic than the engine fumes we breathe, people who build bomb shelters, folks who think computers will solve all of our human failings, folks who think firearms cause crime, and people who watch as their children listen to music played at a louder level than blowing up stumps with dynamite.

The reader of Mitch Jayne's book will finish it convinced that he is a wise and funny friend. And sure enough, he is.

Black House

By Stephen King and Peter Straub

(Random House, 2001)

STANDARD DISCLOSURE: I'm an old friend of one of the authors and an unabashed admirer of the other. Does this prejudice disqualify me from telling you that I found *Black House* to be the most exciting and entertaining novel I've read in many a year?

Just as my enthralled but careful reading of the book left me unable to distinguish between what was written by Stephen King and what was written by Peter Straub, my final judgment of *Black House* has nothing to do with my friendship or admiration for the authors.

Not in recent memory has a novel been as heralded, trumpeted, longawaited, and practically sold out in advance. It deserves all the fanfare. You'll find it firmly entrenched as No. 1 on all bestseller lists before the week is over, and it will remain in that position for a year or more.

If you avoid buying books that are on bestseller lists, you probably also avoid anything by Stephen King on the grounds that anyone that successful couldn't possibly be good. The literary establishment has long turned up its snooty nose at his output of more than thirty books.

The simple, inescapable fact is that Stephen King is the most inventive, clever, and talented writer in America. There is only one writer better, that is, only one writer with more wisdom and stylistic felicity, and that is Peter Straub. Put the two of them together, and you have a veritable blockbuster.

They first collaborated fifteen years ago on a fine novel called *The Talisman*, which concerned the adventures of a pre–Harry Potter lad named Jack Sawyer traveling through a parallel universe called the Territories to save his mother from death and into the bargain to save the world from forces of evil.

That novel, like this sequel to it, was a runaway best seller, but after it, Straub and King went their separate ways, the former to cult status as the most intellectual horror writer in America, the latter to great fame and riches as our premier storyteller.

Now the two masters have joined forces again, have played down their stylistic brilliance and toned down their mythologies, in order to tell straightforwardly and spellbindingly a terrific story. The fun they had doing it translates into great reading pleasure for all of us.

French Landing, Wisconsin, is a tranquil town on the Mississippi, not unlike Mark Twain's Hannibal, downstream a ways, and not unlike La Crosse, which has a French Island. Among its pleasant architecture are two disturbing buildings. One is a nursing home called the Maxton Elder Care Facility, a familiar but unpleasant place.

The other is a totally unfamiliar place, perhaps even a lost place, a strange, ugly, ominous house, all of it, even its windows, painted black. This is Black House, and the reader will not even gain admittance to it until late in the book.

A decrepit resident of that nursing home, Charles Burnside, has been sneaking out to Black House and also sneaking out to do mayhem to some of the town's children, whom he has abducted, murdered, and eaten.

There is little suspense about who the villain is. We know (or are permitted to guess) whodunit very early on. What keeps us on the edge of our chairs throughout the book is waiting to see when the old codger will be discovered, caught, and brought to justice, and who or what has driven him to his evil deeds.

And whether or not his latest victim, a boy named Ty Marshall, the clever, loveable son of a gorgeous woman named Judy and a nice man named Fred, is still alive or not. Judy Marshall appears to have gone insane, even before her son disappeared.

The same Jack Sawyer from *The Talisman*, now grown up and even retired in his thirties from the Los Angeles homicide squad, hoping for peace in the pastoral Wisconsin countryside, free from any memory of his adventures in "the Territories" of *The Talisman*, is drawn into the case of the gruesome child murders.

Several forces bring him out of his premature retirement: his good buddy, the town's police chief; his even better buddy (and the most appeal ing character in the book), a blind disc jockey named Henry Leyden, with multiple personalities; his weird waking dreams of robin's eggs and red feathers; his attraction to the lovely Judy Marshall and his hope of returning her son to her; and his own inevitable plunge back into "the Territories," the alternate or parallel world of *The Talisman.*

The unknown killer has been dubbed "the Fisherman" because of the resemblance of his crimes to those committed years earlier by the real-life psychopath Albert Fish. This allusion is the keystone of so many allusions that a lesser team than Straub and King would flub the attempt to juggle them all.

Some readers not familiar with the Stephen King Universe or the rich and fanciful world of Peter Straub may feel that there are too many allusions to the previous novels of both men. But in fact, these allusions do not require footnotes or explanations: the reader who gets them quickly perceives them as a bonus of entertainment; the reader who doesn't get them at all perceives them as a brilliant tapestry backdrop or arras which never stands in the way of the action.

The action is speedy, brisk, and gripping, abetted by a philosophical motorcycle gang named the Thunder Five but calling themselves the Hegelian Scum, who help Jack Sawyer not only in his quest for the killer but also for the larger, darker forces of evil behind the killer, the *abbalah* or Crimson King.

Harry Potter would wet his pants if he encountered the Crimson King, and the appearance of this archvillain in the book's climax almost renders the reader incontinent as well. This is the kind of novel that you don't merely experience; you *wear* it and feel it in your bones.

An Interview with Peter Straub

Last month, Peter Straub and his wife, Susan, both natives of Wisconsin now living in New York City, flew to Fayetteville to spend a weekend with Donald Harington and his wife, Kim, and to visit some of the sites of Harington's fictions, including Drakes Creek and Eureka Springs. This interview began in Fayetteville and was concluded later by e-mail.

DONALD HARINGTON: What were your impressions of Arkansas? Did you find any reminders of Wisconsin?

PETER STRAUB: What I saw of Arkansas struck me as something like rural Wisconsin, but lusher and more concentrated in its visual effects. In Wisconsin, generally speaking, if you're going to drive up a hill, you can see it coming for miles, but in our travels around Fayetteville, we seemed to take a good many unexpected rises and dips. Weatherbeaten old barns and sheds practically begged to be rendered in watercolors or pastels.

DH: The beauty and tranquility of your Wisconsin settings, particularly for *Black House*, seem to magnify the horror of the events. Is that contrast deliberate?

PS: Can I say yes without sounding manipulative? Part of the point is the tendency of people who inhabit tranquil settings to imagine themselves safe from the disorders associated with urban locations. This sense of immunity can heighten the ordinary human capacity for hypocrisy and denial. Every small town has its unhappy, even shocking, secrets — Stephen King and I merely threw some extra coal into the fire.

DH: In a sense, Stephen King is meeting you on your own territory (and Territories) in *Black House*. Did he have any problems adapting to your setting?

PS: Not really. Steve has a wonderful visual imagination. He could see the landscape very accurately after taking in a small number of details. I don't know, maybe he translated everything to Maine in his head, but whatever he did worked. And that he was unconfined by the actual facts of the landscape and the physical characteristics of the towns we were using allowed us both a greater degree of imaginative freedom than he otherwise would have had.

DH: The setting of *Black House* is yours, and the people of *Black House* are yours. What really was the major contribution of King?

PS: Thanks for the compliment, but the people in the book are certainly as much King's as they are mine. We invented Jack Sawyer and Speedy Parker fifteen years ago, and this time around, we went through pretty much the same process, each adding strokes to what the other had done, then going around and around again until the character strolled fully into view. Apart from that, Steve came up with hundreds of incidents, twists, developments, and inspirations. He thought of calling upon Albert Fish to help define our villain, for example, and that shaped the story as a whole.

DH: The average reader trying to picture the process of your collaboration might think that you guys simply took turns writing sentences, or even paragraphs. "One for you, one for me." How did it actually proceed?

PS: We worked at long distance, supported by the same lovely technology that enables this interview. One of us wrote until he felt he'd come to a natural ending point, then zipped his pages through the ether by

means of an e-mail attachment. The other picked up the narrative
and rolled along with it until it was time to stop, and so on. We were
using a kind of outline, thirty-seven single-spaced pages amounting to
a fast-forward scan of the high points, that kept us moving forward in
a straight line.

DH: Did you ever have fights or arguments?

PS: No, not at all. The entire process from start to finish was wonderfully
friendly and cooperative. Instead of squabbling, we kept marveling at
the pleasures given us by our ongoing book.

DH: What would be the best metaphor for your collaboration? A ten-
nis match? A chess game? Billiards? Or two old geezers sitting on the
porch?

PS: A ping-pong match played on a long, long table, I think.

DH: How was it different this time around, compared with your collaboration on *The Talisman*?

PS: This time, everything went more easily, and the process took about
half the time. Since we're older, we weren't out to knock the other fellow off his feet with our brilliance; we concentrated on telling our story
as well as we could.

DH: Who is your favorite character in *Black House*?

PS: Jack Sawyer would have to be my favorite if only because he has been
inhabiting me, or the other way around, for a good long time now, and
I cannot but love him. However, Henry Leyden has a big claim on me,
too. I wish I could run into him now and then.

DH: Has the phenomenal success of *Black House* (2 million first printing,
BOMC selection, rave reviews) turned your head?

PS: No, of course not. Whenever Zoltan, my chauffeur, takes me out for
a spin in the Rolls, I have him hand out twenty-dollar bills to the wonderful little people who run up to peer in the windows at every stop
light. It's things like this that keep a fellow grounded.

REVIEW

The Annotated Huckleberry Finn

By Mark Twain, edited by Michael Patrick Hearn
(W. W. Norton, 2001)

MOVE OVER, Alice, Lolita, and Dorothy, and make room for the new kid on the annotated block, Huck Finn.
This is my nomination for *the* Christmas book to give someone you love, even (or especially) yourself, ideally someone who has already read *The Adventures of Huckleberry Finn* (as haven't we all?) and would enjoy this close-up dissection, classification, postmortem, exegesis, and decoding.

If you haven't experienced such delights as Alfred Appel's *The Annotated Lolita*, or *The Annotated Wizard of Oz* by the same Michael Patrick Hearn who has brought out this new look at Huck, you probably think of annotations as those pesky marginal small-print excrescences which made reading Shakespeare such a chore and bore in high school.

Well, much of Hearn's supplement to Huck Finn is also pesky marginal small-print excrescence, but if you have already read *Huckleberry Finn*, it will open up whole new approaches and delights.

If Mark Twain were alive today, he'd probably compare the idea of an annotated classic to having to identify and smell the wildflowers while zooming down the interstate.

It really slows you down. Bogs you down, in fact, but it is meant to. This is one of several reasons why *The Annotated Huckleberry Finn* shouldn't be given to a kid who hasn't already read the novel, the other reasons being that the novel itself is notoriously *not* for innocent children. It is shot full of political and sociological incorrectness, particularly use of the N-word, and the illustrations, the same drawings that E. W. Kemble made for the first edition, would seem hopelessly quaint or corny to today's young people.

Also, the older you are, the faster you can skim over many of the annotations, which explain or define things you probably already know, such
as "corn-crib," "Barlow knife," "powwow," or "hoss." But editor Hearn
wisely feels that everything ought to be explained, and he probably knows
that you're going to do judicious skimming anyhow.

Considering *Huckleberry Finn's* stature as one of the two great American novels (the other being *Moby-Dick*), what is surprising about this
volume is that it took so long to get here. But, in fact, it didn't. Editor
Hearn had already compiled an *Annotated Huckleberry Finn*, published in
1981 by Clarkson Potter, and this twentieth anniversary edition is a major
expansion and improvement upon the original, aided by the discovery in
1990 of the first half of the original manuscript of the novel.

The best thing about the present volume is Hearn's book-length introduction, lavishly illustrated and beautifully written, which traces Samuel
Clemens's career through the writing of, the rewriting of, the editing of,
his wife's tampering with, and the publication and reviewing of, this great
American classic.

The introduction also considers in detail the subsequent history of the
novel, its banning and its acceptance or rejection by critics, including
attention to what African-Americans have thought about the book, a subject to which a 1992 book was devoted. How young African-Americans
have been affected by the book is especially noticed.

Novelists nowadays are very cautious and timid in their use of dialect,
particularly the native speech of minority groups like Southern blacks
and rednecks, the very transcription of which can confuse and offend the
modern reader. Mark Twain felt that dialogue was action, and had to be
rendered faithfully and generously.

The annotations help explain forgotten words to the reader, particularly the younger reader who is unfamiliar with the colorful vernacular of
America's Nineteenth-Century Golden Age. Indeed, the annotations help
recapture and preserve a way of life and a way of human communication
which are lost to us today and greatly missed.

I was seventeen when I first read *Huckleberry Finn* at my grandmother's house in Drakes Creek (which became Stay More) at a time when
the last vestiges of Ozark speech were beginning to disappear. Probably,
I didn't appreciate Huck's language then, because it was still in use in
those Ozarks, and I took it for granted. But now this book brings it all
back to me.

Arkansas readers need to be reminded that *Huckleberry Finn* is essentially an Arkansas novel (or "Arkansaw," as it is consistently spelled). The best parts of the story of Huck and N-word Jim's trip down the Mississippi and their onshore adventures take place at three locations in Arkansas: Council Bend ("Vicinity of Pokeville"), Napoleon ("Bricksville"), and Columbia ("Vicinity of Pikesville").

Mark Twain is, of course, a humorist, and his satire and exaggeration aren't very kind to Arkansaw people and their way of life in the Delta boondocks, but his sense of fun is so universal that his better jokes don't really require any annotation.

The funniest part of the novel, to me, was when Huck took inventory of the house in which he was visiting, and noticed a funereal picture with the caption "Shall I Never See Thee More Alas," and shortly thereafter, another one of a girl mourning her dead bird, "I Shall Never Hear Thy Sweet Chirrup More Alas," and finally a third one, "And Art Thou Gone Yes Thou Art Gone Alas."

"These was all nice pictures, I reckon," Huck observes, "but I didn't somehow seem to take to them, because if ever I was down a little, they always give me the fan-tods."

As the annotation explains, "Mourning over dead pets was a theme of prints, paintings, and illustrations of the period. The false and petty pity lavished on this dead bird becomes less ridiculous and far more tragic when one learns of the vast carnage spread by the girl's family and neighbors in the following chapter."

Huck's part in the performance of the hilarious *The King's Camelopard* occurs on Arkansas soil, as does the sketch of Boggs and the loafers. The celebrated rant of the raftsman, "Whoo-oop! I'm the old original iron-jawed, brass-mounted, copper-bellied corpse-maker from the wilds of Arkansaw!" appears in an Appendix of the raft episode that originally appeared in the novel but was later transferred to *Life on the Mississippi*.

If there is one serious flaw in this otherwise excellent volume, it is the absence of an index, which would have been a valuable locator, cross-reference, and research tool.

Not to have read *The Adventures of Huckleberry Finn* is sad. Not to purchase this brilliant annotation and use it and treasure it is excusable but mournful.

The Lives of Kelvin Fletcher: Stories Mostly Short

By Miller Williams
(University of Georgia Press, 2002)

EVERY STORY," declares the author in a characteristically crisp prelude, "is about someone who wants something while someone or something stands for a while or forever in the way."

That's poetic, typical of the author, who happens to be not merely a dyed-in-the-wool Arkansawyer but also the finest living colloquial poet in America.

He goes on to say, "These are about one Kelvin Fletcher, sometime around the middle of the twentieth century, who wanted to be good and wanted to grow up. What stood in the way of either was the other."

As poets are wont to do, that says it all, leaving little need for a book review other than this attempt to show what a fine reading experience is this revelation of the ways Kelvin Fletcher tried to be good and tried to grow up and, as often as not, failed at both.

The title implies that Kelvin has more than one life, and the seven stories and concluding novella are each about one of those lives, independent of the rest, although the revolving of the stories around the growing-up of Kelvin can give the book the continuity of a novel.

Kelvin is a winsome lad who too often is losesome. That is, he loses more often than he wins. His best intentions get in the way of his vicissitudes, or vice versa, frequently with comedy rewarding the reader's sympathy or empathy.

Williams possesses a mimetic memory, almost like that which has resulted in the intimate memoir becoming such a popular nonfiction book these days, but whether or not he is actually recounting his own boyhood experiences he convincingly suggests that he is. (See accompanying interview.)

The book ranges over a dozen years in the lives of Kelvin's boyhood, adolescence, and young manhood, beginning with a touching tale that includes Kelvin's first reflections upon God, a subject that will haunt him all his days. He thinks perhaps God ordered worlds with winds that give milk and trees that dream. Worlds of crows that are words in disguise and houses that remember what happens in them. He decided this was how God made up the world to start with. He wondered what would happen to the world when God stopped thinking about it.

Kelvin never stops thinking about it and must come to grips with his discovery that the newborn puppies he finds and wants to adopt are, his mother declares, baby rats and he must find a way to kill them.

Kelvin is constantly confronted with such dilemmas: how to be religious and masturbate at the same time, how to join his pals in peering through a wall into the girls' dressing room and deal with the principal when he alone gets caught, how to find Jesus in a church camp where his fellow campers are hunting for sex, and, in the story that moved me most, "Cantaloupes," the shortest of the stories, how to deal with his guilt when he and a friend hitchhike with a farmer carrying a load of cantaloupes which his friend, as a prank, tosses all over the landscape.

The concluding novella, "Coley's War," is over twice as long as all the stories put together. Kelvin's friend Coley, along with their college friends Monk and Paul, wants to go to Mexico in search of adventure, possibly even fighting in a revolution like the Americans who fought in the Spanish Civil War. (Miller Williams served as a Fulbright professor of American studies at the National University of Mexico, and he knows intimately the landscape and the people.)

The boys—for they are not fully mature yet and have much growing up to do, in conflict with their wish to be good—get involved in some harrowing experiences, some real battles with real gunfire, and some real romances with Mexican girls. "Coley's War" stands apart from the other stories not only because of its length but also because it seizes the reader with its violence.

Lovers of Miller Williams's great poems will be reminded in these stories of many of their favorite characters, situations, and settings.

The eponymous villain of "The Year Ward West Took Away the Raccoon . . . " is the same bully Taylor Wardlow West who beat up the young author in his seventies poem "Getting Experience." The same story contains the drowning of his friend Walter that was so poignantly expressed in the poem "Remembering Walter" from the 1973 collection, *Halfway from Hoxie.*

Speaking of Hoxie, the northeast Arkansas town that was one of Williams's haunts, it must be pointed out that the stories are for the most part not set in actual places in Arkansas. The center of Kelvin's world is a "Booneville" at the heart of a "four-county region," but it is clearly not the Booneville of Logan County, Arkansas.

Williams points out in the interview that he "didn't want to make the setting so clearly Arkansas that the story might not seem at home any-where else." But the universality or non-regionalism thus gained is at the expense of whatever "local color" might accrue to setting the stories in Arkansas. He could at least have used the mythical "Bascum, Arkansas" of his poems.

That's a minor quibble. My only serious cavil is with the novella "Coley's War," not because its length is disproportionate to the seven stories but because the point of view shifts from the third-person hilari-ous of the stories to the first-person dead-serious, which, while it may be necessary to reinforce the point that Kelvin and his pals did not really grow up, or did so at the expense of goodness, makes a downbeat contrast to the stories.

The central difference between prose fiction and poetry is that the lat-ter, like the finer arts of music, dance, and modern painting, is concerned mostly with *how* something is expressed, the *form* of the thing, whereas stories and novels are concerned primarily with *content*, the subject mat-ter of the thing.

With his coauthor John Ciardi, Miller Williams titled a famous text-book on poetry appreciation *How Does a Poem Mean?*, a catchy and per-haps puzzling way of emphasizing the primacy of form over content.

But why do so many people who read fiction shun poetry? I don't think it's because they lack the intellectual capacity for tackling poetry. I think it's because a story has the power to make us participate more than simply contemplate.

In turning his hand to the writing of stories, Miller Williams seems to have belatedly realized that there are certain strings of the heart that can be plucked only by fiction, not by poetry, and he has proceeded to pour out some lovely prose that not only plucks the heart's strings but strums them with arpeggios.

If that doesn't sound too highfalutin. Considering his love for jazz (his latest collection of poetry is wonderfully titled *Some Jazz a While)*, perhaps I ought better speak of his riffs than his arpeggios, but the point is that Miller Williams here has taken delight in allowing the reader to participate instead of simply contemplate, with the result that *The Lives of Kelvin Fletcher* is an experience to relish and remember.

Donald Harington Interviews Miller Williams

In his anthology *Arkansas, Arkansas,* editor John C. Guilds wrote, "If Miller Williams ranks as the greatest poet born, bred, nurtured, and still living in Arkansas, Donald Harington is by the same standards Arkansas's greatest novelist."

DONALD HARINGTON: First, let's lay to rest the suspicion of the reader who thinks I gave you this good review because I'm an old buddy of yours. I'm not, am I?

MILLER WILLIAMS: Don who?

DH: That settled, I'd point out that if I were truly an old pal, I would have heard you talk about Kelvin Fletcher before. Or about any of his experiences. Now I have to ask, To what extent are you Kelvin?

MW: Every piece of fiction is to some extent autobiographical—a kind of confession—but it doesn't have to be a diary. As Picasso said about all creative work, it lies its way to the truth.

DH: Did you ever mistake baby rats for puppies? Or look through a hole into the girls' dressing room? Or get into deep trouble in Mexico?

MW: Let's say, in the first two instances, that I know someone who did. Where Mexico is concerned, I lived and taught there and came to know and like the country and its culture, but all the deep trouble I've fallen into has been closer to home.

DH: Two related questions: was your upbringing as religious as Kelvin's? And, why does religion disappear as Kelvin grows older and becomes involved in "Coley's War"?

MW: Yes, my upbringing was strongly religious. My father was a preacher seven days a week. He was also, though, a civil-rights worker and a union organizer who didn't make distinctions among the three callings; both my parents taught their kids to live in the real world. But to address your question more specifically, "Coley's War" seems to me a kind of morality play.

DH: What do you perceive as the basic difference between a great narrative poem like your "Rubaiyat for Sue Ella Tucker" and a story like "Truth and Goodness"?

MW: That's a marvelously gracious way to frame the question. The internal structure is a story line, which of course makes it a short story as well as a poem, but there are two basic differences. One is that the unit of the poem is not the scene but the line, which is a unit at the same time of sound, sense, and syntax, most of which ask an implicit question which the next line answers, giving the reader (we hope) a continuing sense of forward motion. The other is that while both poetry and prose fiction call upon the reader's intellect, emotion, and imagination, these are generally involved in different proportions in the reading of the two genres.

DH: Except for passing references to Little Rock and Pine Bluff, there's not much actual Arkansas geography named in the book. Were you striving for non-regional universality?

MW: I didn't want to make the setting so clearly Arkansas that the story might not seem at home anywhere else.

DH: "Coley's War" is not only much longer than the other stories but much more serious and violent and gripping. Was this mandated by the greater length, or vice versa?

MW: It was simply a story that took more time to share, and it's more serious because the kids are grown up now by the calendar but are still not grown up.

DH: Which is your own personal favorite among these stories?

MW: It depends on the time of day and whom I've been with.

DH: May we hope that you'll continue writing fiction, or did you learn a lesson (or two) that will leave you content with poetry?

MW: I don't know what I'll write tomorrow, but I can tell you that I learned something in the telling of these stories, and that's an undying admiration for writers of good fiction.

The Truth About Celia

By Kevin Brockmeier

(Pantheon, 2003)

DON'T LOOK BACK," Satchel Paige once famously warned. "Something might be gaining on you." I ignored his advice, and glanced over my shoulder, and there was Kevin Brockmeier, closing in.

Already celebrated for his debut collection of short stories, *Things That Fall from the Sky*, and worshipped by numbers of children for his novel, *City of Names*, Brockmeier now bursts forth with his first grown-up novel. Arkansas should be proud, ideally before the rest of the nation climbs aboard the bandwagon.

Brockmeier has lived most of his life in Little Rock, although this city appears in only one of his stories, and is merely alluded to in his new novel. Seeking a universality as an antidote to regionalism, he avoids local color, any semblance of dialect, anything "Southern" (or Western or Northern or Eastern). The names he gives to his characters can be found in a phone book anywhere.

Christopher Brooks is the main character in *The Truth About Celia*. Indeed, it might be said that he is the only character, and that all the other people are merely his inventions, he who is but an invention of Kevin Brockmeier.

Brooks is, according to a postscript about-the-author which is not at all about Kevin Brockmeier, "the author of several highly acclaimed works of fantasy and science fiction," a winner of prestigious prizes, "born and raised in the town of Springfield," the setting of the novel, definitely not in Arkansas but not in Colorado, Illinois, Massachusetts, Missouri, or any of the dozen other states which have cities of that name.

Brooks has been living in a National Register house "for more than fourteen years, first with his wife and daughter, then with his wife, and now alone." That is a bare-bones synopsis of the story of this novel.

One day, while he is casually supervising her play in the yard of that house, his seven-year-old daughter Celia disappears. She was a lovely child, and he was deeply devoted to her, and he will always blame himself for her disappearance.

The novel itself, as Brooks tells us in "A Note from the Author" at the beginning, consists of stories which are "a mixture of fact and speculation, and of fact shading into speculation shading into fact. I think I believed that by writing them I could rescue or resurrect my daughter, that the fact might reconstruct her as she used to be and the speculation might call her back from wherever she is today. It is not the book I hoped it would be."

It is spoiling nothing to reveal here that Celia is never found. Readers who turn pages in hopes of a "happy ending" or even an explanation of her disappearance may be disappointed. The novel that Christopher Brooks writes, or rather that Kevin Brockmeier beautifully constructs for Brooks to write, is not built with a cause-and-effect plot, with rising tension and suspense, with motives steadily revealed and solutions falling into place.

No, the pleasure of Brooks/Brockmeier's novel—and it is a deep pleasure indeed—comes from an excruciatingly poignant exploration of the effect of Brooks's loss of his daughter upon his own soul.

For a long time after her disappearance, he naturally suffers from a severe case of writer's block. Then, when he can finally write again, he produces a twelfth-century morality tale, "The Green Children," reprinted here in its entirety (and which also appeared in last year's online *Arkansas Literary Forum* and will appear in *The Year's Best Fantasy and Horror* . . . both times under Brockmeier's, not Brooks's, name).

The only clue to the twenty-page story's relevance to the novel in hand is that the girl's name in the story is spelled "Seel-ya." Academic sleuths will have fun uncovering other connections or symbols, but the main function of the story is to show us what kind of fiction comes from Brooks's mind during his distress.

Again, later in the novel, after we have been exposed to his wife Janet's addiction to movie matinees, Celia's own supposed memoir about her life and her friends, and the disintegration of Brooks's marriage, we are treated to another story from Brooks, "Appearance, Disappearance, Levitation, Transformation, and the Divided Woman," about a magician who takes a woman's son as his apprentice, a lovely story, really, but which has no connection to the Celia novel other than the resemblance of the names "Sheila, or Sally."

I should not say "no connection" because the story demonstrates Brooks's ability to perform magic, which he must do in order to make a novel out of Celia. The final words of *that* story, "the stories were never about what she thought they were about," can be taken to refer, Chinese-box-like, to this story itself.

The novel contains many such Chinese boxes, or Russian dolls, or the idea that inside of any given place or person is another more meaningful place or person. Inside of Christopher Brooks are all of his creations, including Celia, and in his effort to share them with us, he is driven to compose some of the most moving writing in the English language.

This novel is not for everyone, and some prosaic readers will be unable to accept the parts that are sheer fantasy, such as Brooks's conversations on the telephone with his missing daughter.

In the supposed memoir by Celia, she says of her father, "In the evening he stood talking on the lawn with the real people who were our neighbors, and in the morning he wrote books filled with the imaginary ones who lived only in his head, and at times I think that if I wish or pray or concentrate hard enough, I will be able to tell my story through his hands."

Fellow writers can only envy Brockmeier's felicity with prose, his elegiac tones, his lyricism that aspires to great music. *The Truth About Celia* is modest in size but not in scope, and the magnificent prose lingers in memory long after the book is closed.

All the great writers have fifteen letters in their names. Geoffrey Chaucer. Gustave Flaubert. Fedor Dostoevsky. Ernest Hemingway. William Faulkner. Scott Fitzgerald. Vladimir Nabokov. And now Kevin Brockmeier.

Winter's Bone

Daniel Woodrell
(Little, Brown, 2006)

Verdict: Finding beauty in the brutal backwoods.

DANIEL WOODRELL is the inventor and leading practitioner of country noir, a name he gave to it as a subtitle of his fifth novel, *Give Us a Kiss*. Country noir is darkened pastoral, missing the happy charm of close-to-the-soil living, focusing instead on the brutality of the backwoods.

The people in Woodrell's new, eighth novel are close to the soil, but there is not much you can do with soil in the dead of winter, the least pastoral of the Ozarks' rugged seasons. The duration of this brief novel is not simply some weeks of a harsh winter but one of those very rare snowfalls that comes and sticks and chills you to the bone.

This is the ugly Ozarks of poverty and deathly clannishness where the principal crop is nothing to harvest but something to cook: crystal meth. Nearly everyone is involved in this activity. The local bail bondsman's entire clientele is from one extended family, the Dollys.

Sixteen-year-old Ree Dolly is in a predicament that no teenage girl should ever have to face: Her father, a prime chef of meth, has jumped bail, and unless he shows for his court date, his wife and kids will find themselves homeless. The wife is mentally ill, and Ree is virtually a nurse to her, which includes cooking for her and for her young brothers. Now Ree must teach the boys how to fend for themselves while she goes out in a heroic quest for the missing father.

The kinfolk that Ree must encounter in her search for her father are an extended family of Dollys, some good, most bad. There are so many

Dollys with the given name Milton that it is necessary to give each an additional name: Blond Milton, Thump Milton, Catfish Milton—and Spider, Whoop, Rooster, Scrap, Lefty, Dog, and Punch.

The Hatfields had the McCoys to spend their aggression on, but the Dollys have only the Dollys. This profusion of characters, good and bad, is an expression of the central element of Woodrell's art, which in visual art is called expressionism: the emotional exaggeration or distortion of people, places, and things.

Just as Daumier's depiction of the poor of Paris edges up to caricature, Woodrell's people are not merely "more real than real," as critics have observed, but have assumed an invented (thus creative and artistic) reality all their own. This is the essence of expressionism as opposed to mere realism.

The winter gets colder, the story gets blacker and bleaker as Ree's search for her father probes into some of the darkest, most cutthroat elements of the pernicious Dolly clan, where her father is suspected of having been a snitch and is thus a marked man. Ree is viciously beaten by a group of Dolly women.

Jessup Dolly himself doesn't appear in the narrative until a macabre tableau toward the end, but in a sense he is the book's central character, next to his daughter. The novel revolves around him, often with high-speed revolutions that, like van Gogh's swirls, are another aspect of Woodrell's expressionism.

It is easy enough to point to Faulkner as the chief stylistic influence on Woodrell, and thereby to throw him into the camp with Raymond Chandler, Cormac McCarthy, Charles Frazier and other devout believers in the sound as well as the sense of words. But the music coming from Woodrell's banjo cannot be confused with the sounds of any other writer.

The artist that Woodrell most resembles is not a writer but a photographer, Shelby Lee Adams of the Kentucky backwoods. Like Adams, Woodrell is a native of the country he depicts and has no problem winning the trust of his kinsmen so he can get close enough to observe them and listen to them. Although Adams has been widely praised for his realism, he is just as much an expressionist as Woodrell, without even trying, for his people have a kind of built-in exaggeration.

Thus, neither Adams nor Woodrell is a documentarian, although both would seem to be, especially Woodrell with his knowledge of the "crank" drug culture. If marijuana supplanted moonshine in the backwoods culture, then meth has supplanted both of them in our own time. Compared with booze and pot, crank is an ugly drug and thus most suited for a country noir novel.

Daniel Woodrell has selected a frightful subject and populated it with the best and the worst of country people, including a courageous, audacious, resourceful sixteen-year-old girl destined to enter the pantheon of literature's heroines.

III

INTERVIEWS

⚡⚡⚡

⚡⚡⚡

IN HIS FOREWORD TO *Strong Opinions,* his own miscellany of nonfiction pieces, Vladimir Nabokov delivers a screed against the interview format:

[N]obody should ask me to submit to an interview if by "interview" a chat between two normal human beings is implied. It has been tried at least twice in the old days, and once a recording machine was present, and when the tape was rerun and I had finished laughing, I knew that never in my life would I repeat that sort of performance. Nowadays I take every precaution to ensure a dignified beat of the mandarin's fan. The interviewer's questions have to be sent to me in writing, answered by me in writing, and reproduced verbatim. Such are the three absolute conditions.

In one of the interviews included later in the volume, Nabokov also describes his characters as "galley slaves," a description that this supremely gifted control freak of an author could just as meaningfully have applied to his interviewers.

The Nabokov of the Ozarks, Donald Harington, imposed no such pre-emptive conditions on interviewers, but his deafness did generally make it necessary to submit questions to him in writing. Such is the case with the second—and, by far, the shortest—interview presented here, a set of questions that I e-mailed to Harington in the spring of 2004 to accompany my review of *With,* a brief set of exchanges included in this volume primarily for the revelations the author shares about his most successful and (arguably) most important novel. Also, it was precisely the kind of interview with the author that Harington liked to include with his own reviews, when possible, but this time with him supplying the answers instead of the questions, constructing them to suggest that they could have happened in the kind of person-to-person exchange that Nabokov had once derided before he e-mailed them back to me.

The short *With* interview also helps to illuminate tantalizing aspects of the other two, much longer, and more suggestive sets of interviews included here. The first set features Linda Hughes and Larry Vonalt, literature scholars whom Harington had befriended at the University of Missouri–Rolla (now the Missouri University of Science and Technology) when he taught there briefly as a visiting professor in the late 1970s. Sometimes singly and sometimes in tandem, they asked Harington a wide range of questions about each of the four novels that he had published to that point. These transcripts turned up unexpectedly in a search of Harington's hard drive and represent an unusually thorough commentary by the author on his early work, apparently at an early point in his career, relatively close to their publication. But they are also, almost certainly, delightful cheats on the part of the incorrigibly metafictional author, allegedly representing the kind of free-flowing in-person exchange that would have been, quite literally, impossible for the deaf Harington to engage in. He presents them as live conversations captured in a television studio, which they may (in part, anyway) have been, but Hughes (who, like Vonalt, would go on to publish several articles about Harington's work) cannot verify the existence of any such recording; moreover, even if Harington's responses were recorded live, the questions would certainly have had to be written out for him to read and respond to. And most decisively, the interviews themselves serve up plenty of internal evidence of Harington's hand not just as editor but as the playful novelist who likes to allow his characters to know of events to come in the texts before they have happened. Harington frequently indulges himself in this same kind of prescience with his interviewers' questions, as when he offers the following musings in Hughes's first interview with him, about his first published novel, *The Cherry Pit*: "Well, I think in interview number twelve, or is it interview number thirteen, I forget which interview, looking ahead to *Some Other Place. The Right Place.*, you're going to challenge me about why Daniel Lyam Montross sees death as a woman in the end when he's dying." While it's impossible to know the exact circumstances that gave rise to the original interviews, the existence of these text files on Harington's hard drive (a technology unavailable to the vast majority of consumers at the time the interviews were supposedly conducted) and the remarkably thoughtful set of polished exchanges that so thoroughly explain his early novels strongly suggest that the author was not just transcribing or even editing the exchanges but also creating them (or at least significant portions of them), lying his way to the truth.

But to whatever degree they were fictionalized, one particular aspect of these interviews immediately leaps out: Harington's comments on race and racism. Faulkner was famously haunted by race and managed (in many critics' minds) to transfer the tortured legacies of racism as a source of guilty inspiration to all subsequent Southern literature. Styron too (even as a 'non-Southern' writer, another of Harington's great teachers) published some of the most provocative twentieth-century novels on the same torturous American legacies. But as much as both of these writers inspired Harington, only one of his novels, 1965's *The Cherry Pit*, broached the same territory, seemingly unavoidable for a Southern novelist. Harington attended high school in Little Rock in the early 1950s, shortly before the Little Rock Nine helped—against considerable, violent, racist resistance—to integrate Arkansas's public-school system, so when he speaks out against the racism of his father and discusses his own friendships with kids in the black neighborhoods near his, he fills in (at least partly) a curious void in his work.[1]

Finally, the extensive "Stay More Interviews" that conclude this volume (the longest single text included here) serve as a loving cheat of a different sort, a playfully collaborative autobiography (as it were) of America's greatest unknown writer.[2] Those interviews begin with a brief prelude about the methods used in our exchanges; together with my comments in the introduction above (see pp. xi–xiv), that last prelude situates our guestroom novelist's final words in a nest of mirrors thick and teasingly skewed enough to hopefully satisfy (or at least pique) even the most skeptical of readers.

The Linda Hughes
and Larry Vonalt Interviews

The Cherry Pit, Part I

LINDA HUGHES: We're here today at the University of Missouri at Rolla on May 2, 1979, and are continuing the series of interviews with our visiting professor Donald Harington, which we began at the end of April. We'd like to devote this session to some general questions about Donald Harington's work as well as to specific questions about his first novel, *The Cherry Pit*.[1] And I would like to begin by asking a question about how you prepare for the writing of your novels. Do you map out the structure ahead of time, or do you just let the structure and the plot and the theme happen as you write? How do you begin writing each novel?

DONALD HARINGTON: Well, I have just the very least idea of what the book will be about when I start out, and I have a pretty clear idea of who the characters will be, but I just turn them loose and try to keep up with them. They usually outrun me, but I run along after them and try to follow where they're going, but they seem to, very early in the book, develop minds of their own, and it's all I can do simply to run along after them. So most of it is chance, unconscious, accidental writing.

LH: Maybe I should ask then, how do your characters get born?

DH: How do they get born? Well, I anticipate you're probably going to be asking questions about specific characters when we get to them, and I'll just wait until you get to those specific characters and tell you how those particular characters were born.

LH: Okay, fine. I'll go on to the next question then, which is, what are your cardinal rules in writing? I know I've heard you mention certain cardinal rules before. What are these?

DH: That's a tough one. Well, I would say, first of all, be funny, and if you can't be funny, be of good spirit, or of good humor, or I think, despite all of the frequent obscenities in my work, it's in good taste. So if you can't be in good humor or good spirits, you can always be in good taste. Never overwrite to the point that the reader will want to put the book down. A frequent remark made to me about my work by a lot of people who have read it is that they couldn't put it down. They had to stay up all night, and so forth. So I have a sort of built-in warning device that tells me when I have written to the point that the reader might want to put the book down, and at that point, I know that that's the place to end a chapter, or end a paragraph, or end a sentence, or whatever.

LH: What about during the composition of a novel? Do you have cardinal rules for the composition, the writing process?

DH: I don't have them written out on the wall, but I have, in my mind, I have an idea of certain things that I can do and cannot do that pop up from my unconscious when I'm composing. I couldn't recite them off the top of my head right now, but if I were in the act of composing a novel and I did something that violated one of my principles, something would tell me about it.

LH: Okay. Well, let's go on to the next question then, which is, do you think of your novels as a form of communication with the reader, and if so, what readers are you writing to? All of them? Do you write just to some readers? Do you create a certain audience in your mind, or what?

DH: Well, my ideal reader is a nonexistent person somewhere out there in the great wide world who knows as much as I do and would appreciate and enjoy reading the book as much as I would. That person does not exist except as me, but possibly, there are readers out there somewhere who can grasp what I'm trying to say and appreciate it, or if not, simply be entertained by the story. I don't ever write with any fixed reader in mind. I try very hard to blot out, for example, my editor. I don't want to write with my thoughts of my editor in mind. That would hold me back. I don't write with thoughts of any friends or relatives in mind, but just an idealized concept of some perfect reader out there who understands.

LH: Okay, very good. Let's go on then to a first specific question about your first novel, which is *The Cherry Pit*. Could you tell us what was the germ of *The Cherry Pit*? What prompted you to start writing that particular novel?

DH: Well, I wanted to write a novel, and it had to have some story to begin it with, and I had just, under very unfavorable circumstances, been visiting in Little Rock, my hometown, and happened to come across an old friend of mine from my high school days. My wife and I ran into him and a woman I suppose was his wife at one of the favorite gathering places in Little Rock. We walked to his table, and I tried to strike up a conversation with him, and he, in a sense, snubbed me. I was hoping he would invite us to sit down and chew over old times. We had been very close in high school, years before. But his snubbing me provided the inspiration for the fact that Clifford Stone in *The Cherry Pit* gets snubbed by not just one but just about all of his old high school chums. That's the germ of the concept that, not in the sense that Thomas Wolfe put it, you can't go home again because if you do go home again, it will probably lead to disappointment, disillusionment of some sort. Either your old friends won't want to see you . . . you won't want to see them.[2] And that was the theme of what *The Cherry Pit* would be about, Clifford's attempt to go back to Little Rock in search of his roots there and so forth, but he could not go home again.

LH: What you're saying, then, is that Hy Norden was very much based on a real person that you knew back in Little Rock.

DH: Oh, well, I used that person who snubbed me as a character in the book. He's, in fact, the only character in that book who is based on a real person. Everyone else in *The Cherry Pit* is more or less imaginary.

LH: Okay. How long did it take you to write *The Cherry Pit*? Did you know exactly where it was going to go when you began? Did you know it was going to have three parts, or did all this come when you started to write the novel?

DH: Well, I'll answer your first question first. It took me about a year and a half altogether to write the book. I did not know when I started it where it was going to go other than the fact that it would end with Clifford leaving Little Rock. I knew that in a sense the ending would be bittersweet or unhappy. I had not planned for it to be three particular parts. In fact, in the original draft it was something like thirty-six consecutive chapters not divided into parts. It was dramatically revised and reworked before I had finished it. Well, in a sense, to answer the end of your question, it all did come later. The structure of the book *did* come later.

LH: Okay, well let's go on then to a specific question about the first part, which begins with an epigraph that I'd like to ask you about. The epigraph is from Gerstaecker, who says, "Little Rock is . . . one of the dullest towns in the United States." Do you agree with that?

DH: No, I don't. I put that epigraph in for Clifford's sake, not for my own, and since that is the epigraph for the first part, which is "Why Have We Come Here to This Water," the question itself is a question of exasperation or futility or whatever. Why the hell have we come here to this water? Because this particular water happens to be the dullest town in the United States, or it was by . . . that epigraph by Gerstaecker was written in 1840, and back then Little Rock was a very dull town. Like all of my epigraphs . . . all the epigraphs in my books are, in a sense, little jokes, and that epigraph is the first little joke.

LH: Okay, where do you find your epigraphs? How do you go about creating them?

DH: Mostly accidental. For example, in the epigraph to the third part, "Julia and I did lately sit; Playing for sport, at Cherry-Pit," after I had finished the novel, a former student of mine at Bennett College had run across that poem by Robert Herrick in some anthology of English literature, and just sent it to me, and so I put it into the book. In the case of the Gerstaecker that you referred to previously, I was reading *Wild Sports of the Far West* to see what he had said about Arkansas and just happened to come across what he said about Little Rock. Other epigraphs are simply ones that are trite or famous or familiar, like "Cogito, ergo sum" from Descartes is . . . everybody knows that one.[3] "Fear boys with bugs," I simply got out a concordance to Shakespeare and looked under bugs to see if Shakespeare had ever mentioned bugs, and sure enough, in *The Taming of the Shrew*, Shakespeare had mentioned . . . well, the line is quoted completely out of context as you may be aware, but "Fear boys with bugs" implies that the reader should beware of Dawny and his lightning bugs.

LH: Yes. Let's go on a little further. We get all the way to page three before I have my next question. On that page, you say that the events that you cover in the novel, "lead to shame, to frustration, to disillusionment, to, yes, even tragedy." Now when you refer to tragedy, are you speaking only of the tragedy of Slater's death, or are you speaking of perhaps a larger, more subtle tragedy?

DH: Well, from Clifford's point of view, it was . . . it referred, of course, to Slater's death but also to his own tragedy of his being unable to find what he was looking for in Little Rock and having to return to Boston unfulfilled. That, for him, was the main tragedy, so I would say that that's what he's also referring to, as well as to Slater's death.

LH: To you, is that the central tragedy?

DH: Not to me, no. That's . . .

LH: I mean for Clifford.

DH: Keep in mind that, in a sense, the writing in *Cherry Pit* is a working-out of some of my own emotions about my relationship with Little Rock, but it's still Clifford's story, and I don't think of myself as Clifford, and I went to great lengths to keep from being confused with Clifford, although I didn't succeed.

LH: I noticed.

DH: I didn't succeed.

LH: Okay, no. I didn't mean was it your personal tragedy, but in your view of Clifford, is it his inability to find fulfillment that is the central tragedy of the book?

DH: I wouldn't call it exactly the central tragedy. I think I might have thought of that at one time, but under the influence of Drs. Hughes and Vonalt and Patrick,[4] I was persuaded by, the central tragedy for Clifford was his inability to communicate with other people, specifically women. For him, his inability to . . . well, of course, Little Rock is a symbol of Margaret, and his inability to communicate with Margaret is also a suggestion that he can't communicate with Little Rock. So the two tragedies are, in a sense, bound up together.

LH: Okay, let's go on to the next one, which is a slightly broader question. Clifford works for the Cabot Antiquities Foundation, which is dedicated to preserving and kind of resurrecting the vanished American past. Two questions here. First, is Clifford's immersion in VAP, as you call it, vapid? I always think of the word vapid whenever I see VAP. And secondly, is your own work kind of dedicated to the vanished American past?

DH: I'll answer those in reverse order. All of my work is, of course, about the vanished American past, except to the extent that it intrudes on the present in *The Architecture of the Arkansas Ozarks* and will continue into the present in *Farther Along*.[5] In a sense, maybe the title *Farther Along* is an attempt to get away from that obsession with the vanished American past, or the VAP, which can be vapid if you get too hung up on it, and I think Clifford was, perhaps, in his work at the Cabot Antiquities Foundation; he tended to be . . . to see his work as becoming vapid, if you mean, by "vapid," dull and boring and tedious.

LH: Okay, let's go on to another one. Still early in the book, Clifford says at one point that he wants to get away to build a log castle to hold up rather in the deep woods, and whenever I read this, I'm reminded more or less of Thoreau, and I know that you mention Thoreau explicitly in a short story of yours, which is "Artificial Respiration," published in the November 1968 issue of *Esquire*. So my question is, is Thoreau an important influence for you? Do you identify with him?

DH: Well only to the extent that Thoreau himself was very much obsessed with regaining lost values and trying to establish independence. In fact, he was, at least during the time he was at Walden, he was a loner, and the theme of the loner or the hermit appears somewhere in all of my fiction. "Artificial Respiration" is about a hermit who saves a young girl from a drowning accident. Slater in *The Cherry Pit* was essentially a loner. Dawny becomes lost in the woods in *Lightning Bug*, and so on. There are loners and hermits, like Henry Fox in *Some Other Place. The Right Place*. I'm not particular about Thoreau. I've read Thoreau several times and taught Thoreau in college, but I'm not hung up on Thoreau.

LH: Well, I don't think I was asking that. If Thoreau, then, is perhaps not an influence, I might ask, what do you read in your spare time? Do you read fiction, nonfiction, history? What do you read?

DH: I read the newspaper. Or at least . . .

LH: Unlike Thoreau.

DH: I look at the pictures. I look at the pictures in the newspaper. I read magazines. I do read fiction. I read nonfiction. I read biography. I read books on psychology. I read books on nature.

LH: But are there any authors you consider more important for you and your art than other authors?

DH: Well, I've never been asked to rank them, so I have to be careful about how I would begin to . . . in what order I would begin to mention them for fear that it would suggest the one I mention first would be the primary influence on me, and that is not true. Nabokov is perhaps the writer that I have admired most, but that does not mean that Nabokov is the writer I have been inspired by most. If I mention Faulkner, that would suggest that, like other Southern writers, I am hung up on Faulkner, and I'm not. I've never read Faulkner or any other writer while I'm writing for fear that somehow their style might creep into my own. So I've always made, going back to cardinal rules of writing, the cardinal rule that I never read fiction while I'm working on a work of fiction, but I read widely in between books. I have great admiration for, for example, John Barth, William Styron, Tom Robbins, Pynchon, Fowles. I've read most of my contemporaries. Updike. I'm very fond of Updike. I don't think he's a profound writer, but he's very entertaining. I was greatly influenced by Styron. The structure of *The Cherry Pit* is

very closely modeled after *Set This House on Fire* by Styron. So, does
that answer your question?

LH: That answers my question very nicely, yes. Thank you. Let's go on to
the next, then. At one point, Clifford implies that he's very defensive
about being from Little Rock. He mentions how it would mean a great
deal to him if this little guy from Little Rock goes back and shows how
he had been successful. Do you ever feel that being from Little Rock or
being from the "sticks of Arkansas" has stood in your way of becoming
better known more quickly?

DH: That question never bothered me until you asked it, but now that
you mention it, there's probably some truth to the fact that the rest
of the world looks upon me as a provincial writer. And to the extent
that I confine all of my work to Arkansas, that that might have had
some effect on the lack of proper appeal. But possibly to say the same
thing with Faulkner, up to a point, that the reason his works did not
really catch on in his earlier years is because he confined himself to the
small town in Mississippi, but once his critical reputation was established, the thing that attracted so many people to Faulkner was that he
was writing about a part of the country that was unfamiliar to them
and somewhat exotic to them, and exciting because of the strange way
the people acted and talked down there. That's not quite so much the
case today because of the homogenization of the American way of life
that's brought about by radio and television. I don't think people still
feel about Arkies the way they used to feel about Arkies, so I wouldn't
think that that's quite as applicable to me as it would have been to, for
example, the Southern writers of the thirties and forties.

LH: Well, okay. As long as I'm making you feel uncomfortable, I'll ask
another question like that. Clifford at one point says that his problem
is that he's oversexed, and I wonder if you are too?

DH: Well now that you mention it . . . Well, wasn't that something? [He
wipes his brow with his handkerchief].

LH: This is the last one of these.

DH: I anticipated that somebody was going to ask me that, so I did get
prepared for it by bringing it up as a philosophical question with Dr.
Robert Oakes of the Philosophy Department. We had an interesting
conversation to the effect that there is a philosophical distinction of
considerable importance between being oversexed and being highly
sexed, and Dr. Oakes was of the opinion that being highly sexed is a
highly desirable condition whereas being oversexed is an uncomfortable

condition. So let us say that I concur with my colleague Dr. Oakes that I am, yes, I am very highly sexed, but I'm not oversexed.

LH: All right, I'm glad that has been settled forever. We can go on now to something else. Clifford's father's house is located in Little Rock in an integrated neighborhood, half black, half white. And there's also . . . one of the major characters in that first novel is black, Naps Howard, and, I was wondering, growing up in Little Rock, did you yourself have opportunities to know blacks?

DH: Well my . . . I didn't live on a half-black block, but the block I lived on, the next block down the street were all blacks, and most of my best friends in childhood were blacks in Little Rock. So I had, in a sense, a double advantage of during the school year, nine months of the year, people I played with and talked with were blacks, and during the summer, people I played with and talked with were hillbillies. So instead of having a conventional childhood of growing up with kids like myself, I am, in a sense, half black and half hillbilly.

LH: Were you aware of racial tension as you grew up, or did you just think that everybody got along well with blacks?

DH: Oh, I was very aware of racial conflict. My father was a real racist. He hated to hear me, or hear of me, running around with "niggers," and let alone eating at the house with "niggers," and he never lost an opportunity to use the word "*nigger*" around me. He was still doing it when my children were growing up, and the closest I ever came to getting in a fight with my father was after he'd been throwing that word "*nigger*" around in the presence of my children. I grabbed him by the collar and said, "Dad, you can say that all you want to around me, but I don't want my kids hearing it," and he got kind of red in the face and never used the word again. But I was very aware of race, hatred, the racial crisis that existed, and I never felt racist sentiments myself because these were my friends and my playmates. I grew up with them, and I didn't care what color their skin was.

LH: Let's go on to another problem person, let's say, which is . . . we have Wes Stone again who talks about Faubus in the novel. It is very ambivalent. How did you feel about Orval Faubus growing up and now?

DH: Well, in a sense, I've already answered that by saying that I never felt any race prejudice myself, and I despise Faubus for the stand that he took during the racial crisis. As a matter of fact, that was indirectly responsible for my going into exile away from Arkansas. I was so . . . from 1958, when we left Arkansas, the year after the racial crisis, I was so ashamed of what Faubus had done, the disgrace that he brought upon my hometown of Little Rock, the disgrace he brought upon the whole state of Arkansas. I wanted to get just as far away from it as I could, so we left Arkansas and went to Boston. Ironically, twenty years later Boston was having its own racial crisis, but by then, I no longer lived in Boston.

LH: Okay, let's go to a different kind of question, then, which has to do with the style of *Cherry Pit*. There are a lot of Latin phrases throughout the book. Clifford has studied Latin and knows it very well, and it makes me wonder about your own background. Have you studied the Latin language? Have you immersed yourself in the classics, or what?

DH: The only course I ever flunked in school was ninth-grade Latin. I made an F in ninth-grade Latin and never did, never did take any more of it. And all of those Latin phrases that Clifford uses, just to make him more pedantic. All those phrases are out of the paperback *International Guide to Foreign Terms and Expressions*. You know that book?

LH: You've just changed your image entirely.

DH: Well, I don't want to leave the impression that I can spout off Latin the way Clifford could.

LH: Okay, let's go on to another one, then, to a different kind of language matter, which is Clifford's relationship to the word. It's a very curious relationship, almost a solipsistic one. He locks himself up in the bathroom to write in his Ringmaster notebook. He goes to the library and reads his own article; he doesn't read anybody else. He cannot communicate with others, mostly with himself. Do you believe that writing can become a retreat and a separation from the world rather than a connecting link with it, or are you just saying that writing is a very lonely profession?

DH: Well, I would have to say that I feel that, since words are the tools of my trade, that that's really the only way you can communicate in terms of ideas, and so . . . well, words, words are solipsistic to the extent that I hear you talking to me. I hear myself talking to me, but I could just be imagining that, unless . . . I mean these words are just up here in the air, but if you type those words and put them down on the page, then on the page they become less solipsistic. They become more tangible, more believable. That's why, for me, the written word is the most important form of communication.

LH: Because it is more solid and less abstract? Okay, interesting. That leads to a different kind of question. I think maybe you've answered this, but I'll ask it anyway. In a lot of critical circles today, there's much said about the instability of language and of structure. Texts disintegrate or collapse from within, or there is no real structure, we just imagine it. Also that novels really are non-referential. They are self-contained. They have nothing to do with the outside world. What do you have to say to that?

DH: That's a lot of crap. Like your question on, well, your question that called my attention for the first time to the fact that I might have been provincial in my writing only about Arkansas, that's a concept that is news to me, in a sense. I've heard a little bit about it, the concept that William Gass had that the novel's existence depends only on itself and has no reference to any reader. It's like saying that if a tree falls in the forest and no one's around to hear it, that it makes no sound. Well, maybe it does make no sound if there are no ears to hear it, but the ears are the most important thing for the sound. The reader's mind is the most important thing for the work. The work has no validity or existence without a reader to interpret it, to experience . . . if you're talking about fiction, the story has no independent life of its own apart from a reader to visualize and to experience that story. If communication or the use of language is breaking down, that's news to me too, although you can see evidence of it in a lot of trash that people read. And possibly . . . I haven't taught English in college for about fourteen years, so I don't know just how bad student writing is becoming these days, but I've heard rumors to the effect that it's really getting worse and worse. Is that true? Let me ask you a question. Can I ask you a question, Dr. Hughes?

LH: Yes, yes, you may. I'm the eternal optimist, and I think the swing is coming back up around. I think it hit bottom about two years . . .

DH: It bottomed out?

LH: Yes, I think so.

DH: Good.

LH: Let's go on then to another one. You've mentioned . . . you've answered this partly, but I'll, there's more to the question, so I'll ask it anyway. Clifford, at one point, says that Little Rock is a masculine town. He's going back where women are women and men are men, and it's a tough Western town, but as you've pointed out, Margaret is also associated very much with the city of Little Rock. This prompted me to ask, are you saying that the roots of our existence, because this is the hometown of both of them, are always kind of androgynous, or looking

ahead to a later novel, they were bigeminal, the two sexes? Is this what
you're getting at, with calling it both a masculine and a feminine town?

DH: Well, Clifford calls it a masculine city very early in the book. That's
the way he's been thinking of the city, of perhaps tying up the city of
Little Rock in his mind with his father, and the scene with his father
suggests that that's what he thinks of Little Rock as being, masculine.
But in the course of the book, I think he becomes more and more
aware that, as he says on the very last page . . . the masculine reference
is almost right up in the front, and on the very last page, he discovers,
in his leaving Little Rock, that the town itself was the mother that he
was looking for. And suddenly, he realizes that his mother . . . his own
mother's been dead for years, and Margaret accuses him of seeing her
as a mother figure after he accuses her of seeing him as a father figure
and so forth, but he does, in the end, see her as, or see the city of Little
Rock as, a feminine creature. But it's a little bit of both, and there is a
lot of androgyny in all of my fiction, and the whole concept of bigeminal does relate to the fact that this is a building that has two doors. The
one door happens to be male, and the other door happens to be female.
I think there's a little bit of both sexes in all of us.

LH: Okay, well that leads very naturally to my next question then. How do
you view the relationship of men and women in general? Do you think
it's easy for them to communicate? Are there barriers between them?
What do you think?

DH: Well, yes, natural barriers. Always have been, not just between
human men and women. All male and female creatures have natural,
physical barriers between themselves. There are barriers of communication, inability to make oneself understood to the other. I've explored
that in all of my fiction. Barriers of misinterpretation, people not knowing how the other person really feels, and then the biggest barrier of all
is, of course, the barrier of not being willing to reveal all of oneself to
the other. That is what provided Henry Fox's definition of love in *Some
Other Place. The Right Place.* to the effect that love is being willing to
share all of yourself with someone else, to keep no secrets back from the
other person. I think men and women are often much too devious with
one another, much too closed in on themselves. In the case of Clifford,
it's probably a self-protective device. He was conditioned over the years
of opening himself up too much to Pamela; he had to start withholding
himself from Pamela, and that created a vicious circle.

LH: But you are optimistic that men and women can relate?

DH: Well, I think, in recent years, possibly as a result or a side effect of the women's liberation movement, giving women more sense of identity of their own, that things have been looking up ever since. I think that for centuries, up until the 1960s, that was one of the major obstacles to relationships between men and women was the fact that women were expected to remain in the home, raise families, do all the housecleaning. Women were, in effect, slaves, and once they were liberated from that slavery, it gave them the experience of establishing their own identity and having a self-respect that they needed in order to have . . . they could not love their mates unless they were able to respect themselves, and being able to respect themselves enabled them to improve relationships greatly with men. And I think men have profited from that almost as much as women have.

LH: Yes, well, I would hope so.

DH: Would you agree?

LH: Oh, I would hope so. That's the whole point, is to make everybody happier. Let's go on, then, to specifically a female character in your novel. Margaret is the female protagonist of *The Cherry Pit*, and she's suspected of being slightly crazy, or at least, Clifford is afraid that she's slightly crazy, and this made me think of the female protagonist of your next novel, who is Latha Bourne, who is called by another character "crazy as a quilt," and who spends time in an insane asylum for a while. But at the same time they may be called crazy by somebody else, I think they are enormously attractive characters, and so my question is again twofold. Are you dealing with this concept of nonconformity as a kind of heightened insanity? And you're not dealing with the idea of female hysteria, are you?

DH: Oh, no. I wouldn't call it hysteria, but neurosis. This, in a sense, this question is related to your previous question about relationship between the sexes. One thing that woman's place in society did to her was to make her highly susceptible to neurosis. On one hand, it was crippling. On the other hand it also added to the . . . it still does. I don't mean to be using the past tense. It still does add, to a certain extent, to the mystery that the male feels about the female. And to Clifford, to me, Margaret and Latha and other female characters that I have used have been somewhat strange, but not crazy. Crazy is not the word, I don't believe, for Margaret or Latha, but they've been unusual. That's what has drawn the men to those women, is that you can't stereotype Margaret, you can't stereotype Latha, you can't stereotype Diana Stoving, any of the

Ingledew women. And I have . . . back to my cardinal rules, one of
the cardinal rules is to avoid stereotypes, avoid conventional, ordinary
people. So I've tried to make my women a little bit peculiar just to make
them more alluring.

LH: Well, I think they are that. Another question, then, related to the
women. Neither Margaret nor Latha will leave their hometowns. In
both cases, their lovers say, "Come with me. We'll go away from here,"
and they both staunchly refuse. Of course, it shows their strength as
women, their very strong, independent spirits. Are you also implying
that it's necessary for all of us to cling to our roots, to stay where we
know who we are?

DH: Well, both Margaret and Latha are, to some extent, personifications of their towns, so I think, well the . . . I'm not generalizing about
the women as our roots because then that would imply that they could
only be female roots. No. They have to be both . . . roots are both male
and female, but the women can be personifications of their town.

LH: Why?

DH: Well, we've already explored the question of why is Margaret a personification of Little Rock.

LH: But why women rather than men to personify a town?

DH: Well, I think in interview number twelve, or is it interview number
thirteen, I forget which interview, looking ahead to *Some Other Place.
The Right Place.*, you're going to challenge me about why Daniel Lyam
Montross sees death as a woman in the end when he's dying. He sees
death as a woman and all of her emblazoned radiance coming to blind
him so that he could see his way to reach her dazzling breast, blah blah
blah. Well, in interview thirteen, remind me to . . . when I explain how
death is a woman, I will also explain why towns are women. Okay?

LH: Okay, let's take one more question on a female character and then I
think we'll continue this later. The novel ends without our knowing
what becomes of Margaret. Her fate is kind of left hanging in the air.
Do you have, in your own mind, a notion of what happened to her, and
will we ever see her again in any of your work?

DH: Well, I let my characters that are not going to be used again, I let
them live their independent lives thereafter to do what they feel like,
but I did hear that Margaret had married an architect in Little Rock
and had been married to this architect for several years, but it was
not a very happy marriage. Clifford will reappear in a future work of
fiction but will not have any particular desire to look her up again,

even though he has heard something to the effect that she's not very happy with this architect she married. That, of course, is all symbolic, because modern architects recently have really messed up the appearance of Little Rock townscape.

LH: Okay, well, I think we'll conclude for now and take it again.

DH: See you later!

The Cherry Pit, Part II

LH: Today is May 3, 1979, at the University of Missouri at Rolla, and we are continuing the second part of an interview with Donald Harington on *The Cherry Pit*. When we left off last time, we were talking about Margaret, and today, I'd like to move on to some of the other characters in the novel as well as some general questions about your art. One person we haven't mentioned too much is Naps Howard, who is the black major character in your novel, and at one point, we find out a little bit about Naps's name, and I'm wondering if Naps's name is symbolic. He says at one point that he's named after a town that's been washed away, one that's mentioned in Mark Twain's *Life on the Mississippi*. And it suddenly occurs to me, after all, Clifford is dealing with the past of his own that has been lost, washed away, and that can't be recovered. Is there some kind of connection there?

DH: Well, I wasn't thinking of that when I wrote the book. As I pointed out in the book, Naps's name is symbolic of the fact that he is, as his wife sees it, that he is nappy-haired, which was an expression that blacks used to refer to nappy hair, the ulotrichous race, as I put it, but the fact that he was named after the vanished town of Napoleon in Mark Twain's *Life on the Mississippi* does symbolize that Naps represents a vanished way of life that he is still clinging to, just as the vanished American past is past and cannot be recaptured. The way of life that Naps represents, as far as blacks are concerned, is also gone away.

LH: Did you think of Clifford and Naps as a kind of foil for each other?

DH: In a way, yes. Not so much a foil as a kind of complementary. Well, Clifford had known Naps when he was growing up and assimilated parts of Naps's culture, and vice versa. And in the action of the book, they tend to help each other, complement each other, rather than to be a foil.

LH: Okay, thanks. Turning to two other characters, we have Margaret and Dall, D-A-L-L, she calls him Doyle, but there's a curious kind of, what shall I say, parallelism between those two in that they both have something to do with dolls, D-O-L-L-S. Margaret owns a collection of rag dolls, and Doyle, or Dall, has a caricature of a black man, which in the early stages of the book, he is training his dog to attack. Do dolls have some kind of special significance for you? Is there some reason you're interested in them?

DH: Well, they must to the extent that in *Farther Along*, which I'm working on now, a doll, a living doll, plays a significant part in that, and also, one of the characters in *Farther Along*, he thinks of his ten fingers in terms of dolls that represent characters in the book that interreact. I think that's all part of what might in broad terms be called a Chinese box effect in all of my writing, that here I am as the author, here are my characters that I manipulate and think of as dolls, and then my characters in turn have their dolls, and so on down into the Chinese box. That's, well . . . I'll confess that I had, myself, I had, when I was very young, a rag doll that my mother made for me. I was very attached to it. I also entertained myself by playing with paper-doll soldiers that I would cut out and stick a pin through one hand to represent the swords that they were holding, and they would fight with the swords. I would put them around three-dimensionally in a bush and stage battles between these paper-doll soldiers, and that probably was crucial or significant in terms of my learning how to manipulate creatures of my own invention.

LH: That's very interesting. Did you imbue them with a personality? Did your dolls have personalities that you gave to them?

DH: Well, I don't think I made up individual personalities for them, but I did see them as imaginary creations. I was very attached to that rag doll that Mother made me . . . maybe some sort of Oedipal transfer. I couldn't love my mother, so I loved the doll that she made for me, and I gave the doll a personality, and, in a sense, maybe unconsciously these dolls in my work have some relationship to that doll that I had. The doll is an important symbolic metaphor in most of my fiction, not just *The Cherry Pit*.

LH: Yes, yes. Okay, that brings us to another of your creations then, which is James Royal Slater, the dramatist who ends up committing suicide at the end of the novel. And you've been known to say that although you don't exactly admire Slater, maybe not as an artist nor as a man, you do feel a certain affinity with him. Could you explain what you mean by that affinity you feel for Slater?

DH: Well, I have to have an affinity for all of my characters, and in a sense, Slater is the only villain in *The Cherry Pit*. I dislike villains in general, but in order to make a villain convincing, I have to feel some affinity for him, and in the case of Slater, I have to project some of my own bad qualities into him and also to try to imagine what would be the source of his disillusionment or disenchantment with modern life in order to write his suicide note and make it a convincing suicide note. I recall that as I was writing *The Cherry Pit*, I was sending it in, section by section, to my editor, and when I sent in that section with Slater's suicide note, he demanded to know where I had copied that because he refused to believe that I had just simply made it up. It is purely a fabrication. I did not copy Slater's suicide note from anyone else's suicide note. I was trying to imagine, if I were forty-nine years old, had the same problems as that poor son of a bitch did, that . . . what would I say in my last statement to the world to explain my reasons for killing myself? And I did feel, just as Clifford did . . . Clifford, although Slater in his suicide note had said some bad things about Clifford, that he hoped that his own afflictions would be transferred to Clifford, Clifford still felt sorry for him and regretted the fact that he never met him. And by the way, Slater never appears in *The Cherry Pit*. I don't know if anyone ever noticed that, but deliberately, Slater never appears in person in *The Cherry Pit*. Other people talk about him, but he's never there. I dislike death very much, and if anyone's going to die in *The Cherry Pit*, I wanted it to be offstage, so Slater never actually appears.

LH: Okay, well now you've made me have about three or four more questions. First of all, a nasty question. What are your bad qualities?

DH: Well, like Slater, I'm something of a hermit, wrapped up in a world of my own. I think, even though I didn't know the word at the time, I suspect that Slater was also a solipsist like myself, and if you are a solipsist, you can't really relate to other people. Slater was a bit of a fool, and I'm a fool, in many respects. Slater was a dramatist of the absurd, and although I have complete contempt for theater of the absurd and was trying to express that in what I said about Slater, you could make a pretty strong case for the fact that there is an absurd quality about much of my fiction.

LH: Well, I don't see you as a fool. Why are you a fool?

DH: Well, a fool is someone who really can't come to grips with life, someone who is not able to take things in stride and deal with reality in a "realistic" way, and often gets into scrapes or trouble or personal anguish as a result of being unable to deal with the reality of life.

LH: Yes, but fools, as in Shakespeare, often speak the truth as well, yes? Okay, another question related to what you just said. I did notice that Clifford and Slater never appear together. I guess maybe I wasn't catching on to what you said, but is Slater a kind of double for Clifford?

DH: To the extent that I use doubles in all of my fiction, or doppelgängers, then Slater is a doppelgänger for Clifford in a way. That Clifford will, eventually, when he gets older, take on some of Slater's qualities, and as Clifford remarks in the book about Slater's suicide note, "I almost could have written that myself." At the age of twenty-eight, he's not quite ready to write that, but when he gets into his forties, he could possibly have protested in the same way that Slater did, and curiously enough, many of the things that Slater specifically objects to are still around, like Richard Nixon, California, ZIP code, TV, card games. All of the things that Slater detests are still with us fifteen years later.

LH: Okay, one other question. I was going to ask this later, but I'll ask now. Are Slater's afflictions transferred to Clifford as Slater hopes they will be?

DH: Not so much the physical, the specific physical afflictions that Slater has. What were they? Gout, lumbago . . .

LH: Constipation.

DH: Yeah, all of those things. The physical afflictions of Slater are not so much transferred to Clifford, but his general disillusionment with himself, with the modern world, with civilization, all of those things, are transferred to Clifford in *Farther Along*.

LH: Okay, we will watch for that. Let's go on to a different matter then. Why is Clifford's middle name Willow? It occurred to me his middle name might be Willow because his story is sad. Were you thinking about it . . . ? Willows weep, you know, and they're by rivers.

DH: Weeping willows. That was not my intention, at least not consciously. I just needed to give him a middle name, and as usual . . . my habit, naming characters, I think up a first name and then wonder what would go well with that first name and lead up to the last name. The best example of that was in *Some Other Place*. that Daniel Lyam Montross, the three names flow into one another, literally, that the last letter of the first name is the first letter of the second name, and so forth. In the case of Clifford Willow Stone, it's just trying to get a rhythmic name, and I needed . . . Willow just popped into my mind out of the blue, so it doesn't have any special significance.

LH: Okay, what about getting at the first name? How do you arrive at even selecting the first name? Does it just occur to you?

DH: I just wanted a name that seemed to fit that particular personality, and Clifford, which is not a very common name . . . I could have called him Ronald, or Lawrence, or whatever, but Clifford seemed to fit his personality, so that's why I used it. I was not thinking of the significance of cliffs or fjords or any conscious meaning of the name.

LH: Are you saying then that when your characters are born in your mind, they have their personality first and then you name them?

DH: Well it sort of works both ways. They have a vague personality, and then I give them a name, and the name tends to shape their personality as I go along. I have a Latha in *Lightning Bug*. I had just a vague idea of what sort of woman she would be, and I had her name, Latha, but the name itself began to make her into the sort of person that she was.

LH: Okay, well, I'll ask one more question about Clifford's name. I have a feeling the answer is no, but I'll ask it anyway. Because Clifford is concerned with going home again and finding that he can't, it occurred to me to ask, is his last name Stone in any way connected with the epigraph to Thomas Wolfe's *Look Homeward, Angel*, which is "A stone, a leaf, an unfound door," yes?

DH: I had not read *Look Homeward, Angel* at the time I wrote *The Cherry Pit*. I don't have much admiration for Wolfe as a writer, and I certainly did not intend any connection between Stone and . . . well I didn't know the epigraph at the time I named Clifford Stone. There are lots of Stones in the Ozarks. It's a common family name. My great-great-grandmother was a Stone, and that's probably why I picked that particular name, because it is Ozarkian and there's Stone County in the Ozarks.

LH: Okay, well I'll ask a question related to what you just said. Clifford has an Ozark grandmother. Is she anything like your own Ozark grandmother?

DH: No, not at all. Just as I bent over backwards to make myself unlike Clifford by making him a little guy . . . he's very self-conscious about being small, being a pebble or stone, or "little rock" . . . I bent over backwards to make his grandmother . . . she's big, and my grandmother was a very small woman. She's very garrulous and outspoken, and my grandmother was very reticent, so there's really no resemblance between his grandmother and mine.

LH: Okay.

DH: Or for that matter between his father and mine, or his sister and mine. They're all as different from myself as I can make them.

LH: Okay. All right. Another issue that intrigued me was the number of fairytale elements in your fiction. In *The Cherry Pit*, we get references to Hans Christian Andersen's "The Red Shoes," we get a reference to "Rapunzel." In *Lightning Bug*, there's a reference to "Sleeping Beauty." "Cinderella" is also mentioned in *The Cherry Pit*. Have you always had a particular interest in fairy tales? Did you read them a lot when you were young, or do you think they end up popping up in your own fiction because they have certain affinities with folklore?

DH: Well that's like asking, "Have you always had an interest in Thomas Wolfe?" I had not read Thomas Wolfe when I wrote *Cherry Pit*. I had not read any fairy tales when I wrote *Cherry Pit*. My oldest daughter at the time of writing *Cherry Pit* was about one and a half, two years old, not quite old enough to have fairy tales read to her, and I had never read any fairy tales until I started reading fairy tales to her, with the exception of I made a point of reading Hans Christian Andersen's "The Red Shoes" in order to make the reference to "The Red Shoes" in *Cherry Pit* authentic, but I had not read, I did not have fairy tales read to me as a child, and I did not read fairy tales until I was reading them to my children.

LH: Do you think fairy tales do have connections with folklore, or do they seem very different from folklore?

DH: You mean my own fairy tales, or fairy tales in general?

LH: No, fairy tales as a genre, yes.

DH: They are very much a part of folklore, but the fairy tale as we know it, "Jack and the Beanstalk" and so forth, is hardly known in the Ozarks. The Ozark oral tradition of tales can be traced to fairy tales, but they're in completely different form.

LH: Okay. Well let's move on almost to the end of my questions on *Cherry Pit*. Coming back to something you mentioned earlier, which was Slater's suicide note, there's a very curious format with the . . . well, earlier, before he writes the suicide note, he's written a poem, and it kind of prefigures his suicide note, and it's completely comprised of three-letter words, and it almost looks like a computer printout. Is there any particular significance to this poem he writes to himself with just three-letter words? Dall wonders if there is perhaps a secret code embodied in that poem. Is there?

DH: Well, there's not a code or a secret message or anything. He's . . . Slater's just showing off. Another bad quality Slater has is being a showoff, and possibly that's the reason he attributed the poem to

Dall Hawkins. It was at least signed by Dall Hawkins. Of course, Dall Hawkins did not write that three-letter-word poem, and as a matter of fact, James Royal Slater did not write that three-letter-word poem. I wrote the three-letter-word poem. I was just showing off to see if you could write a poem consisting of three-letter words, and I think I brought it off.

LH: Oh, I think you did too. Do you show off a lot?

DH: I'm always showing off in my prose. My prose is a constant tour de force from beginning to end in every book.

LH: Okay, I would agree. All right, well, speaking of secret messages though, I think there are some, somewhere . . . I've always wondered, you always carry three-by-five little cards in your pocket, and you're always writing things down. What do you do with those?

DH: Well, I have, at last count, I had four metal file boxes that I refer to as my incubators, and they're arranged by category, subdivision, days, so forth, and I file them in the incubators. Some of them I never see again. Some of them become specific lines in the book. Some of them are simply philosophical ideas that occur to me or fragments of dialogue that I want to use. Ideas for short stories. I've got about eighty-seven cards of outlined short stories I'll probably never get around to writing, but they all go into the incubator. In the case of *Farther Along*, I completely overdid it. The incubator for *Farther Along* has something like ten thousand cards, and when you get that many cards, it's a distraction. I do much better without so many cards.

LH: But it's kind of like a portable journal then?

DH: Yes, a sortable as well as portable. It's a sortable as well as portable journal.

LH: Could you tell us any of the categories, or are those . . . ?

DH: Plot, characterization, dialogue, future novels, future short stories, that sort of thing.

LH: Okay, very interesting. Well, I'll ask one more question, and then we will really conclude our discussion, and that is quite simply, why did you name the novel *The Cherry Pit*?

DH: Well, like most of my titles it's deliberately ambiguous. All of my titles can have different meanings. *Some Other Place. The Right Place.* can be interpreted as referring to . . . well, it's used within the book in many different contexts. It's repeated throughout the book to mean some other place, the right place, and even in one place in the book, we get some other place, the wrong place. But *The Cherry Pit*, the original idea for *Cherry Pit* was, it came from a quote from William Styron when he was interviewed in Paris right after *Set This House on Fire* came out, and the interviewer asked him, "Why do you think *Set This House on Fire* was attacked?" and he said, "Well, we have in America a saying, 'life is a bowl of cherries', and writers who write about the pits are not very popular." So that was the first source for *The Cherry Pit*, and as a matter of fact, the comic writer Erma Bombeck recently came out with a book with the title *If Life is a Bowl of Cherries, What Am I Doing in the Pits?* So that's, in a sense, the second meaning of the title, that Little Rock is a pit in which Clifford falls into the pit. The other is that the outside of the cherry is sweet, but the pit is hard, and in a sense, Clifford is biting into that sweet cherry in the book, but then he bites into the cherry pit. A third possible meaning is the fact that cherry is slang for virginity, and Margaret still has her virginity, and Clifford never gets her cherry, he only gets the pit. A fourth possible meaning is a reference to the poem that's quoted as the epigraph for the third part from Robert Herrick, "Julia and I did lately sit; Playing for sport, at Cherry-Pit," which was a game during . . . when was Robert Herrick . . . ?

LH: Seventeenth century.

DH: Seventeenth century. Popular game in England, seventeenth century. I don't know how the game was played but, "She cast; I threw; and having cast; She got the Pit, and I the Stone." Actually, in the Herrick poem, it's the other way around, but I deliberately misquoted Herrick to make it fit, that she is left with Little Rock, the pit, and he is left with the stone, and not only the stone of Clifford Stone, but also he's left with stone as slang expression for stone-ache, which he is left with after this game that leaves him unfulfilled.

LH: All right, thank you very much. This concludes our interview on *The Cherry Pit*. We look forward to hearing from you some more on your later novels. Thank you.

Some Other Place. The Right Place.

LARRY VONALT: This is May 8, 1979, and we are going to talk about the third novel of Donald Harington's, called *Some Other Place. The Right Place.* This is the novel. [He holds up a copy of the novel.] Mr. Harington has been talking with us for the past week about his various novels, and this novel, *Some Other Place. The Right Place.*, is probably

Mr. Harington's most risk-taking novel. It is risk-taking because he uses the theme and subject of reincarnation. [He turns towards an empty chair.] When and why did you choose reincarnation as a subject?

LV: That's an extremely interesting answer. Now, related to this theme of reincarnation is, I think, the subject or theme of doubles that you deal with in *The Cherry Pit* and *Lightning Bug*. Dawny is like Every; Dall and Nub Stone share certain characteristics. We might think of Day representing the sun, Diana the moon. Can you comment on what you think of the subject of doubles in *Some Other Place. The Right Place.?*

LV: I had really never thought about doubles that way in the novel before. That really surprises me that you see it that way, but I think you're absolutely right, that doubles work that way. Now, to continue with the theme of doubles and the theme of reincarnation, for much of the book, one of the main symbols in the book is the tree, or trees, and we know from classic mythology that trees are inhabited with spirits and so forth. Do you see in any way how trees and doubles and reincarnation work in this novel, and would you talk about that?

LV: You know, I had forgotten that part of the novel where Charity goes and climbs a tree, and then Day climbs a tree and he's thinking about having a climax when he hangs . . . he's going to hang himself. That's also very interesting. I'm done.

LV: The second novel you wrote, which is unpublished, is called *A Work of Fiction.* It seems to me that *Some Other Place. The Right Place.* could be called *A Work About Fiction.* I say this because you use so many different forms of writing to tell the story: Diana's diary, Day's attempt to write it, Daniel's poems, and then Daniel himself speaks to G, who is to write the story. Do you think that this novel is centrally concerned with the nature of fiction?

[Donald Harington appears on camera,
sits in the chair next to Dr. Vonalt.]

DH: Is that any better, Dr. Vonalt?
LV: Yes, much better, much better.
DH: You'd rather have me here in person . . .
LV: Oh, yes.
DH: . . . than a reincarnation of my spirit?
LV: That's right, that's right. I think it's much better.
DH: You feel more comfortable that way?
LV: Yes, yes, much more comfortable.
DH: You'll get a real answer?

LV: Well, I hope so.

DH: Well, all of my fiction has been concerned with the nature of fiction, and in *Some Other Place.* particularly, the book is about the writing of fiction. The use of all the different voices in the book is an attempt to explore the ways that . . . I had a really hard time getting here. Let me take my coat off. You don't know what I went through to reenter this world.

LV: What was it that called you back?

DH: Well, I had some unpleasant memories of previous incarnations in this particular world, and when the agent came up and said, "Would you go back in reality and be there with him in person?", I said, "Leave me out this time." I said, "Well, what's in it for me?" and the agent said, "Absolutely nothing, except whatever satisfaction you might get out of giving your friends one last look at you in the flesh." I said, "Do you mean I have to take my clothes off?" He said, "No, but you can unbutton your shirt if you get too hot."

LV: You're not getting hot right now, are you?

DH: So do you mind if I unbutton my shirt?

LV: No, I don't mind.

DH: Will the camera pick up all the hair on my chest?

LV: Yes, that's pretty white. I don't know if it will or not. Now, talking about looking at you, seeing you in the flesh, brings me to the question about voyeurism in the novel. That is one of the main thrusts of the book, I think, and I wanted to know if you thought that voyeurism, other than its prurient interests and so forth, is somehow related to your idea of fiction.

DH: Yes, the author himself is the main voyeur into his characters, and in my own fiction, I'm trying to have the reader participate with me in being a voyeur into . . . I think the central pleasure that we get out of fiction comes from the fact that the reader . . . well, voyeurism by definition is the pleasure that you get out of secretly watching other people do things, and in a good work of fiction, the reader is a detached observer. He can open that window and become a Peeping Tom at any time, and in a sense, the pleasure that the author gets from peeping, he tries to communicate to the reader. So, all of the peeping that occurs in *Some Other Place. The Right Place.* is simply a reflection of the peeping that the reader and the author are doing.

LV: Do you think that this peeping, spying, is also related to a concept that we're going to [bring] up and talk about later in our discussion today, and that is of the It, and the relationship of one person's It to another person's It, and in being a spy, one is trying to gain control or gain power over the other person's It?

DH: I don't think I would put it that way, that you're trying to gain control or power over the other person's It, but the idea of the It as the core of your being is . . . in a sense what the It seeks to do is merge itself or surrender itself to the other, and that's a completely different concept from the idea of gaining power or control over the It.

LV: Okay. I wanted to ask you, the book begins with a line from Robert Frost's poem "Directive," and in that poem, Frost speaks of "the children's house of make-believe," and Diana says that her trouble is that she can't find anything to believe in, and she would like very much to find something to believe in. Now, I have a couple of questions. One, can you comment on the relationship of Frost's poem to the novel? For example, why did you use the poem to get you into the action of the novel? And then, secondly, can you comment on the relationship between belief and fiction as you think it's formulated or shaped in the novel?

DH: Well, how did the first line of the book begin, with the words "Back out of all this now too much for us, as the poet Frost once began a piece called 'Directive,' there is a town that is no more a town." That's all a direct quote from Robert Frost and refers to the . . . in a sense, the book is the story of young people who have become disenchanted with the world that they grew up in, the world they live in, and they want to get to that, back out of all this now too much for us, which is a very nice poetic way of expressing the idea of the vanished past, the lost places in the heart, in Diana's search for something to believe in. She can't believe in the here and now. She would like to have something to believe in. She wants to believe that there is a Daniel Lyam Montross. To anticipate your . . . are you going to ask me about solipsism? Sometime you are?

LV: Yes.

DH: Well, to anticipate that question and to join that question to this one, the book can be seen as happening solipsistically to each of the persons in the story, and if you want to, you can say that Diana is just imagining all of this. She wants to believe in something, so she brings up Day to be the reincarnation of her grandfather and to serve as the catalyst, and she chooses him because he has Boy Scout skills, and he's just the perfect person that she needs in order to go through this experience that she can believe in.

LV: Which I was just thinking that she even buys him a violin to play like her grandfather played a violin, so that kind of thing.

DH: Yes.

LV: You mention solipsism. How do you see or how do you understand solipsism, and what does it mean to you? What is solipsism?

DH: Well, the philosophy goes back to, I think I mention in the book, Descartes's famous dictum about "I think, therefore I am." That's the only real philosophical proof of existence, that you know you think, therefore you are. But how can you prove that the other exists? There is no philosophical proof that . . . I think you are, therefore, you exist, but that's just I think you are, therefore, I think the rest of the world exists only in my imagination, and the rest of the world performs, or misperforms, as I would want it to.

LV: I was thinking, I think it's in the Fourth Movement of the book when G. gets chiggers and he says, "I itch, therefore I am."

DH: I itch, therefore I am.

LV: You're sort of playing on that which appeared in, I guess, the Second Movement when the Descartes thing is mentioned.

DH: The only real physical proof of the fact that somebody else exists is that you cannot, I think Jacob Ingledew may have mentioned this in *Architecture*, that a person cannot, as hard as you try, you cannot tickle yourself, but you can tickle somebody else. You can tickle somebody else; therefore, that is proof . . .

LV: That someone else exists.

DH: Yes, but you can't possibly tickle yourself.

LV: The poem of a lost town that Daniel writes talks about "A town is a tournament of two," but before that, there are a couple of lines where he talks about one, and then out of one comes more, comes another, and then another, and another, and in the Fourth Movement, G. is going to become like a ghost town, that somehow he too . . . one person can make a town, and you deal a lot in your fiction with hermits and so forth, but you also deal with communities, mostly dying communities, but what's the relationship between solipsism and community?

DH: Well, I think in that poem you're referring to, it says that a town is but a tournament of two, but it takes at least two to make the community. The solipsist has to find another and be able to accept the existence of that other, and in a way, to give up part of his own identity in order to make a perfect union with the other, and once that happens he is no longer a solipsist, if he can believe that the other . . . well, one of two things . . . either that he can believe that he is not any longer a solipsist or else the other person is also a solipsist.

LV: I was thinking about [Diana] perhaps like the idea of the muse. The artist has his muse, and there's someplace in the book where Diana says to Day, "Well you might be a writer after all," and he says, "Yes, but I would need you there to turn me on."

DH: Right, that's a very good example of . . . well it's right after that, just a few pages after that, when the notion first occurs to Day, when Day is writing his journal, that Diana is simply someone that he dreamed up, that she isn't real, that she is his ideal of the perfect person. But a few pages before that, he had recognized that, in order for him to be a writer, he would need Diana around to turn him on.

LV: I was thinking, too, about . . . while we're still here on the subject of writing and solipsism and so forth, one of the things I found curious in the book was Day's pride in his writing, that at the end of the Third Movement, after we've gone through most of Daniel's poems, Day says, "Well I told it as good as he did in his poems. I told it as well in my own writing of the thing." This need to maintain one's sense of self, I guess, is how I see it, but maybe you see it [in] a different kind of way and want to talk about that a little bit.

DH: Well, everyone is trying to tell Daniel's story. First, the omniscient third-person author, or he mentions first person in a couple of places in the First Movement. Second Movement, Day takes over and tries to tell it. He gets into fights with Diana over his writing after letting her read his journal, and she calls him a bad writer, where Diana herself had been called a pedestrian writer by her writing teacher, and for that reason, Diana never tries to tell the story. Unless there's the possibility that Diana had . . .

LV: . . . told the whole story.

DH: . . . told the whole story as in *A Work of Fiction*, my unpublished novel, that it turns out in the end that although it appeared to have been written by the man, actually the man's wife was the true author of the whole story. And Daniel tries to tell it in his poetry, and Day is simply observing that he thought he did as good a job as Daniel did.

LV: Well, too, I was just thinking that [in] the last movement, the Fourth Movement, we have the character Daniel dictating, in a way, his story to G, who will then eventually write the whole thing up, and so you have the character writing his own story.

DH: Well, G. does presumably write the whole book, but he didn't.

LV: He was simply a recorder who was turned on. In terms of the struc-ture of the book, the structure seems to be musical. You have six parts in it, the Overture, four Movements, and then a Finale. Why did you choose a musical form for this book?

DH: Well, I think all of my books in a way have had a kind of musical form. As I think you pointed out in an article, or in a letter to me, the structure of *Lightning Bug* is very close to the structure of Dvořák's "New World" Symphony.[6] Although that was not deliberate, I was very familiar with that piece and was listening to it as background music when I was typing. I've always been interested in musical structure, but I know nothing about musical structure. I've never studied music or the composition of music, but I like the idea of, in this case, we would have an overture, which like the overture to any piece, it sort of builds you up and gets you ready for . . . I think the idea for the musical struc-ture . . . I started out writing *Some Other Place.* without any definite musical structure in mind, but I got to that point toward the end of the Dudleytown exploration when they're on the search for Daniel Lyam Montross, and at the point where it says, well he'd just finished eating supper, pitched their camp out in the woods, and he asked Diana, "Are you bored?"

"No," she answered. "Are you?"

"Not at all," he said. "I just wondered if maybe you were."

"I haven't been so *un*bored in a long time," she said.

"That's good. There's nothing to do."

"No place to go."

"Nothing happening. This is where it isn't at."

"She laughed. 'I like the way you put that. "This is where it isn't at."' Then after a while she said, 'But you're wrong you know. This is where it *is* at.'"

"Yes," he said. "It surely is."

And she says, "Go to sleep, Day."

All of that movement is very quiet, tranquil, like the fading off of the Overture just before the full orchestra comes in this bombastic voice of Daniel himself speaking, "This is where it is at. Where I am born. That I am born, beslimed and puling, onto the straw tick of life, is not a come-off for joy in the faces of those watching. Black looks from my audience are my first sight in this new world," and so forth. That's Overture building up for the music of the First Movement, and then by the time I got to the Second Movement and knew that Day could not possibly finish it, it would be called the Unfinished, and then the Third Movement would be Here and There. The collected poems would be in a different tone as movements of the symphony would be allegro and adagio, whatever, that each of the movements has its own particular rhythm, sound, tone, and so forth.

LV: Related to the musical structure of the book is also the fact that Diana is a dancer, and Diana and Day dance together, and they listen to the radio and to classical music, especially Ralph Vaughan Williams's *Pastoral Symphony*. The sounds of the forest remind Day of some of these pastorals, Beethoven's Sixth Symphony, and then the John Playford dances in the Fourth Movement sort of characterize that last movement. They're there, and there are various kinds of dances that go on, and dance, [it] seems to me, is another important part of the book.

DH: Well, all of those musical allusions are references to things that I liked and things that I had listened to when I was writing. You saw that Dvořák's "New World" Symphony got somehow into the structure of *Lightning Bug*, but actually, the work that most inspired *Lightning Bug* musically was the John Playford dances. I probably listened to them every day that I worked on *Lightning Bug*, I would listen to that record. And so, all of these pieces that are mentioned in the book are references to specific compositions that have inspired me or that I have listened to.

LV: They also fit very well in terms of some of the other subjects of the book. The *Pastoral* Symphony, Beethoven, and Ralph Vaughan Williams, and even the John Playford dances suggest that pastoral element of the book, and there's that one place where Day and Diana exchange, what is it, the passionate shepherd's request and so forth. How is this book pastoral or nonpastoral?

DH: Well, the book is obviously a very pastoral book, and so the *Pastoral* Symphony is very appropriate for . . . well the other night at UMR, for the historic record, the UMR Symphony Orchestra gave a performance of Beethoven's *Pastoral*, first time I'd ever heard it live, and as I was listening to the part of the tempest and after the storm in that, I could feel once again the way I was trying to pace that afternoon that they first spend in Dudleytown and get caught in the rain and the sort of pastoral quality that existed in the first of the ghost towns and which they would find in all of the ghost towns. That is definitely very pastoral.

LV: Also in relation to the musical theme is the fact that each movement seems to have the same theme, or a variation on that theme. Daniel meets a woman that he loves and loses that woman to some other person. Daniel, at the end of each section, kills a man. That man is named Allen or some variation of it.

DH: Right.

LV: Except in the last movement, where things are reversed and Daniel is killed by a man who is named Ellen, and each one of the towns is dying or dead, except the last one, Stick Around. Is there some reason for that, why you had these particular elements in the—?

DH: Yes. Well, there's so many of these variations . . . well, that's musical structure. What little I know about music is that a composer will pick a theme and then have variations on that theme, and so all of those variations on the killing and so forth is simply one device that I use to unify the various movements by having—

LV: Do you think that all of your fiction has one theme and each of your novels is a variation on that theme?

DH: Yes.

LV: What is that theme?

DH: Well, I think somebody referred to it as duplicity, but it would probably be better to call it pair bonding, or pairings, or couplings, or doubles, or bigeminals, or whatever word you could come up with.

LV: How about love?

DH: Love would do just fine.

LV: Because one of the things, one of the brilliant passages in the book I think is where Henry Fox comes out and says . . . gives Daniel the definition of love. I was going to read that passage, but I'm not going to read it now because we don't have time, but in that passage, you deal with some of the things that you're concerned with throughout your work. "Words are all we have to reach each other with," he says. He gives his concept of the It. He talks about the idea of wanting to share, of Rachel wanting to share herself with Daniel's It. Then . . . one of the things I'm very interested in in your work is the idea of embarrassment, and I want to embarrass you and ask you what you're doing with embarrassment, do you think, in your books?

DH: Well, embarrassment to me, in its very broad term, simply means the breakdown of this pair bonding or the attempt to reach the other, the attempt to believe in the other, the attempt to have a perfect union. Embarrassment is an impediment to true love, and its more specific meaning, in regard to that section, has to do with the fact that Daniel and Rachel can't comfortably share the privy together, but as Henry

Fox put it, the . . . to put it crudely, that the two-hole privy is man's
aspiration to love, but just as few people as are ever really able to use . . .

[The videotape ends.]

The Architecture of the Arkansas Ozarks, Part I

LH: We are about to continue with our series of interviews with Donald
Harington. Today is Sunday, May 6, 1979, at the University of
Missouri at Rolla, and Don has even consented to break up his weekend for us and share some of his thoughts and information about his
most recent novel, which is *The Architecture of the Arkansas Ozarks*,
published in 1975. We'll start at the beginning again, and so I'll ask
you, how long did you have the basic concept of the novel in your
mind before you actually began writing it? Did you know that you
were going to write this even as you were completing *Some Other
Place. The Right Place.*, or did the conception for the novel come later?

DH: Well, as I recall, the basic idea for the novel must have come before
the end of *Some Other Place. The Right Place.*, because it's mentioned
by name in the fourth section of that book, so I must have already been
thinking about the novel, and as I said before, it's my practice to have
a title in mind before writing the book, so I had the title at least while
I was still working on *Some Other Place.*, so that would have come as
early as about 1971.

LH: So this is really incubated a long time, isn't it? [Phrasing from
Harington's original file]

DH: Yes.

LH: What about the notion of the double Taoism that the title forms,
TAOTAO? Was that in your mind from the beginning?

DH: No, no I had almost finished *Architecture* when I wrote my brother
who lived in France and told him the title of the book, and he wrote
back and said, "Did you know that the title of your book forms a double
Tao?" It surprised me. It's just one of those coincidences that make
writing so much fun, and it simply happened to turn out that way.

LH: Okay, well, what kind of research did you do? I guess I would say you
didn't do much research into Taoism before you began. Right?

DH: No, I didn't know anything about Taoism when I wrote the book.

LH: Okay, but what kind of research did you do to prepare for this novel?

DH: Well, I had to research, first of all, the architecture itself; find out
as much as I could about styles of Ozark architecture. I had to select

specific examples of architecture that I would use. I had to do some research into the concept of what vernacular architecture means. Although I've been teaching the subject at Windham College for a number of years, I didn't know all that much about vernacular. But I had to research the history of, well, beginning with the first chapter, I knew nothing about Osage Indians, so I had to read several books from the Osage to inspire that. How they lived, what they looked like, and so forth. Then I had to research the Arkansas involvement in the Civil War. The troops in Newton County were both Federal and Confederate. Throughout the book, I had to research the history of what was happening in the Ozarks and applying it specifically to my mythical town of Stay More.

LH: Were there some of the building types that you used in the novel that you've actually taught in your classes back at Windham?

DH: No, I never taught any of the . . . I never taught any Arkansas architecture to my Windham classes. We were too much concerned with the New England, colonial architecture.

LH: Well, let me continue this notion of research, though, to expand it back to your other novels. Have you done extensive research for all your novels? Is there any novel for which you have not done extensive research?

DH: Not as much as I did for *Architecture*. That was probably the most researched of all my books. *Lightning Bug* was probably the least researched, but I have done research for all of my novels.

LH: How long did it take you to complete your research for *Architecture*?

DH: I never timed myself on my watch, so I'm not sure. It varies. Usually, I'll maybe do a few weeks of research before writing and then continue doing the research as I go along, so I never have any mental concept of just how long I spend researching. I just do what is necessary for what I'm writing on at the time.

LH: Okay.

DH: I can't write around the clock, so I use my working hours that are not put into writing to be reading something in preparation for what I'm writing.

LH: Okay, let's turn to the finished product then. I feel when I read this that you've done some rather distinctively new things in terms of form and genre in the novel. How would you describe the innovations in genre or form or structure that you feel are embodied in *The Architecture of the Arkansas Ozarks*?

DH: Well, in form I don't think it's terribly innovative at all in the sense that it's simply a chronicle of a family, the Ingledew family, in *Stay More*, and it's relatively straightforward. In terms of time, I don't really fool around with time in *Architecture* the way I have in my other novels. It simply has a beginning, long middle, and an end that takes place over one hundred four years. In terms of genre, it's certainly not the first of its type, and it's modeled, not closely, but it's modeled upon *One Hundred Years of Solitude* by Gabriel García Márquez. Márquez's book in turn was modeled on various books by Faulkner. It all goes back to the Bible. The Bible started the idea of telling a family saga, so the genre itself is not really new. The innovations, in my mind, have to do with the use of Eli Willard as a catalyst over all of the generations, that he alone endures almost throughout the entire book. It's innovative in terms of its application of Ozark folk humor to a novel, which I don't think even . . . well, we think of Mark Twain as a very comic writer, but Mark Twain did not really use that many folk sources. So it was, I think, one of the first really successful applications of folklore to fiction. It also has a lot of tricks, things like change, change in tense that occurs toward the end. That occurred in all of my books, but here it changes to the present tense with the chronometer wristwatch that Eli Willard brings, and then later changes to the future tense and ends in the future tense, as *Lightning Bug* did and *Some Other Place.* also end in the future tense, with the book not really ending but continuing on forever. Those are the major innovations that I can think of.

LH: Okay, let's talk about the drawings then for a little bit. Did you complete the drawings before you began writing? Would you do the drawing as you wrote the chapter? Or would you just draw?

DH: I had an idea in mind of what the building would look like, but I didn't do the drawings until after the book was finished. I did the first . . . I did rough sketches of the first four drawings simply to give my editor some idea of what I intended to do, but I polished those up extensively after finishing the book. Or actually as I was writing the last five or six chapters of the book, I was also illustrating earlier chapters, but the last five or six chapters were not illustrated until the book was finished.

LH: How long would it take you to do each drawing?

DH: Well, again, I wasn't looking at my wristwatch, but in my memory of it, I would write during the daytime and then have five or six drinks before supper and then have supper, have five or six more drinks after supper and get out my drawing board and start drawing. That would be about 7:00, and then I would probably finish a drawing by 2:00 in the morning.

LH: What have you done with the originals?

DH: They're all framed in one big, one big golden frame or painting. It's about . . . do we have room for this? No, right? It's about four feet by six feet.

LH: And where is that painting? Where is the frame?

DH: Where was it?

LH: Where is it?

DH: Where is it? To the best of my knowledge, it's probably behind my desk in my study in Putney, Vermont.

LH: Okay, the epigraph also has to do with drawings. It's from Frank Lloyd Wright, who is saying in the quote, which you take from Frank Lloyd Wright, he's saying that humble, indigenous buildings are to the study of the art of architecture what folklore is to literature or folk-song is to music, and he also, if not explicitly, implicitly talks about the organic nature of much of these humble, indigenous dwellings. Did you include that epigraph in order to tell us something about why we're looking at domestic architecture that some people may have ignored before, and were you also trying to tell us something about the mode of your novel, its style, its structure, whatever?

DH: Well, I was trying, since there is so much folklore in the book itself, I was trying to say that the book as a work of fiction is to more polished or sophisticated works of fiction pretty much the same as folklore is to sophisticated literature, or folk song is to classical music or whatever. I just found that epigraph fortuitously after I had started the book, but I thought it was just right in terms of what I was going to do in the book itself.

LH: Do you have your own philosophy of architecture as Frank Lloyd Wright did?

DH: Well, I agree with Frank Lloyd Wright that the best architecture is organic. I don't have an individual philosophy that would depart from Frank Lloyd Wright's philosophy. I think he . . . he was right. Wright was right just about all of the time. Most of the international style opposing Wright was wrong.

LH: Yes, well, I would guess then that you're not entirely pleased with all contemporary domestic architecture, is that right?

DH: To the extent that brutalism has dominated . . . well actually brutalism has not dominated domestic architecture so much as public architecture, but I think brutalism was a disaster in architectural terms, and the influence of the international style in general has been very depersonalizing. There are bold innovations in contemporary domestic architecture that follow the organic pattern of life. I think there's some exciting work in architecture recently.

LH: Okay, two more questions, then, about your drawings before we go on to something else. First of all, are all the buildings that are depicted in your drawings for the novel, are they based on actual, existing buildings in the Ozarks?

DH: Well, there's only one that still exists, that's Jacob's bigeminal house.

LH: That is still there?

DH: That building still exists and was an actual building. It still looks exactly as it appears in the book, and that was my grandmother's house where I spent the summers growing up, and my great uncle Floyd Calico is now living there, but he inhabits the only building existing now in downtown Stay More. The general store of the Ingledews directly across the road from that hotel also was an actual building depicted as it actually looked. The mill behind the general store, or by the Ingledews, more or less looked the way it is in the drawing. I deliberately made it bigeminal, and as I recall it was not. It washed away in a flood. It did not have a wheel but was steam-driven from the beginning. Those three are based on actual buildings in downtown Stay More. Bevis and Emelda's little bigeminal bungalow was based on an actual building in Missouri that resembled very much the bigeminals you find all over Rolla and elsewhere in the Ozarks. Fanshaw's hut, to back up, Fanshaw's hut was based upon an actual Osage hut, but the Osage huts were not bigeminal. The idea of combining two huts together was my imagination. The log cabin of . . . well, both the hewed log cabin and the rounded log cabin were both based roughly on real log cabins. Noah Ingledew's treehouse was completely imaginary.

LH: I wondered about that.

DH: The cat wagon . . . the cat wagon was totally imaginary.

LH: What about the cantilevered barn?

DH: The cantilevered barn? That's based on an actual barn in Tennessee which looks just like that. I got it out of a book about barns. I don't think they had cantilevered barns in Newton County or Stay More, but they could have.

LH: It's a lovely barn, I think my favorite in there. One final question, then, about those drawings. Why are there no people in the actual pictures?

DH: Well, that's probably to . . . I wanted the buildings to establish a setting and leave it up to the reader's imagination to . . . I think readers
like the privilege of being able to visualize in their own minds what
people look like, and if I had put pictures of actual people in the illustrations, it would have interfered with the reader's free imagination. I
know myself that when the jacket was designed, that I did not design
the jacket, but the jacket has a picture of Jacob and Noah and the cow
and dog supposedly, and those two pictures of Jacob and Noah bear no
resemblance to my own image of what Jacob and Noah looked like. I
think they interfere with the reader's imagination.

LH: Let's step off the front porch and walk inside now. I think the narrative voice in *Architecture* is very distinctive. In fact, that's one thing
that I feel is especially remarkable about your works as a whole, that
each novel has a very distinctive narrative voice and the style changes
significantly as we go from work to work. How would you describe the
narrative voice that we find in *Architecture*?

DH: Well, I think of that narrator as a somewhat pedantic or slightly stuffy
professor of architecture who is addressing a class in architecture and
talking about, or pretending to talk about, the buildings when what he
himself is really most interested in is not the buildings so much as what
happened inside after they stepped off the porch and went inside, and
I don't think that narrative voice is really too intrusive. In most of the
narrative, I was trying to let the events and people themselves capture
the reader without the reader being too aware of any style or any voice
behind, but just at the point when I would think the reader might be
in danger of forgetting that that teacher was still there talking, I would
bring in the first person, usually first-person plural, but occasionally
there was the first-person singular to reinforce the fact that that is . . .
the teacher still teaching.

LH: Did you have this voice in mind from the very beginning before you
wrote the first word?

DH: Well, the first word is "We." The first line in the book is "We begin
with an ending," and so the first word in the book establishes that, here
we are, class. Let's begin with the class and so on [and] so forth.

LH: A little later, then, the narrator remarks this: "The Bodark in the
arciform architecture of the Arkansas Ozarks," and remarks that if we
say that phrase, in essence, we're using a phrase in which every single
important word comes from the same root, which, of course, goes back
to the title of your novel as well in which every significant word comes
from the same root. Is the point of that title and of this phrase in the

text that the life that we find in the Ozarks and the architecture are an organic whole, or are you also using it as a metaphor for all literary art in general and yours in particular?

DH: That's kind of a tough one. I don't use metaphors when I can keep from it. But if you want to look at it as a metaphor, then, yes, but I think for the most part it was simply, well again, go back to what I refer to as the Chinese box. There you have a kind of Chinese box that reflects the style and the title, as well as every element in . . . well, every significant word in that sentence comes from the same root is also the root of the title. So we could say that it is a form of oneness and its diversity.

LH: Okay . . .

DH: It is organic of course.

LH: Yes, yes.

DH: As I said in the book, it is an organic form.

LH: Well, I would say that you have to use one metaphor throughout the book, though, and you even call it as simple at times, and that's bigeminal architecture. What does bigeminality signify or symbolize to you?

DH: Well, I thought it was very obvious in the book, to anyone who's read the book, that bigeminality symbolizes the division of all creatures into male and female. That although they are equal, that all of the bigeminal elements in *Architecture* are equal, Fanshaw's squaw's part of the hut is the same size as his part of the hut, the doors in bigeminal houses are the same size, emphasize the equality of male and female, the separation of male and female into different creatures in a way. Also, above all, the coming together of male and female.

LH: Do you associate bigeminality as well with a kind of dialectic, or would you say . . .?

DH: I don't know what that word means. Dialectic?

LH: Well, you know, this then this, this then this. That kind of—

DH: Dualism?

LH: Kind of. That would do.

DH: Well, bigeminality has infinite extensions away from the basic metaphor of male/female. You think of yin and yang, sun and moon. The cosmos is full of pairings.

LH: And were these in your mind when you were using the term as well? I mean the larger pairings as well as the specific pairings?

DH: Sure.

LH: Okay. All right. I want to digress just a moment away from the text because this question about bigeminality and your symbolic use of it in a literary text raises another question to me about genre and form, and that is, what would you say is the difference, if we're speaking of artistic forms, between pictorial art and architecture on one hand and fiction on the other? Are they more alike or unlike each other?

DH: I haven't given too much thought to the relationship between pictorial art and fiction until Dr. Vonalt forced it upon me in one of the classes that I was teaching for him on George Caleb Bingham, and it dawned on me that [in] pictorial art and architecture, the artist or architect is dealing essentially with a two-dimensional surface that moves vertically, horizontally, diagonally, whatever, whereas a work of fiction is almost completely linear. It has [a] beginning, [a] middle, and the end and moves in a straight line. It moves through time more than pictorial art. The poet Goethe once spoke of architecture as being frozen music, which . . . that's an interesting metaphor, but I don't . . . I see what he means, but still, music is linear through time.[1] It has a beginning, and intervals, and spaces between notes, and goes to a conclusion. Architecture and pictorial art do not. They exist. You can look at it in an instant and you look away and you've seen it, in a way.

LH: Do you see any similarity between the structure of a novel in which, yes, one has to go through a novel in linear terms, but when one is done and can step back from the novel and see it as a structural whole . . . do you see any resemblance between that and the structuring of a building?

DH: Well, in *Architecture* I was trying, in a way, to make the structure of the chapters similar to the structure of architecture, and I remarked at one point that we are now going up the slope of the roof and down the back slope of the roof. I was speaking in terms of the structure of the novel. The novel had reached the point at which we have ascended the facade of the structure, climbed the roof, then gone down the back slope to the denouement. I thought of each chapter in a way as vaguely reflecting the structure of, well, the content and structure, of that.

LH: Were you also thinking of the physical book? I mean, I was holding my book like this when you were talking about having Vernon search for Jelena, and I could see him going up one slope and down the other, and you said the base was heavier . . . well, I'd read a lot of pages, and the base was heavier, that would be here, then it was on my right. Were you specifically thinking of the physical . . . yes?

DH: It is a physical book, and it turns on itself, and since Vernon was able to reenter the book in search of clues as to where Jelena might be, and it even refers to specific lines, page numbers, that was another part of the tour de force of what I was trying to do structurally in the end of that book.

LH: Is that the first time any novelist has used the physical shape and structure of the book and the physical book in a novel?

DH: I hope so.

LH: I think so.

DH: I hope so.

LH: I'd never seen it before.

DH: I don't know if . . . I certainly didn't copy the idea from anyone else.

LH: Oh no, I wasn't implying that.

DH: Possibly some other writer . . . I haven't read all that much fiction, but it's very possible that someone else had already thought of it before I did. I don't know.

LH: Well, I didn't think of it. Let's turn now to some of the characters in the novel. One of the things that struck me in the early sections of the book is that almost all of the white male settlers who came to Stay More have biblical names: Jacob, and Noah, Isaac, there's an Elijah running around somewhere in there too. Were you playing off the Bible to suggest the idea of genesis, since this is the beginning of the Stay Morons and also the fathering of tribes because we see the population building up, or were you simply using the kinds of names that nineteenth-century people used?

DH: Well, those names were very common in the nineteenth century, and as I've pointed out before, the founders of Drakes Creek, the model for Stay More, were Jacob and Isaac Drake. Those were very common names in the nineteenth century, and I didn't intend any allusion to Genesis in the Bible in general.

LH: Do you think those biblical overtones work, though?

DH: Sure, if you want to see an allusion to the biblical Jacob in Jacob Ingledew as Jacob was the progenitor of the Ingledew clan in Stay More, and so if you want to connect that Jacob to the biblical Jacob, that's fine.

LH: But you claim no responsibility for our doing that, is that what you're saying?

DH: Right, right.

LH: Okay.

DH: I have only a certain responsibility to myself and to the book, and what you want to do with it after that, you have complete freedom to take it anywhere you want to.

LH: Do you really believe that? Wouldn't you get angry if you had a reader who, in your opinion, read the book incorrectly or was cavalier about the book? Wouldn't that provoke a response?

DH: I wouldn't get angry. It's happened all the time, with all of my books, that the books have been completely misread. Are you going to ask me about the frakes, eventually?

LH: Yes, yes.

DH: Well, I had a very bad misreading and had a very bad review from a critic. I think, at the time, he was teaching at Lehigh University, and his name was James R. Frakes, and back then, I had a relatively thin skin, and he wrote . . . if it had appeared in the *Philadelphia Inquirer* or a newspaper like that, it wouldn't have been so bad, but it was in the *New York Times*, which is the most prestigious, most influential of all the book reviews, and to get such a terrible misreading of *Some Other Place.The Right Place* . . . he couldn't have spent more than thirty minutes with that book, but to neglect it that way and then write a putdown of it in the *New York Times*, that infuriated me. So I named my mythical disease, the frakes, after James R. Frakes.[2]

LH: Have you ever had the frakes since encountering Frakes?

DH: I have them right now, yes, but they're not contagious, so don't worry.

LH: Well, I want to ask one more thing about this business of you versus the reader. When you're finished with a book and you've sent it off, is that, in your mind, the end of your connection with the book? I mean, is that it?

DH: There's nothing else I can do after that. I've written the book, it's going to be published, there's nothing I can say that will help the book. There's probably a lot I can say that may harm the book, but it's no longer my business. It becomes the property of the world, and my duty to the book has ended when I have finished writing it.

LH: Let's try the converse. Does it please you when people give the book what you consider a good reading?

DH: I'm sorry?

LH: Does it please you when people give the book a good reading?

DH: Oh, of course, of course. Naturally, I'm happy when people understand what I was trying to do, and I'm disappointed when they don't understand, but there's nothing I can do beyond that point to help anyone understand.

LH: Okay, and now I'm going to ask you to help me understand. I'm going to go to a question about Eli Willard. When Eli Willard . . .

DH: Why do you think I'm giving you all of this time? Why would I be giving you all of this time of mine if I didn't believe that there was still possibly something I might be able to do to help the books after they're written?

LH: The answer is obvious. Obvious answer . . . because you're a very nice man. I wish the camera could pick up your blush. Oh well, that's okay. No, I know what you're saying. I agree. Let's go back to Eli Willard, how's that? Can we go back to Eli?

DH: Okay.

LH: Okay, or did you have anything more to say about this last subject?

DH: Well, you wanted to know what frakes was, I anticipated, so I've told you what frakes were.

LH: Okay, so let's go to Eli Willard, who, when he first comes to Stay More, sells Jake a clock. Now the question is, is that clock in itself symbolic, and if it is, do each of the items that Willard sells to the population of Stay More, do they each acquire a more highly charged symbolic meaning, or is it simply that he's a peddler and he has to sell something?[3]

DH: Well, the clock, the first clock he sells Eli doesn't work, it's too slow.[3] The second clock is too fast. So the clocks are symbolizing that the time in this novel . . . the time is going to be confused. Either you're going to think that time is passing too rapidly or else you're going to think that time is slowing down too much, which is pretty much the way people perceive time in the Ozarks. Either there is never enough time to get done all the things that have to be done or else there's such an abundance of time that everybody has what I call the sourhours . . . boredom.

LH: What about the other items that Eli sells?

DH: Well, I think each of them has some sort of symbolic significance. For example, after he brings Sharps rifles for the Civil War, and then after the war, he brings balms and unguents, and I think each of the items that he brings has some sort of significance. And then he . . . the last item that he brings, after bringing two faulty clocks in the very beginning, the last thing he brings is a chronometer watch that keeps perfect time, which in a sense is spoiling things for Vernon to have a clock that would keep absolutely perfect time, but probably the reason Vernon doesn't like using it, well, the main reason he doesn't like using it is because he is shy and embarrassed by the power of the watch to bring the audience into his problems. But another reason is that perfect time is very dull. Perfect time is extremely monotonous.

LH: Well, why does Eli give it to Vernon, then?

DH: I think probably as a symbol that the old time of the Ozarks is gone, and we're now living on standard, American, central, dull, tedious time. That the old life of the Ozarks is vanished. The old folk speech is gone. The old customs and habits have died out. Everybody in the Ozarks nowadays is just about like everybody else. We all watch the same thing on TV, we all eat at the same fast-food places. There's no individuality left, and as a consequence, time itself has become not the same time that people enjoyed back in the old days, so we see the time, the chronometer wristwatch, as a symbol of the modern time.

LH: I still have some other questions about Eli. One of the things that interested me as I was reading is that Eli is an outsider. He comes from the East, and he keeps intruding into the lives of Stay Morons. And it occurred to me . . . well, at one point, Eli even mentions that he doesn't fully understand Stay Morons. He feels he's not like them. Is it possible that you're using Eli as a kind of center or counterpart for the reader who is also an outsider who enters into the town of Stay More through your book?

DH: Well, Eli Willard is my agent. I didn't intend Eli as a reflection directly of myself. As I put it in one point, when young Hank is try-ing to join the circus and asks Eli if he is the boss, Eli says no, he isn't the boss, but he [is] an agent for the boss. The boss he's talking about there is the boss who is writing the novel, and Eli is an agent for me who comes from New England, and as one critic remarked about my work, one of the best things about it is that it's written about the Ozarks but from a New England perspective, the same way that . . . well, not the same way but similar to the way that Samuel Clemens wrote about Missouri from the standpoint of Connecticut. And maybe I had, in the back of my mind, I had Clemens as a Connecticut Yankee, then Clemens's book *The Connecticut Yankee*, and then the Connecticut Yankee of my own invention, Eli Willard. I had all three of them sort of tied up in the back of my mind as performing the function of the Eastern outsider who brings the American civilization into Stay More and in the process corrupts them, in a way.

LH: All right, good, but is it the same kind of thing for the reader? Is Eli also kind of parallel to the reader who also enters from the outside, or do we not get him? Does he belong only to you?

DH: Oh, I hadn't thought of that. I don't think the typical reader . . . in order for that to be true, the typical reader would have to identify with

Eli, and unless I'm mistaken, I think the typical reader feels that he's on the side of the Stay Morons, and that when Eli comes, Eli is intruding into his . . . I might be wrong, but I think the reader would probably feel closer to the Stay Morons than to Eli.

LH: Yes, that's true too. Backing up just a second before we go on, you were talking about writing from the New England perspective. Did you write this in Putney, Vermont, *Architecture*? Is there a definite kind of relationship in your mind between Putney and Stay More? Do they have anything in common, or is it really mostly a distancing kind of thing?

DH: Putney is simply an accident of destiny as a place where I live. I see no connection whatever between . . . except that hanging on the door of my study in Putney is a sign that says "Stay More, Ark. Pop. 1" and so, to me, to the extent that Stay More does exist outside a real physical place in Newton County, Arkansas, it's simply the confines of my study in a house that's in Putney, Vermont.

LH: Well, I've never been to Putney. I guess I was curious, were there rolling hills by Putney? It's kind of alike . . . ?

DH: It looks physically . . . I wouldn't be living there unless it had a very close physical resemblance to Stay More. We don't have chiggers, we don't have ticks, we don't have . . . can't grow okra, can't grow black-eyed peas, we don't have poisonous snakes. A lot of advantages and disadvantages to living in Putney. I probably would have remained in the Ozarks if it had been financially possible, but Putney just simply happened to be the place where I have lived for fifteen years.

LH: Would you resettle in the Ozarks now if you could?

DH: Oh, in a minute. In a minute.

LH: Okay, that's interesting. Do you think you could still continue writing? Do you think you could still continue to write in the Ozarks?

DH: Oh, yes.

LH: That would be no problem?

DH: Regardless of where I have to live, I'll always be writing about the Ozarks.

LH: So you don't necessarily need the geographic distance. It's all right, but you don't require . . . ?

DH: I don't think I need it anymore. I needed it when I was starting out, but I think I could live in the Ozarks now and keep writing about them.

LH: Okay, well, let's turn to something completely different for a while, which is education. Jacob Ingledew founds, and is the first teacher in, the elementary school there in Stay More and is a very unusual teacher because he excludes reading and writing from the school in favor of having philosophical debates and discussions. Two questions on this. First of all, do you think this is a good kind of school, and depending on if you say yes or no, do you think it's kind of odd that a writer would have a school in which the word is excluded?

DH: Well, what a writer writes about is not always what he approves of. I mean, for example, I've never beheaded anyone in any of my books, but if I beheaded somebody, does that mean that I'm in favor of beheading? The fact that Jacob doesn't teach . . . well, as a matter of fact, I did, I did put that in on purpose because, to an extent, literacy spoiled the Ozarks. Back in the old days when nobody could read and write, there was a certain innocence or certain lack of being corrupted by the word. The word had to be interpreted to you by a preacher or whoever. But best of all, there was an oral tradition of stories handed down from generation to generation, spoken or sung, and just about everyone knew the oral tradition. Nowadays, or after the coming of literacy, the oral tradition began dying out, and what was left of the oral tradition was totally killed off by radio and television.

LH: So you're saying that you don't necessarily believe we shouldn't learn to read and write, but you do see this as a problem?

DH: I would be out of business. I would be out of business if people couldn't read. I was saying that Jacob deliberately did not include reading and writing in the curriculum because he knew it would spoil.

LH: What about your own curriculum? I know that you're a teacher. Are you anything like Jacob as a teacher, or are you pretty different?

DH: I didn't see any . . . I wasn't making Jacob a self-portrait in terms of pedagogical methods. I didn't see . . . I didn't see Jacob as, in any way, like myself as a teacher.

LH: I guess I was wondering if you like to focus on philosophical issues when you teach?

DH: Not necessarily. I can do it when the occasion demands, but I'm not hung up on philosophical issues.

LH: Okay. How about political issues? One of the things that happen to Jacob is that he's involved in politics a great deal. First, he's mayor of Stay More, then he's sent as a delegate to a state convention held when they want to decide if they're going to succeed, and eventually, he's governor of Arkansas. Again, two questions here. One of the things that struck me as I read about Jacob, it's actually a very nice mixture, is that he's involved in politics, he's a leader, and yet, he's kind of detached from the whole thing. I wonder if you could discuss that, and then tell us whether you consider yourself a political animal or whether you think you're apolitical.

DH: Well, I'm not political at all, and I didn't . . . to whatever extent Jacob does have a kind of detachment from the politics that he becomes involved in, that might be a reflection of my views, but I've never been involved in politics. Well, I voted Democrat for many years, but that doesn't mean that I'm necessarily a Democrat. I don't take very much interest anymore. I used to be more interested, but I've become kind of disenchanted with national politics ever since Jimmy Carter became president.

LH: Why?

DH: I just try to ignore . . . I try to ignore politics as much as possible now.

LH: Well, what about when you were writing the Civil War passages in that novel? There are remarks in there about the sheer stupidity and futility of war, and I wondered if you were at all influenced by the Vietnam conflict when you were writing those Civil War passages?

DH: Quite possibly. I wasn't consciously thinking of [the] Vietnam War, but I was fed up to here with the whole business, and the whole concept of war itself is extremely repugnant to me, and so, possibly, I was . . . well, *Architecture* as a whole is an attempt to comment upon, or make fun of, just about everything: education, religion, politics, sports, war. I was trying to, in a sense, say the only thing that can be said about war. Everyone is agreed that war is bad, but that doesn't keep it from happening, so all you can say about it is that it's ridiculous. Poke fun at it. The whole idea of people out shooting each other, especially their own kinfolks, the only thing to do with it is, as Joseph Heller did in *Catch-22*, just lampoon it. Show how ridiculous and stupid the whole business is.

LH: Well, I would guess that one of the ways you try to do that is through a peculiar quirk of the Stay Morons, at first, in the early stages of the war, when Jacob and the Union contingent are fighting Noah and the Rebel contingent and they won't kill each other. They're such good marksmen that they can fire and not shoot to kill. Would you say that Ozarks people are really this kind and nonviolent? Do you think you were reflecting a trait as well as poking fun at war? Or in making the Ozark people so nonviolent and nonaggressive, do you think you are idealizing them at the same time?

DH: Well, I think when I got to that point in the book, I deliberately introduced the villain, Ike Whitter, who goes around beating people up and finally gets beaten up in turn by Isaac. I put that in because I was probably feeling that maybe the reader was getting the impression that Stay Morons were totally nonviolent, and I wanted to show at least one example of somebody who was really violent and received violence in return. I don't think Ozarkers are all that kind and nice and nonviolent, but I think that the Stay Morons in general . . . since Stay More is a kind of a pastoral utopia, and you think of a pastoral utopia as a place where there isn't much bloodshed and bruises and gore or whatever.

LH: One of the people who ends up showing up in the book is not a Stay Moron at all, and that's the woman whom we cannot name. How did you come to include her in the novel?

DH: Well, Isaac Murphy was the Madison County hillbilly who was the governor of Arkansas during Reconstruction, and all of those things that happened to Jacob Ingledew happened to Isaac Murphy. He was the lone person who voted against secession, and when he voted against secession, a woman up in the balcony threw a bouquet of flowers at his feet. That's all we know from the historic record, but I simply took that fact and elaborated on it that that woman, whoever she was, and I suspected that she must have been from elegant Little Rock society, and therefore, assuming anybody did know her name . . . she's not named in historical record . . . but if somebody did know her name, it would be the name of a family still prominent in Little Rock society today; therefore, we cannot . . . she is the woman whom we cannot name. That was . . . well, that's partly a joke. I'm making up fiction and I have the right to name anybody I want to, but we cannot. That makes her more real. The fact that she cannot be named enhances her reality.

LH: Will you ever turn the joke around and name her after all?

DH: I'm going to turn the joke around farther along. I'm going to have a book in which nobody has a name except the woman whom we cannot name. She will have a name in that book and be the only person who is named in it.

LH: Okay. We'll look forward to that. Let's turn to another big issue, which is the religious passages in the novel. The Ingledews are extremely interesting because none of them believe in God or a hereafter, have nothing to do with churches. There are several preachers who come through and so on and so forth. Are you saying that the Stay Morons are naturally or naturalistically religious without preachers and sermons, or what? What are you doing with religion in this novel?

DH: Well, again, just as I attack politics and war and everything I can possibly attack, I'm attacking religion in that by implying that, just [because] that Stay Morons are nicer or less mean than other people, that they are any less religious. A lot of places in the Ozarks where religion is simply not taken seriously at all. For example, after writing the book, I learned that the town of Mountainburg, Arkansas, had a really rowdy revival back in the twenties sometime that got completely out of hand, and as a result of that, there was no more religious service whatever in the town of Mountainburg for the rest of the twentieth century. I was just making up the fact that Stay Morons were opposed to religion, except as it applies to Brother Long Jack Stapleton.

LH: Now he's an interesting character too. Why did you include him in. the novel?

DH: Long Jack Stapleton? Well, he is clearly a metaphor for the author in [a] Chinese box of . . . he preaches from Song of Solomon. Whoever wrote that was a great writer with the power of creativity. Brother Stapleton has the power to create images in your mind's eye. The author behind Stapleton, so it's the Chinese box again. Were you the one who asked me which of my characters am I most like?

LH: We talked about it one day. Why don't you repeat the answer for the camera?

DH: I think I'm most . . . I'm most like Stapleton of my characters that simply flattering.[4]

LH: Does that include Stapleton's religious beliefs? I mean do you have any religious beliefs yourself?

DH: Stapleton didn't have any religious beliefs.

LH: Yes, is that . . . ?

DH: He just had the ability to create love stories from the Bible.

LH: Right. Well, is that like you? Do you have no . . . ?

DH: Yes, I have the ability to create love stories.

LH: I know that.

DH: But I have no religious beliefs.

LH: No religious beliefs. None whatsoever, of any kind?

DH: No religious beliefs.

LH: Okay. Has it always been this way?

DH: Oh no. I told you about my experience as a preacher. I was Church of Christ preacher as a teenager.

LH: When did you quit believing in religion?

DH: Well, I was dying for a smoke. I was also dying for a drink, and the Church of Christ did not believe in either one.

LH: So a permanent parting of the way.

DH: I walked out to have a smoke . . . excommunicated myself.

LH: All right, well, what about the Taoism then? Is that, too, satiric, or is it just there by chance, or whatever?

DH: Well, as I demonstrated for one of the philosophy classes I taught here at UMR, it's possible to make a convincing case that there is a similarity between the way of life in Stay More and Taoism. You can, but for that matter, Taoism is such a vague, generalized way of life and religion or whatever that you can probably apply Tao to just about any system, any way of life.

LH: Kind of like the Bible itself.

DH: I had not read Tao before I learned that I was going to use that double Tao for my title in the book. Then I had to research Tao. I find it intriguing philosophy, but that doesn't mean I believe it.

LH: Okay. Well let's take another big issue, which is that of progress. And one of the things that is curious in your novel is that you always spell "progress" a very distinctive way. It's always all caps, and you separate with a space the first syllable and the second syllable.

DH: Bigeminal.

LH: Okay. Now, are you implying something about the meaning of the word too when you separate it like that?

DH: Well, in the first place, I'm simply separating it in order for it to be pronounced as people in the Ozarks . . . they say PROG RESS. They don't accent either syllable. They don't say *prog*ress or prog*ress*. PROG RESS is the way they say that word, and they also usually say it a little bit louder than they say other words because most Ozarkers have a, or at least the old-time Ozarkers, have a great deal of contempt for PROG RESS, and so that's simply the reason it's spelled that way.

LH: Do you have contempt for PROG RESS?

DH: I sure do.

LH: Well, explain.

DH: Well, I think it's a matter of future shock, that things have happened to us in this century much too rapidly, that we have completely lost touch with the better aspects of life as it used to be, even though I know that life in the good old days was often terrible, but a lot of the good in the good old days we have been almost running, running out of breath to escape from the past, and we go much too fast, much too quickly, and [have] wound up where we are now, running out of oil, living in constant fear of nuclear accidents, either deliberate or planned, having diseases accelerating, like cancer, that were not so bad in the good old days. Even though we have made a lot of PROG RESS in terms of creature comforts and having what we want, I think we've totally lost sight of what we're doing with ourselves.

LH: What would you say are the good things in the good old days? You said we're running away from those good things. What are they?

DH: Well, hard work. Hard work never bothered anyone in the good old days. Everybody took for granted you get up at dawn and really sweat all day long in order to earn a living, but ever since then men and women have been accumulating labor-saving devices, which do save a lot of labor, but also, they are polluting and destructive. I don't want to start preaching a sermon. Let's go on to . . .

[The video tape ends.]

The Architecture of the Arkansas Ozarks, Part II

LH: Today is May 8, 1979, and we're ready to finish up our interview on *The Architecture of the Arkansas Ozarks*. When we finished up, we were about to receive a sermon on progress and what it really means, which was cut off for several reasons. And we're going to pick back up and finish some questions, and this idea of progress is still in my mind. It's that sermon staying with me. One of the things that happen in the progress of the story of Stay More is that literacy eventually does come to Stay More during the Decade of Light. And the narrator comments that, quote, "During the Decade of Light the people of Stay More acquired not only a post office but a means of patronizing both ends of it, sending and receiving. And once they became literate they spent all their spare time writing letters, a worthless enterprise." End quote. A lot of us here happen to know that you are a very gifted writer of letters.

DH: Thank you.

LH: And I'm curious, do you really consider it worthless? Are you going to break all our hearts or not?

DH: Well, there again, as I often do in my work, I'm simply poking fun at myself. I often write more letters than are good for me, and I'm trying to suggest that writing letters is not as worthwhile as writing fiction. I ought to spend more time writing fiction, less time writing letters, so I'm just making a little dig at myself when I do that. I don't mean to imply that literacy or the word is worthless.

LH: Do you enjoy writing letters?

DH: Oh, sure. It's fun. You get a more immediate response. If you write a letter, somebody answers it, you can expect to have a response, but when you write a work of fiction it's going to be a long, long time before you have any feedback.

LH: Well, there are two characters in the novel who do have immediate feedback, and these are Bevis and Emelda Ingledew. They have a very curious way of relating. They never need to speak to each other, they just simply read each other's minds spontaneously. And one of the comments that the narrator makes is that there's absolutely no possibility of misunderstanding or lying if you're reading each other's minds. Does this strike you as a kind of ideal that we should all strive for? Is that what you were working with here?

DH: Well, you know, there's a theory that before language was invented, the people communicated by telepathy. The human beings are the only creatures who use language as a form of communication. It's thought that possibly other creatures are telepathic. I know, for example, that cats, cats can read human beings' minds.

LH: How do you know?

DH: Yes.

LH: How do you know?

DH: Well, if you're talking . . . if you're talking about a cat, the cat can't understand your language but the cat will get fidgety and restless or start licking and fluff to indicate that he knows that he's being talked about. It was . . . there's also a theory that the purpose of the invention of modern language after . . . for thousands of years, human beings had communicated telepathically, and then . . . but, with telepathy, it's impossible to deceive anyone. So the whole purpose of the invention of language was for deception. That put the writer in a bad spot too, as far as the use of the word is concerned, because if words are to deceive, then fiction is essentially a deception for the purpose of entertainment. That would be one definition of a work of fiction, to deceive the reader into believing that what is happening actually happened. I have never experienced telepathy myself, but other people have been telepathic toward me. In other words, they could pick me up, but I couldn't pick them up. They could read my mind, but I couldn't read theirs, which was a very uncomfortable position to be in.

LH: Would you say perhaps that readers of your fiction are in essence experiencing a kind of telepathy? They're reading your mind as they read your words.

DH: I think so. I hope so, that they get more from the work of fiction than I actually put into the words, or to use the expression, they read between the lines perhaps and find things there that I did not actually put there in words. I hope the reader, the good reader, can pick up things that are in my mind.

LH: I hope they can too. Let's turn to the later part of the story now. At a certain point, you say that the decline of Stay More begins. What would you say is the point at which the decline begins, and is it caused by a person, is it caused by history, by time, or is it simply a matter of geography?

DH: Well, as I recall, I gave the impression that the decline of Stay More began after Every Dill had robbed the bank. That was one economic factor involved, but that was not the main cause. Geographically, Stay More was isolated and people began to leave during the Depression. Well towns, towns all over the Ozarks, started their decline back in the twenties and thirties, mostly as a result of isolation and movement of people into the city and movement of people out of the state. I think that was probably the main reason for the decline.

LH: When you're saying that, are you speaking of population decline or are you speaking about a cultural decline?

DH: Well, a little bit of both. I think they probably went hand in hand to the extent that as the culture declined, people . . . I think a lot of people in the Ozarks became too aware of their isolation. As civilization advanced, one reason they had enjoyed life for so many generations in the Ozarks was because of that isolation, but once the outside world began to make them aware of their isolation, they felt a kind of inferiority complex about it, which, on one hand, caused them to give up their culture and, on the other hand, caused a lot of them to try to get out of that isolation.

LH: Well, some of them did indeed get out, and they went to California, which is always a bad place in your fiction, not just in *Architecture*. Why? Why do you have it in for California?

DH: Well, any number of reasons. The main reason is that California stole my people. That my people went to California in search of a better life, and that's what stifled off the population from the Ozarks. Another reason is that California is simply a lousy place. Well, just look at recent events. The [Guyana?] massacre was over mostly Californians or people who had come from Arkansas, Missouri, and gone to California to join Jones's cause. And then, shortly after that, the mayor of San Francisco and his superintendent were murdered. Something goofy is always happening in California. They passed Proposition 13, stupid thing to do. They elected Jerry Brown as governor. You can always expect anything flaky to come from California.

LH: We had a president, too, that I don't think you liked who came from California.

DH: Yeah, yeah, we had a . . . I forget that guy's name. What was that son of a bitch? He went back to California after the . . . they managed, finally managed to get rid of him. Dick somebody. I only think of Tricky Dick when I think of him. I think his last name sort of rhymes with his first name. It'll come to me in a minute. Next question.

LH: Alright, during the declining part of Stay More, we start having more and more funerals, and the song that is always sung at each funeral is "Farther Along," farther along we'll understand all about it. At one point, there's a funeral for two twin sisters, Jelena and Doris. And Doc Swain, who is the one in charge of this funeral, says, "Heck, we know all about this one." Is that a kind of clue that, all along, we really do understand all about it, or do we really have to wait until farther along to understand the meaning of what's in here?

DH: Well, I think what Doc Swain meant in that was . . . well of course the implication is all it is. Farther along we'll understand why people have to die. We'll understand death, the meaning of death, and what Doc Swain meant there was simply that we already knew pretty damn well why those sisters had committed suicide. We didn't have to wait until farther along to understand their death.

LH: Do we have to wait until farther along to understand *Architecture*?

DH: Maybe, maybe that's implied, but there are a lot of hidden sermons or hidden meanings in "Farther Along" about the general meaning of civilization, the cosmos, metaphysical speculations that are concealed. I think you might have to wait farther along to really understand fully what was said in that book. I will too. I'll have to wait farther along to know just what I was really saying.

LH: Do you feel that that's true for all your novels? That you wait to find out, maybe sometimes years to find out, what you yourself have said?

DH: Well, that's certainly true in the case of . . . to give you a specific example, the way people at UMR, yourself, Dr. Vonalt, and faculty have interpreted my work and shown me things about it that I did not realize I was doing at the time I was writing. So in that respect, I've had to wait for fifteen years to understand *The Cherry Pit*. Farther along, I might understand the rest of them a little bit more.

LH: Well, excluding us, I don't want to get us in here. What about for yourself? Do you . . . after writing a novel, do you understand just in terms of your own psychic economy why you've written that novel?

DH: Well, I think it was a great Italian novelist . . . twentieth-century Italian novelist. Names don't come to me easily in these circumstances, but he remarked that one writes a novel in order to understand why one has written it. That was his definition of the purpose of writing. To a large extent that's true, that I write a novel to understand farther along what motivated me to tell that story, or what that story means in terms of my own life. And even though my work is not at all autobiographical, still I make up symbols and situations, or I fantasize. I write about things that I would like to do but have never done. I'm playing . . . playing house with myself in a way.

LH: Is there anytime you've never understood why you played house with yourself?

DH: Well, farther along, farther along, I'll understand why.

LH: Alright, alright, enough said! One of the things that some people don't always understand is Eli Willard's death in the novel. He's the world's oldest man. He recapitulates his entire story, and just when he's about to finish, he dies in the midst of it, and is never formally buried because he's not a Stay Moron. Instead he's put in a glass display case and stored at various places in Stay More; he's never buried. Question . . . two questions here. Is this based at all on a real incident, and second, is there a strong symbolic significance of Eli Willard's death and inability to get buried?

DH: Well, I'll take those questions in order. The first, my editor had sent me, before I had written *Architecture*, he had sent me a newspaper clipping about a guy in North Carolina, who was . . . I think his name was Mr. . . . he was an Italian, they nicknamed him Mr. Spaghetti or something like that. He had been embalmed and put into a showcase and shown to the public until the state found out about it after twenty years and insisted that he be given a proper burial.[1] So that was the genesis of that story, and after writing *Architecture*, I've been deluged with newspaper clippings that people have sent me from all parts of the country about people who have not been buried. They've been embalmed and left in a box, or put into a glass case, or left lying in bed or whatever. It just somewhat reminded me of the fact that . . . I wasn't aware of it when I was writing *Architecture*, but that Lenin is in a glass case in the Kremlin, and I might have been unconsciously thinking of Lenin. As far as your second question's concerned, that is the real example of "farther along we will understand." I don't know what to do at this point with the body of Eli Willard. It's a . . . it's a millstone around my neck. I've left him there in that glass showcase, I've got to do something with him. That building is going to deteriorate and collapse eventually, and we have to get Eli Willard out of there. But what he's doing in that case is, why since he's a symbol, that although he's dead, he's still there. The town of Stay More is dead, but it's still there. That's the primary symbol. So what do we do with the town? Do we try to restore the town? If so, we have a permanent place to display Eli Willard. If we don't restore the town, we have to bury Eli Willard, and recently Dr. Patrick suggested the perfect solution would be that Clifford Stone, who's living as a bluff-dweller, would give Eli Willard a bluff-dweller's ceremonial funeral and bury him in the fashion that the bluff-dwellers buried their people. I think that would be . . . that's probably the way it will turn out.[2]

LH: Okay, we'll wait and see . . . farther along. Vernon is the one who inherits the watch from Eli Willard, and it's also curious that Vernon is one of the most successful of the Stay Morons in terms of economic success, material success. Does this make him happier than Jacob and Noah Ingledew, or do you think it's more a burden?

DH: I think probably a burden, but no one could ever recapture the life of Jacob. Jacob . . . Jacob not only dominates the book, but Jacob establishes himself as a character that none of his successors can duplicate. But even Isaac, for all of his heroic deeds and legends and so forth, Isaac is not the colorful, flamboyant character that Jacob is. And [with] each successive generation of Ingledews, as I pointed out before, the architecture of the book gets progressively worse, and since each successive chapter becomes shorter, each successive generation of Ingledews is a little bit less happy or colorful, or less of a character. And Vernon, despite his great intelligence and despite his great wealth, is . . . I don't think Vernon is the man that his father was, and he's a long way from being the man that his great-great-grandfather Jacob was.

LH: Now you made me just understand something else. It's no coincidence that Jacob's story covers almost the first half of the novel, and that we get all the others pushed into the second half. That was very deliberate and intentional on your part.

DH: That was very deliberate. The stories of the successive generations of Ingledews become shorter, and the amount of space taken up by Vernon's story is just a fraction of that taken up by Jacob's story.

LH: In the "Afterword," you tell your readers that despite what they might think, a lot of the more fantastic incidents in the novel are based on historical fact. Could you tell us which ones you were thinking of? Are you thinking about Fanshaw and his dialect? Are you thinking about Jacob and his governorship? What are some of the incidents that are actually based on historical fact?

DH: Well, Fanshaw's dialect was, that was just made up, so I don't know. It's logical, it's credible, that George W. Featherstone, in traveling through the Ozarks, encountered the Osage Indians, and he might have become very chummy with one who admired his British accent and tried to imitate it.[3] Jacob . . . Jacob was based on the actual character Isaac Murphy, and the events that happened to Isaac Murphy . . . becoming governor during Reconstruction, fighting in the Civil War . . . all of those were based on reality. By fantastical, incredible incidents I was thinking of things like the Battle of Whiteley's Mill, when two hundred and fifty Union and Confederate forces fought a two-hour pitched battle and not a one of them got killed. That was true, that happened.

LH: What about the robbery of Isaac's mill, or the attempted robbery of Isaac's mill?

DH: Well, the mill at Drakes Creek was robbed by Jesse James and his gang. Jesse James . . . well they have no actual proof that it was Jesse James, but one of the workers in the mill recognized, or thought he recognized Jesse James, and a story about it appeared in *Arkansas Gazette* newspaper years after the event. And I used the circumstances of that story, I followed it pretty closely, except the part about Isaac Ingledew beating them up. That was made up.

LH: Okay, this actually raises a question, I think, about all your fiction. Could you discuss what you think is the relative proportion of fact to fiction in all your works, and do you think that it's necessary to have both . . . to have a kind of tension between fact and fiction to have effective novels?

DH: Well, *Architecture* was actually the only one that I was . . . that used a lot of historical fact, and even then the proportion of historical fact to what was made up is relatively low. In my other books, there's hardly any fact at all, so I mean there's really no tension between fact and fiction to the extent that there's no fact in most of my books, it's mostly fiction.

LH: Well, let's step back, then, a moment and look at *Architecture* as a whole. We've talked about the characters all the way through, we've talked about the plot and the decline, the rise and fall of Stay More. I'd like to ask a couple final questions about the overall rhythm and structure of the novel and its readership. First of all, we've kind of established before that we can use the term *bigeminal* in terms of all kinds of contrasts, almost a dialectic. Would you say that this applies to the rhythm and structuring of the novel as well? I noticed especially in the opening chapters that, for example, in Chapter One there's a loss . . . Fanshaw leaves. Then in the next chapter, Sarah comes and is joined with Jacob. In the third chapter, I believe it is, Jacob's first son Benjamin is killed . . . there's a loss. And then in the fourth chapter, there's a kind of gain.

DH: We begin with an ending, and we end with a beginning. We have a flood and a drought; there is a kind of bigeminal structure in terms of the whole book.

LH: Within chapters, and from chapter to chapter, and from beginning to end. Would you also say that at any given time in the history of Stay More, even if there is a decline going on, a kind of devolution — a coined term and not a very good one — that there is also a growth simultaneously? Is there any point at which it's all decline, or is there always a source of hope even when there is source for despair?

DH: There's always . . . there is always a source of hope, and even the author himself remarks in the end that "I hope that Vernon and Jelena will invite me to their garden the next time I return to Stay More, and I will be very glad to furnish an epitaph for Eli Willard if they give him a proper burial in Stay More cemetery." There's always the hope, but that hope is never realized. It's like the ambivalent end, in a way, to all my books. We hope in the end of *Lightning Bug* that Dawny will be found. We go on hoping that. He's lost at the time, but there's always the hope that he could be found because the novel never really ends. *Architecture* never really ends. In *Cherry Pit*, we hope that Clifford will somehow find himself, or find his way out of what his problems are. The hope is there, but it's not expressed in the end. In the end of *Some Other Place. The Right Place.*, we hope that Day and Diana are going to live happily ever after, and that they will be good friends with somebody in Stay More, although we don't know at that point that it will be Vernon and Jelena. We hope that "G" will go back home and be reunited with his family and have a nice garden that year and so forth.

LH: What would you say of yourself personally? Are you a more optimistic or a pessimistic person?

DH: I'm extremely optimistic. I would have to be in order to put up with all the crap that I have to go through. I've always been an incorrigible optimist.

LH: I rather think that's . . .

DH: In the face of terrible adversity, I've never given up hope.

LH: I think that is reflected in your novels. One of the things that strikes me about them is that they're very affirmative, despite facing an awful lot of problems, that they always somehow affirm humanity instead of washing its hands collectively.

DH: Well, the Harington family motto written on my coat of arms is translated literally from the Latin meaning that even though we are stripped bare, we never give up hope.

LH: One last question about your Ozark readers in particular. How have they responded to seeing themselves depicted in *Architecture*? Do you have a lot of Ozark readers, and how do they respond?

DH: Well, I probably have a lot, but I haven't heard from very many. The ones I've heard from have all been more or less in agreement that I had depicted the Ozarks as they knew it or as they had heard about it, that *Architecture* is an authentic picture of life in the Ozarks as it was, they felt. *Architecture* is a very nostalgic book. For that matter, nostalgia is a big element in all of my fiction, and *Architecture* was a nostalgic reading experience for them. I haven't received any unfavorable responses from people who have grown up in the Ozarks, except there was the very worst review the book ever got was in the *Ozarks Mountaineer* by Townsend Godsey, who is a teacher at School of the Ozarks, Point Lookout, and he's also a close friend of Vance Randolph's, but he's unlike . . . they're about the same age almost, but unlike Vance, who said that *Architecture* was the best book since *Huckleberry Finn*, Townsend Godsey, he was, is, a very religious person and was offended by all of the sex in the book, and said that I was poking fun at Ozarkers, that I was making fun of Ozark life and I was not. I was simply caricaturing it, in a way.

LH: That raises one last question. Are you a good friend of Vance Randolph's?

DH: Very, very good friend of Vance.

LH: How long have you known him?

DH: Well, I only met him [for the] first time in '76, about three years ago this spring. He is not really able to correspond, so I haven't had any letters from him. I've written letters to him. But every time I go to Fayetteville, and I've been there just about every year, sometimes twice a year, I always go by his nursing home where he lives to chat with him. I reviewed his latest book, *Pissing in the Snow*, for the Fayetteville *Grapevine*. He was very grateful for that, and I'm very grateful to him for having reviewed *Architecture* in Volume II of his annotated bibliography of Ozark folklore and saying that it was the best . . . best regional novel since *Huckleberry Finn*.

LH: Do you have anything else to say to us about *Architecture*?

DH: About *Architecture*?

LH: Or anything else?

DH: Read the book.

LH: Alright, and I have one last thing to say, which is thank you very, very much for having given us so much of your time and for having been so interesting at the same time.

DH: The pleasure has been all mine.

LH: Thank you.

Brian Walter
with Donald Harington

—2004—

BRIAN WALTER: How did you get the idea for *With?*

DONALD HARINGTON: The media are constantly befouled with stories about the abduction of children, particularly young girls. Here in Arkansas there was one particular case that had quite a lot of publicity and left me wondering, with my novelist's imagination, what might have happened to the child if she were still alive somewhere. But there are no similarities between that girl and my character Robin.

BW: You once described *Ekaterina* as an "apotheosis" of Nabokov's *Lolita*; how would you describe the relationship between *With* and *Lolita?*

DH: While it is very true that *Ekaterina* was in homage to, and even in emulation of, Nabokov, I cannot honestly recall once thinking of *Lolita* when I composed *With,* and a careful search of the rather extensive journal that I kept while writing it failed to turn up any mention of *Lolita,* and there were only two mentions of Nabokov: first, when I discovered that allowing Adam to become a narrator midway through the novel gave a somewhat Nabokovian voice to the book, and secondly, when I listed the various sexy books that teenage Adam read in California, and included "one by some Russian named Nabokov about a girl and a man." That allusion in itself is Nabokovian.

I see no similarity whatever between my heroine Robin and Dolores Haze. Sog Alan does not belong to the same species as Humbert Humbert.

BW: It took Nabokov several years and numerous rejections to get *Lolita* published; what challenges did you face in getting *With* into print?

DH: It didn't take me several years, only a year and a half . . . but in a modern age when it is possible to send out manuscripts quickly by e-mail . . . and to be rejected promptly. I fully expect someday to write an essay, "On a Book Entitled *With,*" in which I shall reveal the sordid history of my attempts to find a publisher for the book, and the great variety of ludicrous reasons given for its rejection. I'm not sure whether or not I should brag about having broken Malcolm Lowry's record for the number of rejections of *Under the Volcano.*

BW: Apart from *Lolita,* what other novels does *With* deliberately invoke?

DH: Of course my heroine's name, Robin, offers a clue to the primary source, *Robinson Crusoe.* But her man Friday is an invisible relic of the past. Some of her experiences are almost a match for those of *Alice in Wonderland,* the first novel I read when I was in the third grade at Little Rock's Parham Elementary. But perhaps my direct target as far as invocation is concerned is W. H. Hudson's *Green Mansions.* I honestly wanted Robin to have some of the allure and mystery, not to mention the singing ability, of Rima the bird girl.

BW: Like Faulkner in *As I Lay Dying,* you use a variety of narrators in *With,* shifting to a different character with each new chapter; what are the special benefits and challenges of this strategy?

DH: Actually there's only one first-person narrator, and that's Adam. Quite a number of chapters are narrated from the point of view of Robin, Sog, and the various animals, but they are not narrators themselves. Some rejecting editors complained about my "talking dogs." None of the dogs talk, nor do they narrate, but the happenings of the book are sometimes seen from their point of view.

When I first began the novel, I toyed briefly with the idea of having Hreapha the Wonder Dog narrate the first chapter in the first person. But I quickly realized that wouldn't be convincing, so I simply switched to narrating it myself but from the point of view of Hreapha.

I think my primary motive for all the different points of view in the novel is a kind of foil for Robin's loneliness. Having so many different points of view also broadens the reader's perspective of what is happening, helping to answer that persistent question, "Why is this happening?" The more the merrier.

BW: Nabokov apparently [reportedly] hitched rides on school buses to learn schoolgirl slang; how did you prepare to adopt and present seven-year-old Robin's viewpoint?

DH: I did nothing, really, to prepare, other than having fathered three daughters myself and knowing pretty well how the young female mind works and the female voice speaks at the various stages of childhood and adolescence. That perhaps was my only advantage over Nabokov: he had a son but no daughters.

BW: Why *"With"*?

DH: After a bunch of long titles, such as *Some Other Place. The Right Place.* and *The Architecture of the Arkansas Ozarks* and *Thirteen Albatrosses (or, Falling Off the Mountain)*, it was time to catch my breath with a quick monosyllable.

And yet, that one word is loaded with meanings, significance, and utility. Each of the five section titles of the book is a variation or a play upon that handy preposition. I trust the title will stick in the reader's mind, and in the public's mind.

BW: Ghosts have had an important presence in several of your books; how is the *in-habit* in *With* different?

DH: Kindly realize that *in-habits* are not ghosts. They are the spirits of living persons who could not bear to leave a beloved haunt. Ghosts do haunt; *in-habits* dwell in haunts.

BW: How did the idea for Robin's menagerie of animal companions develop? Did anything about her animal companions surprise you?

DH: I started with the one dog necessary to the plot, and it simply expanded from there. Exponentially. The animals didn't surprise me, but they delighted me.

BW: What would you say to a reader who is reluctant to try a book about the abduction of a seven-year-old girl?

DH: Exactly what I said to a few of the editors who rejected the novel with words like "I have a young daughter myself and I found this unbearable to read." My only response was to wonder just how far into the book they managed to endure the unbearable, because *With* rather quickly reaches a point where it is no longer about a nasty man stealing a little girl but about a little girl outwitting a nasty man and growing up in the wilderness *with* a wonderful series of adventures and life-affirming experiences.

BW: What sort of reviews has *With* had so far?

DH: It's fabulous. In addition to starred rave reviews in all four of the advance review media, and its selection as a Book Sense 76 best book, *With* is steadily amassing a respectable series of fine national reviews. You can watch for a review coming out soon (if not today) in your favorite magazine or newspaper.

The Stay More Interviews

—2006 & 2007—

Prologue

ETWEEN AUGUST 2006 and June 2007, I visited the home of
Donald and Kim Harington in Fayetteville, Arkansas, three
times to capture a video record of the novelist discussing his life
and work, which had (among other honors) earned him both the *Oxford
American*'s lifetime achievement award for contributions to Southern
literature and the (technically unofficial) title of "America's greatest
unknown writer" from *Entertainment Weekly*.

The Haringtons had hosted me in their home on numerous occasions
over the years, going back to my first e-mail exchanges with the novelist in
the fall of 1996, but these interview visits a decade later immediately took
on a different tone for reasons that had little to do with the presence of
the camera. In the spring of 2006, Harington had been one of the keynote
eulogists for Larry Vonalt, his best friend and the dedicatee of *Butterfly
Weed*, and had, shortly thereafter, been involved in a car accident that
broke his ankle and led to the discovery of a near-fatal case of pneumonia
and other physical complications that ultimately robbed him of his ability to eat and drink. As the Fate Thing would have it, the accident and
consequent medical revelations all occurred shortly after he had begun
work on *Enduring*, or END, as he liked (portentously) to shorthand the
novel that would, in fact, appear just a couple of months before his death,
in early November 2009.

To accommodate his near-deafness, I transferred my questions to a
rubber-banded stack of white three-by-five-inch notecards of the kind
that he always carried in his breast pocket and which he had been using
for decades in his day job as a professor of art history to take student

questions in the classroom. As I had done from our first meeting, I rotated the cards ninety degrees to the perpendicular and wrote my questions in narrow strips down the long unlined sides (a habit that Harington had always considered mildly perverse). Many years before, I had accidentally left one of these cards inside my first copy of *Ekaterina*, a Harvest paperback that I eventually sent out (with several other Harington paperbacks that he had signed) for hard-covering, and the card had been bound into the newly fortified book—an apocryphal text incorporated into perhaps the most ingeniously layered Harington text of all.

The three sessions produced some nine hours of material in total, with Harington not only addressing questions about his life, his work, and his art in general, but also reading long excerpts from several of his novels. We also captured images of him visiting Drakes Creek and Wesley Cemetery (where his parents, grandparents, and, eventually, he himself were interred), "feeding" himself through his gastric tube with the nutritional liquid on which he survived, and even, at the end, turning the tables to interview the interviewer in front of a favorite Carroll Cloar print hanging in the Harington library, directly across from his collections of Nabokov, Styron, and Faulkner (not to mention a veritable museum of Harington editions from across the decades).

When we visited the cemetery where he would be buried just a few years later, I asked him and his beloved wife, Kim, to recreate the painting *Et in Arcadia ego* by his parents' headstone, a favorite theme from his work that I had often discussed with him in person and in the articles I had written about his work over the years. Harington gamely took up position on the south side of the tomb, instructing Kim in the pose she should strike opposite him, a comedian of inspired loss and death-haunted beauty who was, even then, writing the novel he had already declared his last. In the interviews, he (once again) lavished plenty of acerbic wit on his frustrations with the publishing world and the life of the writer, but his unmistakable sense that he was rapidly approaching an end seemed to make him a little less mock-combative than he had often been with my lovingly mischievous attempts over the years to pique him with questions about life, the universe, and everything.

Writer's Life

BRIAN WALTER: If you knew you had only five minutes to live, what would you do with that time?

DONALD HARINGTON: I would sit here on the sofa with Kim and hold her hand and tell her how much she meant to me. But five minutes would not be nearly enough.

BW: If you could go back fifty years—to 1956 or so—what could your twenty-year-old self have definitely predicted about his life in 2006? What could he never have predicted back then?

DH: I could probably have predicted that I would be a novelist. I doubt that I could have predicted that I would have written fourteen novels.[1] I could have predicted that I would have something to do with art, but I could never have predicted that I would be teaching art history in the same classroom where I first studied it.

BW: Could you have predicted anything about the content or storylines of your novels?

DH: Yes, I could have definitely predicted that they would have concerned the Ozarks. I wouldn't know about Stay More specifically, but in 1953, I first read a copy of Vance Randolph's *Down in the Holler*, which was a guide to Ozark folk speech, folk language. I fell in love with that book. And from '53 on, I probably knew that I would somehow incorporate that book into my novels. If I ever got around to writing novels. I'm sure that the content would have had to do not only with the Ozarks as a setting, but also with my favorite theme of love—human relationships.

BW: What do you now see and understand as a teacher in the same room that you went to as a student that you couldn't see or understand then?

DH: Well, it's really amazing how much I have learned from myself and from my students over the years about art that I probably had no inkling of at that time. I recall that, in one of the tests given to the MFA students, the art history teacher simply showed two hundred slides and asked us to identify as many of them as possible. I got, I think, something like thirty-eight, which was a good bit more than the other two MFA candidates, and it was only passing score. If I had taken the same test today, I would have scored two hundred, easily. And I not only know a lot more about identifying works of art, but I also know a lot more about just what goes into a picture. For example, I have come to the conclusion that all art springs from the heart or from the head. I didn't know that back then. I had to learn it over the years and develop the idea that all art is either emotional, therefore expressionistic, or it is cerebral, intellectual.

BW: What about your art?

DH: My art? I think my art inclines more to the intellectual than to the emotional, but I try to have a balance of the two in my work. But my art itself could be about very emotional subjects and still be done in a more intellectual manner to produce emotions in the reader. But the art itself is essentially from the mind and for the mind.

BW: What sorts of things that make you laugh or cry? Do any artworks make you laugh or cry?

DH: I have never, to my knowledge, wept or giggled at a work of art. I have a very low trigger point for laughter. I think I have laughed at my own writing maybe twice, three times. Things that people tell me are hilarious—I might enjoy them, but I don't laugh out loud, I don't giggle, I don't feel outward mirth. And the same with crying. When was the last time I cried, Kim?

KIM HARINGTON: I think that you cried when you were writing that part of *When Angels Rest* when [important character] died.

DH: I think that's possible. But the only thing from life that I can remember crying about is when I learned that [my daughter] Jennifer had lost her baby; I think I cried for her. That's the last time I can remember crying. I'm trying to remember when a book made me laugh or made me cry. I just don't . . . I just don't show my emotions. And it could be a kind of . . . repression. When I was a child, a very small boy, I cried at the slightest thing—the least thing would set me boo-hooing all over the place. It was so bad that the next-door neighbor once offered me fifty cents if I could go for a whole day without crying. I was never able to collect. And maybe so much was made of my crying when I was a child that I have just, over the years, steeled myself never, ever to cry again.

BW: Do you consider yourself a stoic?

DH: Not consciously a stoic. But to have endured the things that I have endured, I would have to be a stoic simply by temperament rather than by choice.

BW: Name some of those things that you have endured.

DH: Well, all of those things that made me cry when I was a child. Then at the age of twelve, I was stricken with meningococcal meningitis, which left me hospitalized for most of the summer. And then, throughout my life, I've had things that were very painful, upsetting, time-consuming . . . things that would make a person have to be naturally stoic simply to get through them.

BW: What's the funniest thing you've ever written?

DH: Probably Doc Swain's visit to Saint Louis [in *Butterfly Weed*]. Doc Swain went up to Saint Louis to try to get his medical diploma after sending off fifty dollars of his hard-earned money to the company that printed them up. And when he got there and discovered that it was just a printing press, he thought he might as well see what medicine was like in a big town like Saint Louis. Doc Swain was extremely intelligent; he knew everything about medicine. I think the first big laugh occurs when he describes the doctors in these hospitals, that they wore these striped dresses and little striped hats on their heads, and they were really nurses, not doctors, but he thought they were doctors. That whole passage is full of yuks.

BW: What distinguishes comedy from tragedy? Which takes precedence in your work, and why?

DH: I don't believe that there's just a thin line distinguishing one from the other. I believe that tragedy is about something that is definitely very sad, gloomy, upsetting—tragic. Comedy is about something that elevates the emotions or tries to see mankind and the world in such a perspective as to capture its foibles and its humorous aspects. I definitely prefer that in my work. I don't think of myself as a comic writer; I certainly am not a tragic writer. But I feel that to have a book that is nothing but comedy, without any tragic relief, would be very tedious. So, I try to always throw a little tragic relief into my comedy and a little comic relief into my tragedy. But they are clearly distinct.

BW: What are some of your favorite comedies and tragedies?

DH: [Wryly] Well, let's start with Shakespeare. Probably the funniest novel that I've ever read was *A Confederacy of Dunces*, by John Kennedy Toole. Right behind it would be John Barth's *Sot-Weed Factor*. Those are both hilarious novels. Tragedies, I would have to put, at the top of the list, William Styron's *Sophie's Choice* and right behind it, James Agee's *A Death in the Family*.

BW: Why do you still write novels?

DH: That assumes that I might have any reason for *not* writing novels. I can't think of any reason not to write novels, unless I had written one so God-awfully bad that I was ashamed of having become a novelist. I've done some novels that weren't as good as my others, but I've never written a really bad novel. As long as I can still write a novel that people will find readable, enjoyable, and maybe get something out of . . . I've always told my art students that, by definition, art is an escape from reality, so that when we return from reality after being immersed in art, we can somehow find reality more bearable, more enjoyable, or more understandable. And I have felt that way about all of my novels, that they should do one of those things for the reader, and as long as I can still do that, I have no reason to stop writing novels. I expect to write my last novel at the age of eighty-six.

BW: Why eighty-six?

DH: That's when I'll die, probably.

BW: Why not ninety-six?

DH: If I don't die until I'm one hundred, then I'll be like Hokusai, the famous Japanese printmaker,[2] who said, "Oh, if I could only live to be one hundred, I might learn something about art." If I could live to be one hundred, I might learn something about writing novels.

BW: What are some of your favorite myths and mythological figures?

DH: Many of my books, like *Butterfly Weed*, are filled with actual Greek myths in modern disguise. I couldn't tell you which one is my favorite. The myth of Venus being born fully formed from the head of Zeus, I like that, particularly as it is depicted by Botticelli in his *Birth of Venus*.

BW: What does Botticelli's depiction of Venus being born from the sea mean?

DH: As I interpret it, and it's been subjected to many different interpretations, Venus or Aphrodite was a goddess of love. All of the other gods and goddesses were born from the bodies of various other gods and goddesses. Love was conceived from the foam of the sea or from the brow of Zeus, her father—the implication being that Zeus, the supreme god, had to conceive of such a far-fetched idea as love, that love could not have an ordinary birth like the other gods and goddesses.

BW: What would an Aphrodite of the Ozarks look like? What would be the story of her origin?

DH: I don't think there would be an Aphrodite of the Ozarks, unless there's a little bit of Aphrodite in Latha Bourne, my heroine. The recent Toby paperback of *When Angels Rest* has a woman on the cover that looks very much like Aphrodite, as seen by Botticelli and others. She's an Ozark Aphrodite, but I don't think of Aphrodite as being Ozarkian. The Ozarks are too down-to-earth and commonplace to have a true mythology of their own. Vance Randolph is playing a kind of joke on Donald Harington, the author, when he introduced all of these stories about the history of the Ozarks and the Ozark people that he took directly from mythology. He was probably trying to elevate

Ozark tales to the level of mythology, which he never did in any of his
own writings.

BW: What kind of dreams do you have? Have they changed or evolved
over the decades? Since your accident?[3]

DH: Since my accident, I have not dreamt at all. But over the years,
probably the most common, number-one dream that I dream over and
over again is about a house that has been abandoned for a long time or
is in need of being taken care of or restored, and I feel an obligation to
do something—get my belongings out of it—or do something about
the house to preserve it. That's the most common dream I've had; I
don't know how far back I can trace it. When I was much younger, I
used to have dreams of flying, but such dreams supposedly are a kind
of symbol of transcendence, of wanting to escape from a terrible situation that you're in. I don't recall having one of those flying dreams for
a long time. But as I said, since the accident, I cannot recall a single
dream that I have had.

BW: How do you connect yourself to Sir John Harington? What affinities,
if any, do you have with him?

DH: Harington was a kind of court jester in the court of Elizabeth I. He
was very quick-witted, fast with a joke; he could make people laugh
very easily. And Queen Elizabeth, who adopted him as her godson, she
simply liked to have him around because of his good humor and his
wit, and maybe he was a good-looking dude too, for that matter. But
she elevated him to a kind of stature that the others around her, like
Sir Walter Raleigh, did not have. There's even a vague bit of innuendo
that there might have been something going on between Elizabeth and
John Harington. "Jack," she called him, "Boy Jack." She was much
older than he was. With her encouragement, he wrote and published
his poetry. His poetry made him a small reputation, and then, without
the queen's knowledge, he wrote *The Metamorphosis of Ajax*, which,
in Britain, would be pronounced, "Metamorphosis of A-Jakes." And
"jakes" is British slang for privy, or toilet. *Metamorphosis* was the whole
story of how to make an indoor privy, in which the stuff would be
flushed away. And for that reason, Sir John Harington is given credit
with being the inventor of the flush toilet, and the "john," as we call
it, the john is named after him. He also did a translation of *Orlando
Furioso* that goes on and on and on, but it's considered one of the masterpieces of its time.[4] He wrote countless epigrams, epigraphs, and
various other manifestations of his personal wit. I like to think that I

inherited part of his sense of humor, or I have an affinity with a lot of his work, but sad to say, I have not read the complete works of Sir John Harington. My daughter Jennifer is working on a novel based upon his life, and I expect to read it. I haven't even read *Metamorphosis of Ajax*; I've just read chapters here and there. The only thing of his that I've really tried to read was called *In Praise of Thee*. It's about celebrating the later years of life. I'd have to look that up and get back to you tomorrow with the actual title, but it's a very interesting book.

BW: What do you most hope your future biographers will understand and convey about you? What do you fear that they would most likely misunderstand?

DH: Robert Frost put on his tombstone a line from one of his poems: he had a lover's quarrel with the world. I don't have a lover's quarrel with the world, but I have a relationship with the world that is very weird and unusual and not, by any means, a lover's relationship of any sort. I do love the idea that people were meant to interact with each other and to produce stories that they could tell to each other to create a sense of enjoyment in life. I think whoever created humankind had a great sense of humor. But I do feel that I may be misunderstood as just writing about country yokels. I've written about a mythical place, Stay More, which exists only in the mind of the reader. There is no such place except in the mind of the reader. And that place may seem to be populated by hillbillies, but those hillbillies are actually the parts of oneself that one recognizes in the process of encountering them and thereby laughs at them, learns from them, has some kind of interaction with one's own self. In one of my very early novels, *Some Other Place. The Right Place.*, which is one of Kim's favorites, the narrator, Day, pauses at one point and says, "This is a story, you know it, don't you? Not the story of ghost-towns where actual people lived and died, but a story of lost places in the heart." And it's been my job as a novelist to seek out those lost places in the heart, and because I can't just shove them into your face and say, "Look at these lost places," I do it indirectly by having you discover these lost places in the people and the places that populate my book.

BW: Why art history?

DH: My answer to that would be: why not art history? A novelist should not—ever—have the teaching of writing as a career. Teaching of writing interferes too much with one's own writing. I think I knew that or intuited it from the very beginning. I knew that, if I had to have some kind of career, it would not be in the English Department.

I had begun college as a journalism major and decided that journalism was too ephemeral, so I didn't want to be a journalist. And after a trip to New York in my sophomore year, which exposed me to a lot of great art in the museums of New York City, I came home determined to be an art major. And for two years, I took a lot of painting, drawing, sculpture, all of the arts, and then got into the MFA program to work on a master's degree in printmaking, primarily woodcuts, also lithographs, etchings, engravings, silk-screens, but printmaking was my concentration for the MFA program. But while I was doing that, I had to take so many hours of art history, and we had a very good art history teacher, Ed Albin. Under Ed Albin, I discovered a love for art history that made me decide, after getting my MFA, I would try to get a Master's in Art History, and then a PhD. I knew that, to get a teaching job, you had to have a PhD. So, I got accepted at Boston University, got my master's in one year in art history. At the same time, I applied for admission at Harvard, the best school for art historians, and I was accepted there. I went for one year in the PhD program at Harvard, even up to the point of discussing possible topics for my dissertation. But one of the best teachers, Daniel Catton Rich — I probably named Daniel Lyam Montross after him — was the director of the Worcester Art Museum, and he taught modern art in the art history program. I wrote a brilliant paper on Degas, and in his notes that he handed back to me, he said, "Mr. Harington, this is a very lively paper. It's very breezy and novelistic. In fact, too much so for scholarship." And since he had called it "novelistic," a light bulb flashed on over my head, and I thought, "Maybe I ought to be writing novels." So, when I dropped out of the Harvard program and got my first teaching job, at a small college in New York called Bennett, the first thing I did was I started a novel. And I kept it up and kept it up. I finally finished a novel called *Land's Ramble*. Meanwhile, I had made friends with William Styron, but that's another story.

BW: What was the first painting you fell in love with? Which paintings have you fallen in love with since?

DH: That's another one of those imaginative questions that will take research on my part, a lot of thought and memory. It all comes back to Giorgione's *Tempest*,[5] which I was very fond of when I first saw it. Since Giorgione's *Tempest*, I've fallen in love with just about everything that Thomas Hart Benton did.[6] Many American painters — the Hudson River School, I'm very fond of. It's hard for me to pinpoint particular painters and say that I love this painting, because I love them all.

BW: Whom would you choose to paint Kim's portrait or yours?

DH: You mean famous artists? It would take Botticelli to do justice to Kim. I would like to have George Caleb Bingham to do my portrait.[7]

BW: Which paintings would you most like to enter and remain in forever upon death? As in Yeats's "Sailing to Byzantium"?

DH: That wasn't a painting—that was a whole world that Yeats wanted to enter into. I would like to enter into the whole world of Bingham's frontier Missouri. Bingham's *Shooting for the Beef, County Election, Raftsmen of the Missouri.* That whole world of Bingham, I would like to enter into and remain in forever until death—upon death. Upon death.

BW: What would art history professor Don Harington have to say about artist Don Harington? What could the teacher tell about the artist only from his painting?

DH: He would observe that his biggest flaw was inconsistency. He never found a style. To be successful as an artist, you have to find a specific style and stick with it and do a certain body of work in that particular style. I was too restless, too experimental. I was constantly shifting my admiration from one artist to another. In some of my woodcuts, I'm imitating Menchon;[8] in other of my woodcuts, I'm imitating Antonio Frasconi.[9] I never could make up my mind which style to stick with and never developed a style of mine own. If I had, I might have remained an artist; as it was, I did so many prints and paintings that they all looked like they had been done by a different artist.

⚡⚡⚡

BW: What was the best sermon—or who was the best preacher—you ever heard?

DH: I cannot remember a specific sermon, but I can certainly remember the preacher. His name was Leary—not Larry—but Leary Ball. He lived in Johnson, Arkansas, but he was a kind of circuit rider, and at least once a month, he came out and preached at Drakes Creek. In the vicinity of Drakes Creek is a famous stream called Ball Creek, named after the Balls who lived around it. And I have a suspicion—although I never knew—that Leary Ball might have been descended from those Balls, and that's why he favored Drakes Creek and liked to come out and preach in our church even if he didn't get the proceeds of the collection plate.

He wasn't a fiery preacher, but he was a very good preacher, very warm. I took a shine to him. He was my personal hero in the way that most kids that age had action comic-book heroes, like Captain Marvel, Superman, whatever. Leary Ball was my hero. And I got to the point where, going through a phase of my life in which my mind seemed to be getting away from me, I would be having such a wild, weird succession of thoughts that I would feel as if I were going crazy. Whenever that happened, I would simply summon up the name "Leary Ball," and it would bring me back from the brink of insanity. I worked that into *Lightning Bug*, in which Dawny says that he thinks of Every Dill, and the name "Every Dill" is a play upon "Leary Ball." Just the thought of the name "Every Dill" would bring him back from madness and save him.

BW: What are some of your favorite Bible passages or stories?

DH: Keep in mind it's been forty years since I was a Church of Christ preacher.

KH: But you weren't really a Church of Christ preacher.

DH: I most certainly was. You didn't know that?

KH: Were you ordained?

DH: No Church of Christ preacher was ordained. To the extent anyone can be a Church of Christ preacher, and none of them had been ordained or had any special schooling. I was a Church of Christ preacher in the sense that, every Sunday, I got up and preached.

BW: Please offer your personal definitions of the following terms.

DH: One, *salvation*. Salvation is the promise of going to heaven after death, which is offered to people who repent, confess, and believe in the Lord Jesus Christ. *Rapture* was a term never used in the Church of Christ, so I can't give you the Church of Christ's view of rapture. But it means *to be taken*; the word's related to *rape*, rapture and rape. To be taken by the Lord, removed from the sins of this world. *Fornication* is when one bee gets on top of the other bee and deposits his . . . fornication is any sexual act between two people who are not married to one another. *Original sin* was a sin of disobedience. Adam and Eve were put in the Garden of Eden and told: "You may eat anything here, except don't eat this particular fruit." And Satan appeared in the guise of a serpent and tempted Eve into eating the forbidden fruit. And after she had eaten it, she persuaded Adam to do likewise. So, they both violated the Lord's commandment not to eat the fruit. I don't know what was so special about that goddamn fruit! But God didn't want anybody eating it. Maybe it was just a test, a test of their obedience. And they violated it, and thereby committed the original sin for which mankind continued to pay the price — until the Lord came along and redeemed mankind from its original sin. And finally, *morality*. Morality is a code of ethics, usually drawn up by religious people, who have the need, just as God had the need, to tell people: "Don't you go eating any of that fruit." There is a necessity for religious leaders, including God himself, to tell people what to do, what not to do. Moses said, "Don't eat any pigs, because they're contaminated." And ever since he said that, no Jews have eaten any pigs. Well, this necessity to tell people what to do and what not to do set up a code of ethics governing human conduct. Anything which followed the code was moral, and anything that did not follow the code was immoral. And morality applied to the whole system of what you better not do if you know what's good for you.

⚡⚡⚡

KH: Brian would like me to ask you the questions in this next category.

DH: Our next topic is sex, but we don't say "sex," we say "eros." Eros was the Greek god of love, the son of Venus or Aphrodite. So, we get our word *erotic* from Eros. And Eros provides the name for Russell, who was the son of Venus in *Butterfly Weed*.

KH: What was the genre of your first time making love? Comedy? Tragedy? Drama? Farce? Melodrama? Romance? Or history play? Please elaborate.

DH: You mean . . . us? First time ever? Okay. The one that I would apply to it is missing — recreation. That's not on the list. There was nothing comic, tragic, farcical, melodramatic, romantic, or historical about it. Two people just got in bed to see what happened.

KH: How old were you?

DH: Seventeen. Maybe sixteen. I would have to research that.

KH: Little Rock? Drakes Creek?

DH: I was in a house right across from Fayetteville High School in Fayetteville, Arkansas. I don't want to go into personal details and tell who the woman was; I don't think that should be a matter of record. It was an older woman, and it was in her private home. I happened to be living there, in her house. And I had been there for quite some time before we finally got around to, uh . . . with the help of several beers . . . I went up behind her and gave her a hug, and I said, "Do you know what I want to do?" And she simply nodded her head. That was the last spoken word; the rest of it was just recreation.

KH: In *Some Other Place. The Right Place.*, doesn't Day say to Diana, "Do you know what I want to do?"

DH: Yes. There's something from my life that creeps into practically all of my books. I do remember that.

KH: What do you remember about the first time you tried to describe the act of making love in writing? What circumstances inspired the attempt?

DH: The first making love in any of my books was a hand job. Margaret in *The Cherry Pit* and Clifford are sitting on the sofa, just talking and getting flirtatious, and she decides she can't make love to him, but she will give him a hand job. But at the last moment, she takes out her delicately scented hankie and wraps it around his penis to collect the semen.

That passage in *The Cherry Pit* was my first attempt to describe a sexual act in any of my books. The first act of intercourse was when Latha makes love to Doyle[10] in the cave above Banty Creek. He's met her while he's out fishing.

KH: What circumstances inspired the attempt?

DH: I don't know. I'm just horny, and I wanted to put some sex in my novels, as I usually do. So, I put that part in about their making love in the cave, that's where I wanted to get in a good line about every time . . . Dahl . . . Doyle . . . His name wasn't Doyle; I'm thinking of Dahl in *The Cherry Pit*. What was the man's name? I even put him in the end of *The Pitcher Shower* . . . Dolph—Dolph Rivett! Notice, by the way: Doyle, Dolph, Diana, Dawny—they all start with D. They are parts of myself.

Dolph makes love to Latha in the cave. This is the passage that Mary Steenburgen read at the Porter Prize.[11] They've been flirting around and he's been teasing her and her scant sexual history is reviewed; she doesn't have much of a chance to make love in Stay More. She says, "Life is full of dangers . . . "

I wrote this passage in hypothetical tenses: could have, would have, perhaps, and so on. Throughout my work, I use peculiar tenses. As you know, I start all books off in the past tense, and then I shift to the present tense, and, finally, to the future tense. I started the custom in *Lightning Bug*, and in it, I also used—I don't know the grammatical term for those tenses—future perfect, present perfect, which suggest that it *might* have happened, and it might *not* have happened. Dawny is telling the story; Dawny did not witness Dolph Rivett making love to Latha Bourne in the cave. He had to imagine it. So, those tenses simply suggest that this is coming out of his imagination rather than something that he was an eyewitness to.

KH: How many terms, off the top of your head, can you come up with for *making love?* What are some of your favorite colloquialisms for *orgasm?*

DH: When I'm writing a book, and I want a synonym for *making love* or for *orgasm*, I look it up in one of my books or collections or *Roget's Thesaurus.* I have a thesaurus of slang, a thesaurus of sexual slang; I have all of these thesauri that I constantly refer to when I am writing off the top of my head.

Synonyms for making love, from *The Thesaurus of Slang*, by Esther and Albert Lewin. Fuck, screw, lay, hump, ball, bang, boff, dork, jazz, shag, shtup, jumping one's bones, make it, make out, go all the way, do the dirty deed, go to bed with, spread, get it on, get to first base, put the moves to, hide the salami, parallel park . . . [To Kim] I hadn't heard that one before, "parallel park." Get one's banana peeled, bump bones, poke, work, trim, tumble, hit, tip, pound, cush, cook, crawl, change one's luck, wham-bam-thank-you-ma'am, slam bam. There are hundreds; they come from different parts of the country. The ones that I got out of Vance Randolph I incorporated into my copy of *Roget's Thesaurus*, which is on the floor in my study.

Favorite Colloquialisms, this is a book in which I got favorite colloquialisms for *orgasm.* One was *going over the mountain;* I'd never heard that before, but I got it out of this book and put it into *The Choiring of the Trees.* Come, blow, get it off, get off, get one's rocks off, shoot one's wad, score, shoot, get over the mountain.

KH: And *falling off a mountain.*

DH: No, *falling off the mountain* is a reference to that passage in Vance Randolph about the joke of the farmers falling off their mountain when they're trying to plow. *Falling off the mountain* has no sexual connotation. I wonder if Tom thought it did and that's why he wanted to change the title to *Thirteen Albatrosses.*[12]

KH: Who are the best writers of sex, and why? Which writers, apart from yourself, would you most want scripting your foreplay?

DH: Probably one of the very best writers of sex is William Styron, who has inspired me in so many other ways. But I've read them all. Learned something from Henry Miller. Learned a lot from John Updike. Who

else? As you notice, the top of my head is very plain, and blank, and
undistinguished looking. I'd rather script my own foreplay.
KH: Not surprising.

ϟ ϟ ϟ

BW: Please offer your personal definitions of the following terms: woman,
man, longing, presence, absence.
DH: Woman is the opposite of man. Men are from Mars, women are
from Venus. Without woman, man would commit suicide. Man needs
woman to stay alive. Woman needs to take out the garbage, mow the
lawn, do other little odd jobs around the house. And, on very rare occasions, perform in bed to conceive his children.[13] Longing, well, if we
are talking about the longing in *Lightning Bug*, there are many different
levels of longing. There's Dawny's longing for Latha; there's Latha's
longing just for something that is not here. Longing is the desire to
possess or be in contact with something you do not have, usually inaccessible. Presence, absence — I guess you're referring to *Lightning Bug*,
but I use presence and absence in all of my novels. Presence is when
you have something and are no longer longing for it. Absence is when
you don't have it and you have to long for it. I once made notes to write
an essay in which I would compare all art to the children's game of
hide-and-seek. Children like to play hide-and-seek because when you
hide you are not available. When you seek, you are expressing your
longing for what is not available. And that, in a sense, is all art, even
music. In music, the silent notes are hidden. The sounded notes are
unhidden, are found. And just as all digital is a matter of one-zero, one-
zero, one-zero, all art, music, literature is a matter of hide, seek, find.
Hide. Seek. Find. But I can't tell you which of my novels you should
go to to understand the concept of each of these terms. They appear
in all of my novels.
BW: What presence does music have in your novels, the work of a deaf
man? Pick any of your novels.
DH: First, a correction. I'm deaf, but I can hear music, and I have written all of my novels with music on the phonograph playing. Some of
my favorites are Beethoven's Fifth Piano Concerto, Tchaikovsky's First
Piano Concerto, Dvorak's "New World" Symphony. I've written many
passages in my novels to those. Linda Hughes, the scholar at TCU,
wrote a paper on how *Some Other Place. The Right Place.* reflects the

structure and the timbre of Dvorak's "New World" Symphony. Be that as it may, you can probably find echoes of the music I listen to in the structure, the thematic complexity, the melody . . . I like to think that all of my writing has a melody to it. Even my prose rhythms sometimes have a kind of lilting—or lulling, as the case may be—melody. So music has a very important impact on this deaf man.

BW: To what degree is your writer—like Nabokov's—a metaphysical seeker, detective, and intriguer? Do you agree with Nabokov's Adam Krug in the end that "the glory of God is to hide a thing, and the glory of man is to find it"?[14] How well does this description apply to your relationship with your readers?

DH: I'll answer the first question first. My writer is, of course, it goes without saying, a metaphysical seeker, detective, intriguer. He's all of those things and many things besides. I did not know that Krug thought the glory of God is to hide a thing, and the glory of man is to find it, maybe because I'm an atheist. I believe it is the glory of *man* to hide things—the glory of man, the writer and his readers, to find them. I'm always hiding things for my readers to find, as so many people have told me. I'll give yourself as an example. You read *Some Other Place. The Right Place.* on a train under bad circumstances coming from Oregon, and it didn't make much of an impression on you. And when you reread it recently, you found all kinds of stuff in it that you had missed on the first reading. And the first reading does not have to be under unfavorable circumstances; it could be under the best circumstances. But still, if you read the novel a second time, you will find all kinds of things that you missed during the first reading, because I hid them.

BW: An example?

DH: Off the top of my head? My structuring of my novels is intuitive. I don't make plans or plots. I don't make lists. I don't think out, "I'm going to end this chapter, I'm going to hide this here, I'm going to hide that there." It just happens because of my sense of layering the plot and the subplot. And anytime you read one of my plots or subplots, one of these things will spring up to your consciousness, and you will wonder: "Why didn't I notice that the first time I read it?" But it's not something that I consciously plan; it just happens.

BW: Do you, like many of your fictional avatars—for example, G. in *Some Other Place.*, Harrigan in *Let Us Build*, or Ingraham in *Ekaterina*— find writing work to be an especially healthful activity?

DH: I was not aware that any of those avatars felt that writing was a healthful activity. It gets all of them into a certain degree of trouble, a certain degree of dissatisfaction. My avatars are a way of letting off steam, letting off some of my own frustrations. Letting off my own sense of lack of recognition, lack of achievement. I don't think any of them ever did it for their health.

BW: What is the connection between writing and alcoholism?

DH: Alcoholism is a disease, and despite what certain people believe, I am not an alcoholic. Alcoholics have no tolerance whatsoever for the chemical alcohol. Many writers become alcoholics because they cannot assimilate the chemical into their systems safely. At certain points in my life, I was an extremely heavy drinker. Heavy drinking—as opposed to alcoholism—can open up your perspective on your own soul; it can unlock pathways that you did not know about. It can simply make you feel good enough to tackle the arduous business of writing, but as I have adequately demonstrated, it is not necessary to produce books. So many great writers practically did away with themselves with alcohol, which I would have done if Kim had not come along and made me sober up. So many of them have destroyed themselves with drinking; drinking is supposed to be a badge of honor for the creative writer. But I simply drank because I enjoyed the taste of it. I never wrote while I was drinking; all of my drinking was done at the day's end, after my workday was over.

BW: If you were planning a writers' feast, which writer would be responsible for which dish?

DH: I object to this question not because I am totally unable to eat myself and getting into that at length would make me summon up visions of tempting food. That's not what bothers me. What bothers me is that it demands a knowledge of other writers' taste in food that I simply do not possess. I have been very fond of food myself, and I look forward to the possibility that medical science might find a cure for my dysphagia, or eating disorder, that keeps me from being able to eat. I look forward to being able again to have barbecue, fried chicken, some of the dishes that I love.

Cooking with Southern Celebrities has Bill Clinton when he was running for president and Donald Harington and my carefully worked-out recipe for barbecue butterflied leg of lamb, which has been my specialty dish for many years. I find a butcher who knows what butterfly means, this is the hard part; most supermarket butchers do not understand the term, which is basically simple: removing the bone from a leg of lamb so the meat is a flat slab roughly the shape of papillon. And then all of the various ingredients for slow cooking it on the grill with various seasonings. It makes my mouth water to think of that recipe, and I hope to have it again someday.

BW: What could the writers who have most influenced you have learned from you? Usual suspects: Faulkner, Nabokov, Styron, others?

DH: Here again, we have a question that takes into account other writers, and I cannot see things from their perspective; I can only see it from my perspective. I cannot say what you will find in my work that you will not find in their work that they ought to have had. Sorry, that's another one of those imaginative questions which strikes me as a kind of a trick question because it involves other writers. With time, I might be able to think of something.

BW: If *Ekaterina*'s Ingraham is right that creative writing cannot be taught, only learned, how did you learn?

DH: By reading books—that's really the only way to learn how to do anything creative. Despite the fact that I'm an art teacher, I would say that the only way to learn how to be a painter is to look at paintings, not have some teacher come in and say, "Oh, your shading is a little bit too mild in this corner; I think you should put more color in that corner." Teachers cannot teach creativity. I learned how to write simply by reading other writers.

BW: Such as?

DH: We named most of them. Nabokov, Faulkner, Styron, James Agee. When I was very young, I read Mickey Spillane and probably learned a lot from him. I read Erskine Caldwell, who's discredited today but knows a lot about narratives. I read a lot of John Steinbeck, who most people think did not deserve to have the Nobel Prize. I've read everything by Hemingway, everything by Fitzgerald, everything by Faulkner. I've just read a lot.

BW: How do you write a novel? How have your methods evolved over the decades?

DH: My methods have not evolved at all; they've been consistent throughout. I think of an idea. For example, in my first novel, the idea is to have a character go home to his hometown and see what happens. I started writing page one: Olyphant is the name of the tiny jerkwater town in northeast Arkansas where the Missouri Pacific train I was riding broke down, etc. You start your first sentence and hope it gets you to the end

of the paragraph, and that that paragraph may suggest another paragraph, and then you just keep on writing. That has been my method for
all of my novels, to simply have a rough idea of what my novel is going
to be about and begin writing it and let the sentences write themselves.
I'm having a bad day.

BW: What about the research? How about the technology? Computers,
internet, and so on?

DH: So many of my novels were written before the internet or computers were invented. I simply went off to the library. I wrote my first five
books on an old IBM Selectric typewriter. It wasn't old when I got it; it
was brand new. And the idea of the typeballs—that I could change the
font; that was the reason that *Lightning Bug* has those different type-
faces throughout. If I wanted to find out something for *Lightning Bug*
or *The Cherry Pit*, I would go off to the library. And it remained my
habit to write in the mornings and spend my afternoons at the library.
It got so bad that, at one point, Kim started following me over to the
library to see if I was really going to the library and not sneaking off to
see my lover or something. I quit going to the library. I discovered that
anything I wanted to find out, I could probably find out on the internet.

That is not strictly true. In my study right now, I have six or seven
books on women in mental institutions, which I'm reading in preparation for the passage of *Enduring* in which Latha is committed to the
state hospital in Little Rock. They are filled with information I could
not have found on the internet; it's just never been put on the internet.
So, my research is a combination of what I have to get from the library
and what I can find on the internet. But the internet has made it infinitely easier for me to find out information.

BW: What's in the notebooks for each novel? Samples?

DH: No, there are no samples, you mean samples of the writing? None
of the notebooks contain any of the passages that would go into the
novels. All of those notebooks are research material. Usually, I get a
book that I can't keep because it's on interlibrary loan. So I take it over
to school and run it through the copy machine and punch three holes
in the pages and put it in one of those ring binders. All of those notebooks [and] ring binders are just filled with research material for the
various books. For example, in the case for *Ekaterina*, I wanted to know
as much as possible about Svanetia, her homeland, and the Caucasus.
I probably have enough material in those notebooks on *Ekaterina* to
write two or three more novels set in Svanetia. But all of that was just

intended for me to have some knowledge of what her homeland was like, and I probably—as I usually do—I overdid it. I over-researched, which is simply a flaw of mine that I am not able to overcome.

BW: How was Stay More born? What happened between the *The Cherry Pit* and *Lightning Bug* to allow Stay More to emerge so fully formed in your second novel?

DH: My second novel actually has not been published; it's called *A Work of Fiction*. It's based upon a real-life novelist of the nineteenth century, whose name was Arrington, not Harington, but Alfred W. Arrington, who went off in search of the real General Pike, General Albert Pike, and found him in seclusion in Arkansas.[15] That novel, for various reasons, was never published. But in the process of doing it, I decided that I had a pretty good ear for regional speech, for mountain speech, for the way people in the hill country talk. So, when I began to write *Lightning Bug*, I thought it would be my swan song to the region, that I had to get the Ozarks out of my system, so I would write *Lightning Bug* and then I could go on write more conventional novels, less regional novels. But after writing *Lightning Bug*, I discovered that I was just hooked; there was no way I could escape from the Ozarks. So, I might as well settle down and realize that I had to devote the rest of my life to Stay More.

The [name] "Stay More" comes right out of Vance Randolph. I'd read Vance Randolph's *Down in the Holler*, and its lexicon at the end has *stay more* as common language of the Ozarks: "Don't be rushin' off, Dawny, stay more and have supper with us."

BW: Which of your novels proved the most challenging to write, the one that sparked the most self-doubt?

DH: The one that sparked the most self-doubt also has not been published; it was called *Farther Along*. It went through several different versions. Finally, it reached a version that Kim and her mother and many readers think is just splendid, but I've never been able to find a publisher for it. Probably if I did find a publisher, I would have to rewrite it extensively.[16] But the most challenging novel to write was probably *The Architecture of the Arkansas Ozarks*, because I had to have not only all of the research information about the actual architecture; I also had to devise a parallel between the lives of the people and the buildings that they inhabited. And worst of all, I had to keep the thing lively from beginning to end; it had to be, in a sense, my funniest novel. And it had to be clearly a novel, despite the fact that it consisted of twenty separate chapters, which were supposedly devoted to architecture.

BW: Why "supposedly"?

DH: Because those chapters are not devoted to architecture. Those chapters are devoted to the people who lived in those buildings or worked in those buildings.

BW: How do you keep track of the names and interrelations of Stay Morons through time? Do you have family trees, chronologies, maps, etc., like Faulkner?

DH: I think Faulkner was reputed to keep family trees of all the Compsons and the Snopes and everyone else. I've never done that. I started out to do that once. I listed all of the names on some sheets of lined paper, and then I realized that I could just never come up with all of the names of the people of each one of the families. So, I have, for the most part, confined the populace of Stay More to those people who have already been mentioned in the earlier books. When I was writing *Architecture of the Arkansas Ozarks*, I got all of their names out of the names that had already been mentioned in *Lightning Bug*. I could probably easily be caught out, and people could find that I had somebody married to somebody who was actually that person's grandmother. Or some very illogical family relationships that was the result of my failure to keep records of the people. But I just don't see that record keeping; I have to go off of what's in my head, what's in my books already written.

BW: This one will need more time, but I'll show it to you. Whom would you pick to direct each of your novels? Whom would you cast as the main characters?

DH: Here again, we have one of those big questions that would take research. Let me say that I'm totally indifferent to Hollywood. I have had so many bad experiences with Hollywood; I've seen so much disappointment from the writers who did work with Hollywood that I just decided not to seek Hollywood as a goal in any respect. Think of some of the greatest modern books which have been made into movies, like William Styron's *Sophie's Choice*. That was a brilliant movie; I took Kim to see it on one of our first dates. *Nobody* sees that anymore. You can go in the video store and see all the videos on the shelf; nobody ever checks them out. Great books might or might not be made into great movies. Usually, they aren't; usually, the greater the book, the worse the movie. But, in any case, it is totally ephemeral; it will not last, it will not endure. And I would rather not be involved with it. There's a Hollywood deal in progress right now to make *With* into a movie, with options being signed and so forth.[17] I'd rather just not know about any of that stuff.

BW: What mysteries in your work has no one—to your knowledge— ever noticed or illuminated?

DH: Nobody knows who the woman whom we cannot name—nobody knows just who she is. I made a stab at it in *Farther Along*. I can't think of other mysteries. [To Kim] Can you think of anything?

KH: Maybe. In *Architecture*, what did Sarah whisper to Jacob?

DH: Nobody's bothered to illuminate that, but I happen to know what it was in case anybody ever asked. She explained to him that if she had slept with him on a regular basis, he would not have been driven to accomplish his great deeds, that depriving him of sex, she motivated him to do what he accomplished. He had asked on her deathbed, "Why hadn't you put out for me more?" And that's what she told him. And I think really intelligent readers might even be able to guess, but I wasn't going to spell it out.

BW: Who is the one we cannot name, and why can't she be named outside the work? In an interview, can she be named?

DH: She was a Little Rock society woman from a great Little Rock family, and, supposedly, we cannot name her in the book because it would have created a blot upon the honor of her great family. In *Farther Along*, I identify her as Elizabeth Cunningham, or Liz. I could, if I wanted to, trace the whole family history of the Cunninghams through early Little Rock. But she is whom we cannot name. She has a certain . . . *cachet*, and I mean *cachet* ambiguously. *Cachée* means "hidden" in French;[18] she is hidden, and being hidden gives her a special quality we can't shed.

BW: How many aliases or pseudonyms or masks do you have for yourself in your novels? And why do you find it so useful or needful to make the author so much a character within the fiction?

DH: I'd like to make a distinction between people who are transparently Donald Harington—like G., whose circumstances, age, condition, loss of hearing, all of that, are clearly Harington.[19] Then there are Harington surrogates, starting with Clifford in *The Cherry Pit*. Clifford is not like myself at all; he's a little guy. I tried to make him as unlike me physically as possible, but he has a lot of my characteristics and attitudes.

Every one of my books has either a Harington surrogate or a
Harington in disguise. I would have to take some time to count them
all up, but I've written fourteen books, so you can assume there are at
least fourteen Harington stand-ins. I do it, simply, to make the book
more immediate for the reader. If the reader can feel that here is this
man who's telling me all of this because he was not only there, he was
involved in it, then his involvement in it makes *me* feel more involved.

BW: What is metafiction, and to which of your novels does the term best
apply?

DH: *Meta* means around, and fiction means . . . fiction that goes around
and around to find a way to keep from being conventional fiction — to
be non-fiction, un-fiction, strange fiction in one way or another. As I
see it, *metafiction* applies to everything I've written. I have never written a conventional novel. All of my novels have some kinds of tricks,
devices, shifts in time, playing around with . . . reality.

The most conspicuous characteristic of metafiction is self-
referentiality. By that, I don't mean they are about the characters that
I base on myself, but the novel is, in a sense, turned in on its own self.
The novel becomes aware of itself. The novel takes on an existence
independent of just being a novel; that makes it metafictional, and to
that extent, all of my books are metafictional.

The one that is most metafictional is thought to be nonfiction. *Let
Us Build Us a City* is supposedly the story of how a guy named Don
Harington and a girl named Kim Gunn got together and explored
these lost towns of Arkansas. Those lost towns are actual places filled
with actual people, and Kim interviews those actual people, and Don
transcribes her interviews and puts them into the book. But *Let Us
Build Us a City* is, basically, a novel; it's a love story, but it's a novel in
the form of a nonfiction travelogue.

BW: Who is Daniel Lyam Montross? Who is Latha Bourne? Who is
Dawny?

DH: These are all fictional characters in my books. Not any of them is
based even remotely on a real person, except you could say that young
Dawny, at that particular age — five going on six — might have had
characteristics similar to mine.[20] [To Kim] Have you shown Brian the
T-shirt that has a photograph of me? That's Dawny on the T-shirt; he
looks just like me. But nothing that happened to Dawny happened to
me. I did not know anybody like Latha Bourne; I certainly didn't know

anyone like Daniel Lyam Montross. They were simply inventions of mine.

BW: Who were they within your work?

DH: Can you explain that question to me? Latha is the goddess—the demigoddess, as I call her—of the world of Stay More. Daniel Lyam Montross is the tutelary spirit. Dawny is the observer. You need those three to have a story.

BW: Can you provide a brief synopsis of *The Cherry Pit*?

DH: The answer is no. All of my publishers have asked me to synopsize the books that I have submitted to them. I refuse to do it.

BW: What advice would you have for the author of *The Cherry Pit*? What advice would *The Cherry Pit*'s author have for his 2006 counterpart?

DH: The 2006 author would find much to admire in *The Cherry Pit*'s author, a certain fire that he could not recapture, because he's too old. When *The Cherry Pit* was written, he was in his thirties, and it's full of youthful zest and wildness and experimentation. That author would not be able to impart any of that to the later author.

KH: You were in your twenties when you wrote *The Cherry Pit*.

DH: Yes, I was in my twenties. And if I then had been given the privilege of saying something to myself now, it would be more in the way of congratulations than it would be in the way of advice. And myself now, I could not tell that kid anything other than, "Don't be so disappointed when you and Cormac McCarthy come up together for the Faulkner prize and McCarthy wins it. Don't let it get you down."[21] My advice for him would not be about writing, but about living the life of the writer without getting too discouraged.

Dawny

BW: What do you remember about the first time you lost someone or something you dearly loved?

DH: Well, I had a dog all the years I was growing up. Her name was Dinah-mite, but it was like a girl's name: Dinah, and mite, meaning small. And Dinah-mite was just a cur, but I had her for at least thirteen years of my life. She just wandered off one day and never came back again. And if she had been run over by a car, I might have been able to experience it immediately, directly, but I just had to gradually get used to the idea that the place was lost. Growing up in Drakes Creek,

I very early came to the conclusion that Drakes Creek was lost, that it had once been much bigger than it was. It had a big general store, it had a hotel, it had a doctor's office, it had a bank. It was filled with buildings that had once been very active and busy, but now, it was just a lost place, a lost place in the road. So, I think it might have been the loss of Drakes Creek that affected me more than the loss of any person.

BW: How did you lose your hearing and when? Was it a gradual process or a sudden shock?

DH: When I was twelve, I worked all day long in the farmers' market,[22] called the Curb Market, selling produce to whoever wanted to buy produce. It was a very hot July day, and there was a big basket of peaches. If I had had the sense—just as if I had had the sense not to make that left turn that caused my accident nine weeks ago tonight [see pp. 270-272 below]—if I had had the sense to take that peach over to the water faucet, and turn on the faucet and rinse it off, I might possibly have spared myself contracting meningococcal meningitis. But the next thing I knew, I woke up in the hospital, and I had been unconscious for several days. The doctors told me there was an epidemic of the disease in Little Rock. Several children had been killed or blinded by it, so I should consider myself lucky, because the only thing wrong with me was that I had lost my hearing. Back to your question about being stoic? That was the first big thing to be stoic about, that I was no longer able to hear. And I went for a long time not able to hear a thing. I had tinnitus in my ears, which allowed me to hear imaginary sounds, and the imaginary sounds I heard were crickets, cicadas, the sounds of the night in Drakes Creek. So when I went back to Drakes Creek after recovering from my illness, I could not hear anything, *except* I could distinctly hear those sounds of the summer night that I have tried to capture in my work.

BW: How has your tinnitus changed or evolved over the decades?

DH: My tinnitus changes from day to day. I have no control over it. Sometimes, when everything is going right, I can hear all of my favorite symphonies and concertos in my tinnitus. Other days, when things aren't going right, my tinnitus is just a constant, monotonous, screeching, drowning roar. If I listen to it right now . . . I hear a kind of melody that I can't identify. I don't think it's really changed all that much over the decades. I've become more and more accustomed to it. Some people are practically driven mad by their tinnitus. I've had letters and read stories about people who developed tinnitus later in life, and it just drove them out of their wits. But I guess I had my tinnitus early enough to get used to it, and now, I practically take it for granted.

BW: What did you do during your recovery from the meningitis?

DH: Well, it took me about as long to recover from the meningitis as it took me to recover from this accident that I had. As soon as I was able, at my request, I went to Drakes Creek and spent what remained of the summer at Drakes Creek, just taking it easy and watching people come around and try to talk. The local kids teased me a lot, because they couldn't understand what deafness was, and they had been told that they could come up and call me anything they wanted to, and I wouldn't hear them. So I was the butt of a lot of jokes that summer. But I mostly just relaxed, enjoyed country life, watched the world go by, and listened to the crickets and cicadas.

BW: What did you gain from losing your hearing that you couldn't have gained any other way? What can those of us blessed or saddled with normal hearing never hope to understand or appreciate?

DH: Well, I've always believed that I was destined to lose my hearing at exactly the point where the Ozarks folk speech was undergoing the transition to modern speech. And all the old Ozark words and pronunciations and accents and meanings were being lost and forgotten. That's another item that should go onto the list of things that were lost that I have mourned the loss of. I heard the Ozarks language as it was before it disappeared, and I embedded it more firmly into my memory, because I could no longer hear it, nor could anyone else. Kim is always telling me about things that I should be glad I can't hear, like the refrigerator when it goes on in the middle of the night. I've never heard that or all the little sounds and squeaks and peeps and chirps and little noises that are part of your everyday life. And they can get annoying. Any person who is blessed or saddled with normal hearing has to endure a lot of things that I don't have to endure. And you can't turn it off.

BW: How did the young Donald Harington develop his love for Newton County and the Ozarks? What was a summer evening like for the real Dawny?

DH: The two creeks in Drakes Creek were Drakes Creek itself and Hocks Creek, which ran into it. In Stay More, the main creek is called Swains Creek, and the creek that runs into it is Banty Creek. I went fishing and swimming in both Hocks Creek and Drakes Creek and developed a great love for fresh water, freshwater fish, swimming in the creek. But all of that in Drakes Creek is in *Madison* County, not Newton County. I didn't discover Newton County until I was in college, when I happened to be driving over there and saw how much more spectacular the mountain scenery was than it was back in Madison County. So, when I came to invent Stay More—just as William Faulkner had moved Yoknapatawpha one county east from the actual Jefferson County—I moved Newton County, keeping its actual name, one county east from the actual Madison County.

BW: What was your father like? When and how did you lose him? If he had lived to read all of your books today, which would have been his favorite, and why?

DH: My father was a very severe man. He had a good sense of humor, which I probably inherited from him. He had absolutely no patience. He was very mean to my older brother and to me. My younger sister said that she developed a severe psychological problem, which her psychologist got her to realize was the result of the fact that, by mercilessly beating on me and my brother, my father was showing us some attention that he denied her. She had always felt victimized by being denied the attention that my father's meanness to me and my brother had been displaying. But despite a very abrasive, rough relationship, whenever I was away from home, we kept up a constant correspondence. I have hundreds and hundreds of his letters. I don't know what happened to mine to him; they were probably thrown away. But I have all of his letters, and I know that they are a mixture of poor attempts at humor and just bits of news about the rest of the family. They were my main link with home when I was at the university, when I went away east to college.[23] So, I missed those letters after he died. I was forty-one when he died, and I went to pieces. It made me realize that I probably had loved him a lot more than I was willing to admit or realize. I really did cry. He was buried out at Wesley Cemetery, which is the cemetery for Drakes Creek. He knew that when my mother died, she would want to be buried there beside him, and that was her country. So, he asked to be buried in Wesley Cemetery, and at his funeral, I just went all to pieces. It took me weeks to recover from his funeral.

He pretended not to have read my books. That was the big pretense that he had to stick to—that he was glad to see this new book of mine, or, why, this one's so big that we're using it for a doorstop, and so on and so forth. He never admitted to reading one. My sister told me that he had read them all and loved them, was very proud of them. I had only written four at the time he died. I think he was especially fond of *The Architecture of the Arkansas Ozarks*. But I think if he had lived, he probably would have liked *With*. *With* would probably have been his favorite book, because it's a combination of real-life things that seem to be real but just could not be . . . could not be possible. Like dogs communicating with each other in some way, and the whole idea of this child molester taking this girl up to the mountain top and never harming a hair of her head. *With* is shot through, as we will discover in tomorrow's interview, with enigmas and riddles and incongruities, illogical things. I think he would have liked all of that.

BW: What was your mother like?

DH: My mother was just an Ozark country girl. Since my father liked to terrorize people, my mother was his primary victim. He never abused her, to my knowledge. He never struck her. He spoke a lot of harsh words to her. He made her cry pretty often, but she was totally under his thumb. And I remember the point at which I stopped being such a loving son to her. I had my little red wagon out on the front sidewalk, and I was giving it a fresh coat of red paint. And I had neglected to spread newspapers under it, and I had gotten a couple of drops of red paint on the sidewalk. My father came home, and he was so outraged that he took off his belt; his belt was his favorite instrument of punishment. He took off his belt and began lashing me with it as hard as he could all the way up the front steps of the house, into the house, through the living room. I was crying as hard as I could back to the kitchen in hopes that, in the kitchen, my mother would see what he was doing and make him stop. And I finally got back to the kitchen, and she would not lift a finger to make him stop. At that point, I ceased loving my mother, and I think I never regained true son's love.

My mother was a sweet lady, very frail. She had a lot of Ozark characteristics. She had a lot of common sense, which I may have inherited from her. She had a lot of charity. She was deeply religious and tried to make me religious too, but I gradually weaned myself from religion, to her dismay. In my later years, I was a great disappointment to my mother. I don't remember that my father ever read a book of mine, but I know definitely that my mother read *Lightning Bug*. And the only thing she ever said about it was, "Dawny, you have a place in *Lightning Bug* where the cats openly *make love*. Dawny, I will have you know that cats do not do that in the open — they crawl under the porch to do it." That's the only comment my mother ever made about any of my writing.

She outlived my father by seven years. She spent a lot of her later years in a nursing home. I tried to be a dutiful son, visit her as often as I could. But I have had a very guilty conscience for not paying more attention to her during her last years. She was becoming senile and incontinent and just deteriorating the way that old people do. And when she died, she was buried right beside my father with a double tombstone at Wesley Cemetery in Drakes Creek. And I went to her funeral . . . [To Kim] You went to her funeral too. Did I cry at her funeral? I did not cry at her funeral.

BW: What passage from your novels would you have wanted to be read in celebration of your birth?

DH: That's a really tough one. You gave that to me in advance, and I thought about it and thought about it and tried to think of any passages from my novels that would be appropriate to read in celebration of my birth, and I'm sorry to confess that I simply cannot think of one. If you backed me up against the wall and said, "You better think of something, or I'm going to pull the trigger," I would probably say the passage from *Some Other Place. The Right Place.* that is about the birth of Daniel Lyam Montross. Montross supposedly comes into this world fully cognitive, fully aware of everything that's going on, fully knowledgeable about who all of these strange people are around him, and from that point on, he knows it all. I'd probably have that passage from Daniel Lyam Montross's birth read.

BW: The Stay More novels teem with ghosts, haunts, and spirits, but who are your personal ghosts? Whose spirits continue to visit your consciousness, and how have their deaths and communications changed over the years?

DH: There really are no spirits or haunts in the conventional sense of the word. Kim and I are convinced that everything on Earth is somehow under the sway or control of a force or being whom we have chosen to call the Fate Thing. And to the extent that the Fate Thing is a spirit—and it certainly is a spirit, and it's a real spirit that I believe in, though I've never seen the Fate Thing—I devoutly believe that the Fate Thing is out there, or in here. There's a Fate Thing that's watching over everything that happens to me, and to Kim, and to you, and the Fate Thing is controlling our destiny. I'll give you the most recent example. The Fate Thing usually comes to our rescue; when we're in a bad predicament, the Fate Thing bails us out, makes money come in from some unknown source, makes something good happen when things are bad. That invariably happens. So, I asked Kim why the hell would the Fate Thing allow me to get into an automobile wreck and break my ankle? And Kim thought about that and realized that the important thing about this recent accident was that it hospitalized me so that the doctors could discover what bad condition I was in, particularly my lungs, which were riddled with pneumonia, and a bladder problem that was life threatening. I could very easily have died from one of these other conditions *if* the Fate Thing had not put me in the hospital by simply cracking my ankle—no big deal.

The Right Place

BW: How did you get your first novel published?

DH: *The Cherry Pit* was my first novel, first published novel, published by Random House in 1965 through the offices of my good friend William Styron. But my first attempted novel was called *Land's Ramble*, which I wrote when I was teaching college in New York,[24] and I sent it first to Styron, with whom I had made friends very early, right after *Set This House on Fire* came out.[25] I hated to reveal to him that I had written a novel myself; it was kind of sneaky: to make friends with him, write him lots of letters of full of admiration, and then tell him that I was an aspiring novelist myself. But it didn't bother him at all, and he said that he would send it to his publisher and see what happened. And he sent *Land's Ramble* to Robert Loomis at Random House, and Loomis wrote back to say he didn't think that Random House could publish the book. *Land's Ramble* was, and remains today, strictly unpublishable.[26]

But Loomis also said that he would certainly be interested in seeing anything new that I was working on. I just happened to have finished the first hundred pages of *The Cherry Pit*, so I sent those to him, and he gave me a contract for it, and from that point on, I sent in each chapter as I wrote it, and he would jump all over it. I have a thick correspondence between myself and Loomis trying to make corrections or substitutions or eliminations from my manuscripts. I finally got the thing finished when I was living in William Styron's guesthouse in Roxbury, Connecticut, and sent it to Loomis. He suggested extensive revisions, which I had to make before he could accept it. So I wrote *The*

Cherry Pit partly under Loomis's guidance, or rather his severe criticism. Loomis did not have Styron's sense of humor—or mine—and he missed a lot of my intentions in *The Cherry Pit*, but the final *Cherry Pit* was a compromise between the book that he saw and the book that I saw. It was finally accepted in the fall of '64 and published the following spring.

BW: How would *The Cherry Pit* have been different had you never met Styron?

DH: It wouldn't have been published because, not only did he help me find Loomis at Random House, he also read the book himself when it was in manuscript and made quite a number of important suggestions and criticisms of things that were wrong with it that I took out. I cut it practically in half at Styron's suggestion. Also, I came up with the idea from an interview that Styron had done at that time, in which he said, "There's an expression: Life is a bowl of cherries, and those who write about the pits are in for it." So I got the idea of *The Cherry Pit* from that quotation of Styron's. *The Cherry Pit* would never been published had Styron not read it.

BW: What did you learn from Styron's work?

DH: The love of words. Styron has tremendous appreciation for the English language, which he claims he got from reading Flaubert and Fitzgerald. I don't know where he got it, but it's mostly Styron, as far as I'm concerned, and I tried to emulate it. In *The Cherry Pit*, I even based various characters on characters in his *Set This House on Fire*. The policeman Luigi in *Set This House on Fire* is clearly the model for Sergeant Dall Hawkins in *Cherry Pit*. And the narrator is the model for Clifford Stone. Many other characters and situations in *Set This House on Fire* inspired their counterparts in *The Cherry Pit*. I also learned a few things from Styron on how to endure criticism.

BW: How autobiographical is *The Cherry Pit*?

DH: The main character, Clifford Stone, is not autobiographical; I tried in every way to make him different from myself. In the original draft, there was an autobiographical character who was like myself. He was tall, and he'd been a classmate of Clifford's in college. I took him out eventually; he was intended to be a main character of the book. As I've said, the book, in many respects, follows the plot and characterizations of Styron's novel *Set This House on Fire*, which had a considerable impact on me at the time.

BW: What is the Vanished American Past? How did you discover it?

DH: Well, I would think that's almost self-explanatory. *Vanished* is another one of those words referring to the lost. America's past is over, it's lost, it's vanished. Clifford was a specialist in investigating aspects of the vanished past which ought to still be with us, and the acronym VAP, for Vanished American Past, might suggest "evaporated," which was what happened to the American past. Faulkner said the past isn't past, it's not even . . . How did he put it? No, the past is not over; it's not even past.[27] Well, he's welcome to feel that, but what you did, you can never recapture.

BW: What has been lost? What has vanished? Can you be specific? What sorts of things?

DH: In the lost American past? A whole way of life. Our customs. Our artifacts. Our morality. Just every aspect of American life is gone.

BW: When you think about your first published novel now—four decades and a dozen novels later—what seems most important or telling about the challenges you faced in getting it published?

DH: The final shape of the novel was considerably different from what I had first started out writing. I had no idea what I was going to write about; it was experimental. I wanted to write a novel, and I wrote it as I went along. When I was all finished with it, Loomis had to revise it. I sent it to Styron himself, and he read it and made a number of suggestions for changes, which I incorporated into it. But his letter of criticism ended with the words, "They will build to you someday monuments even in Little Rock"—meant to be encouraging. I had no trouble once we had agreed on a final version; Random House published it. But I lost my agent; he quit the agency just before it was published. So, I was without an agent during a crucial time for the appearance of the book. And it just flopped. I think two thousand copies were printed, and we sold about half of them. But it was nominated for the Faulkner Prize for Best First Novel, and it was runner-up to Cormac McCarthy's *Orchard Keeper.*

BW: And the next novel you wrote has never been published?

DH: My second novel was called *A Work of Fiction.* It was meant to be the life story of Albert Pike, an actual Arkansas hero, the founder of the Scottish Rite of Freemasonry and a Civil War general. The narrator was an actual Arkansas novelist named Arrington—no H, just starts with an A—and was the first appearance of my persona in one of my books. But Loomis rejected it. My agent at the time, Ivan Van Auw, had been an agent for Faulkner and Fitzgerald and several big names, and he had handled several of my short stories that were published in *Esquire*. He read *A Work of Fiction* and said it reminded him too much of John Barth, so he didn't think he could do anything with it. So I lost my second agent. I got a third agent, Candida Donadio, who was called the "den mother of black humor" and represented Joseph Heller and a whole lot of big names. She was wild about *A Work of Fiction* and said she would send it right out. She sent it to an editor at Harper & Row. He said he loved it; he'd draw up a contract any day.

I waited and waited and waited. My family was hungry. I had no salary during the summertime. Finally, I heard that he was getting a divorce and had changed his mind about publishing *A Work of Fiction*. A few months after that, he died of a heart attack, but it was too late for him to take *A Work of Fiction*.[28] Candida Donadio sent it off to several other publishers. They all turned it down.

BW: How did *Lightning Bug*, your second published novel, come together?

DH: While we were looking for a publisher for *A Work of Fiction*, I had finished my third novel, which I called *Lightning Bug* from the beginning. The title came from Kurt Vonnegut's *Cat's Cradle*. But, of course, "lightning bug" is a common expression in the Ozarks for firefly. This was meant to be my swan song to the Ozarks. I was going to write one Ozarks novel and then turn my back on the Ozarks. So I sent the manuscript off to Candida Donadio, and after she'd pretty much given up on *A Work of Fiction*, she tried to find a publisher for *Lightning Bug*. And finally, Seymour Lawrence at Delacorte called. Seymour Lawrence was a pretty well-known publisher of young, experimental novelists. Lawrence took it and decided to publish it.

BW: What happened in the years between *Pit* and *Bug* to make the latter possible? In what ways did it differ from the previous novels?

DH: While I was trying to get *A Work of Fiction* published, I was writing *Bug*; it took a couple of years to write it. I've always had to write in the summertime when I'm not teaching school. So, it took me two full summers to finish *Lightning Bug*.

In the original version of *Lightning Bug*, I meant for one section of it to be in reverse, instead of forward, like a movie going backwards; I meant for this entire section to run backwards. And I discovered that it just wasn't going to work, so I straightened it out and ran it forward instead of backwards. In the final shape, it was pretty much what I expected and wanted, and Delacorte published it with very few changes. It got a great review in *Time* magazine, which caused Sam

Lawrence to increase the print order by three thousand. None of them sold. Like *The Cherry Pit*, it just did not take off, despite the good review in *Time*.

I have often called *Bug* my favorite novel. I've been rereading it lately in the process of writing *Enduring*, the life story of Latha Bourne, because a lot of *Lightning Bug* is just cannibalized directly into . . . I wouldn't say a lot, but large sections are taken exactly as they appear in *Lightning Bug* and put into *Enduring*. In the process of reading it, I stop and ask myself, "Why can't I write like this anymore?" I think, in so many ways, it's the most imaginative of all of my novels. It's the *sweetest* of all of my novels. It's the most powerful love story of all of my novels. It's always been very close to my heart, and it was probably my great disappointment in its failure that made me determine to keep on writing about Stay More until somebody noticed.

BW: What are the origins of Latha's and Every's names and characters? Did Latha, whom you have called the "demigoddess of Stay More," just spring fully-formed from your mind, like Athena from Zeus's?

DH: No. Latha was based on two people. A woman from Drakes Creek was confined to the Arkansas State Hospital in Little Rock, a mad woman. But she had visiting privileges, and she came out to our house in Little Rock when I was a kid and visited. We had a pretty good visit, and she didn't seem crazy to me, but I was just a kid. As she was leaving, she fell down on her knees and said to my mother, "Jimmy, *please* keep me! Don't take me back to that place. I will do anything for you. I will cook for you. I'll sweep for you. I'll do anything you ask me. Please don't take me back to that *bughouse!*" Of course, my mother had to ignore her, but that quotation of hers finds it way into *Lightning Bug*, and it's about to find its way into *Enduring*.

She was also based partly on a favorite cousin, a second cousin, my mother's first cousin. Her name was Georgia Callico,[29] and she was sort of an artist's model for the image of Latha. She wasn't nearly as beautiful as Latha. For Latha, I wanted a name that was pretty, and I probably found it in a book of girls' names. Every, I knew was probably — if his name had been Everett, which it was not, they would probably have called him Every. And I probably remembered reading *Everyman*, the medieval morality play. I read that, and I taught that in college. But the model for Every was a Church of Christ preacher I had when I was growing up; his name was Leary Ball. And I wanted

Every to have a name similar to Leary's, because Leary was the model for Every in the way that Georgia was the model for Latha.

BW: How did you come up with the name "Stay More"?

DH: The title "Stay More" came from Vance Randolph, who says *stay more* is a common expression in the Ozarks. I needed a name for my town, so I just took it out right out of Vance Randolph.

BW: Why did you need a town?

DH: Well, *Lightning Bug* takes place in a town. Latha Bourne is the postmistress of the town. She has correspondence with the post office department, in which the post office misspells the name of the town; the name of the town figures prominently in the book.

BW: What happens to Dawny in the end?

DH: He's lost in the woods. He was lost in the woods. He's still lost in the woods. Don't ask me what happened to him. I guess he's still out there in the woods trying to find his way home. I don't know.

BW: What challenges did you face in getting your next novel, *Some Other Place. The Right Place.*, into print?

DH: I had written about half of *Some Other Place. The Right Place.* when *Lightning Bug* appeared. I needed just one more spring to write the poetry section and then the summer to write the final prose section. So I had that ready to go by the fall of '71. I sent it off to Seymour Lawrence, who had published *Lightning Bug*, and he did not want it. Candida Donadio tried it out on three or four other publishers. The story once again was not that there was anything wrong with the book; it was that I had published two novels which were complete failures commercially, and no publisher wants to take a chance on somebody with a record like that. So that's why Sam Lawrence rejected *Some Other Place*, and it probably had a lot to do with why I was rejected at the other places where Candida sent it.

I was so proud of the book when I finishing it that late that summer, I kept writing Candida and saying, "I'm almost done with my masterpiece. Let me know when you're going on your summer vacation so I can be sure that the manuscript gets to you when you are *not* on vacation." I got no answer to that. Wrote her again, said the same thing; no answer. Wrote her a third time; same result. So I finally just sent her the manuscript and said, "Here it is, it's finished; I'm proud of it." And I got a postcard from her assistant saying, "Mrs. Donadio has gone on a month's vacation, and you may expect to hear from her when she returns." I really . . . went

through the roof. I wrote back to the assistant and said, "This manuscript has to be read at once." So, the assistant read it and said, "Well, I
think it's a great book, but I have to wait for her to get back." And I was so
pissed off at her when she finally did return that I was hardly cooperative
when she tried to send it out to several different publishers.

    Meanwhile, Sam Lawrence's first reader, who had accepted *Lightning
Bug*, had left Sam Lawrence to become a first reader for Little, Brown.
He came to visit me one day because a friend of his had read *Bug* and
thought it was the greatest novel he ever read and had to meet me. And
they came up and spent a pleasant afternoon visiting. His name was
McDonough, Richard McDonough. And he said, "Well, what are you
working on these days?" And I said, "Well, I just finished a novel called
Some Other Place. The Right Place. Would you like to take a look at it?"
And he said, "Oh, I'd be delighted." I had it in a grocery bag. It was a
huge manuscript, seven hundred pages of manuscript in a grocery bag,
and I just gave it to Dick. He took it home with him. In two weeks, I
heard from Llewellyn Howland III, senior editor at Little, Brown, saying they absolutely had to publish it. The rest is history, as they say.

BW: Did he require extensive edits, like Loomis with *The Cherry Pit*?

DH: Louie, as he was called, made very few changes. He cleaned up some
of the sex; the sex was too bold for him. As it turned out, the Little,
Brown printer was just down the road from my house in Putney. I forget the name of the printers, but the head of the printing company was
practically my nextdoor neighbor. So when they set the type—in those
days, they had to set type by the typesetting machine—for the poetry
pages, they invited me to come down and make sure that everything
was absolutely correct. I thought that was fate; the Fate Thing had had
something to do with getting me a printer in the neighborhood. But it
was published mostly in the form in which I wrote it.

BW: How did early readers respond to this book, which is so much longer
and more narratively complex than your previous books?

DH: I had given a copy to my friend and neighbor, John Irving.[30] He read
it and was so consumed with envy that he wrote a hideous diatribe
trying to attack it, in which he said, "Who wants to read novels *about
kids*?" That was before he, himself, had written five or six novels about
kids; just about every criticism he made of it is something he himself
has done in a later novel. His criticism was sort of the end of our close
friendship, but it did not deter my determination to get it published.

But even though it was a Book of the Month Club alternate selection, it did not sell well enough to pay off the advance. And so Little, Brown was skeptical about taking my next novel.

BW: Why, in the author's opinion, is *SOP.TRP.* Kim's favorite?

DH: It was the first book of mine that she had read. I can see why she would like *SOP.TRP.* There's a Porsche on the cover. There's also the very romantic story about how she met the author as she knew she had read this great novel but could not remember the author's name — couldn't even remember the title; all she could remember was that there was a red Porsche on the cover. So, she went to the library in Beebe, looked through all of the books, looking for a book that had a red Porsche on the cover so she could write a fan letter to the author, and that was the beginning of our relationship.[31] So, for that reason alone, it probably remains her favorite book. She used to reread it every year. She quit rereading it after about the fifth or sixth violent argument that we had. We used to have — well, we still do — these really violent arguments, and . . . [To Kim] When did you quit reading it? You used to reread it every year. When and why did you stop?

KH: I did not stop reading it because of any argument you and I had.

DH: I'm just trying to make a joke, trying to inject some levity into this somber interview.

BW: What personal experience have you had with hypnosis?[32]

DH: My only personal experience with hypnosis came when I was seeing a counselor at one time about fifteen years ago. I asked him if he had a lot of experience hypnotizing, and he offered to hypnotize me. But I said I was concerned because of my deafness; I could hear him put me under, but I would not be able to hear him bring me out — I'd have my eyes closed. So, I was too nervous to permit myself to be hypnotized, and therefore I have had no personal experience with being hypnotized. [To Kim] I never told you Clare wanted to hypnotize me?[33]

KH: Clare? Really? Why did he want to? For what reason?

DH: To be hypnotized. He suggested it — to find out things about me that I could not reveal with my conscious mind.

KH: I would love to hear that.

DH: [*Chuckling*] Well, yeah. But I could not permit myself to be hypnotized; I hope you understand why.

KH: I do.

BW: How would you describe the "It's" of Diana, Day, and Daniel?

DH: Well, they all have an It. An It is pretty clearly defined by Henry Fox in *Some Other Place. The Right Place.* And to the extent that an It is a presence which is extremely sexual, Diana and Day and Daniel, all three, had it in pretty much equal measure. I would not differentiate among the It's of Diana, Day, and Daniel—you notice, of course, that all three of those names begin with the same initial that mine does, so they all three are, in a sense, personae of myself.

BW: If Day resembles G.,[34] in what ways does he resemble you? In what ways does he most differ?

DH: Well, he most differs in the sense that he was an Eagle Scout, and I never got beyond the Cub Scouts. I did have a scout handbook, and I enjoyed reading it, but I never could pass the tests that were required to graduate from Cub Scouts to Boy Scouts. So, I'm not like him in that respect. Day was an only child; I had a brother and a sister. Day grew up in urban New Jersey; I grew up in, you could say, urban Little Rock and the backwoods of the Ozarks. I never knew anyone like Diana when I was Day's age. So, there are many ways in which he differs from me. But I wrote the second part in the first person, so I had to identify with Day, which I had already done pretty much in the first part, just imagining that the story was something that might have happened to me.

Someone once asked me if I thought it was possible that all of those poems by Daniel Lyam Montross could actually have been written by Day. I did write those poems myself. But I don't think at Day's age, I could have written those poems.

BW: Do you have a favorite Daniel Lyam Montross poem in the novel?

DH: It'll take me a minute to find it, it's been so long since I looked at this. "The Dreaming." It's the last poem.

We dream our lives, and live our sleep's extremes.
The one is to the other not as real.
We fabricate our future in our dreams.

The present moment isn't what it seems.
Experience is only what we feel.
Our lives are dreamt. In sleep we live extremes.

The past is prologue, as the Bard proclaims.
It made us what we are. Let's turn the deal
By fabricating future in our dreams.

Our night will wake to day from sound of screams.
But so our day will yearn for night to heal.
We dream our days, and live our night's extremes.

The future enters us in bits and gleams
In order that its brightness may reveal
How we can learn to make it in our dreams.

The past is history's. The present, schemes
Of chance or temporality can steal.
We dreamt our lives, and lived our sleep's extremes.
We'll fabricate our future in our dreams.

That's a villanelle, of course, a strict form. I don't know if I mentioned it, but all of the poetry is modeled, in terms of mechanics and structure, on the collected poems of Theodore Roethke. And he has a couple of villanelles in his collected poems, so I have a couple of villanelles in mine. And at one point in his collected poems, he drops rhyme and versification and becomes wildly free verse. And the same thing happens here.

BW: How do you answer Diana's defining question, "Do you think why I am me?"

DH: That was a question she asked her father in challenge. I think she felt that the answer was that he didn't think of her. Her father spent very little time thinking about her or thinking about why she existed. The question was originally asked of me by my oldest daughter, Jennifer. She simply wrote on a piece of paper, "Daddy, do you ever think why I am me?" And I put her on my knee and explained to her at length of how often I thought of why she was her. So, I decided to put it in Diana's mouth in *Some Other Place*.

BW: Whose book is *Some Other Place. The Right Place.*—Diana's, Day's, Daniel's, or Dawny's?

DH: It's Donald's, but Donald pretending that he is Diana, that he is Day, that he is Daniel. I never thought of any one of those three, or four, as the primary creator of the book.

BW: Had you already started on your next novel (as with your previous novels) before *Some Other Place.* came out?

DH: I actually waited for *Some Other Place.* to come out to see what kind of reception it would get, whether the Book of the Month Club selection would make any money. But I had thought of a title in advance just as I did with *Some Other Place.: The Architecture of the Arkansas Ozarks.* The title came first, before I wrote any of the text. It was just meant to be a wise-ass title, because it's not really about architecture, but the repetition of that sound, "arc-arc-arc," is like a dog barking. And it's about my home state and about two of my favorite subjects: architecture and country people. I had written *Lightning Bug* as a swan song to the Ozarks, but in *Some Other Place.*, when I got to Part Four—I had not intended for Part Four to be in the Ozarks—but by the time I got to it, I decided to make it the Arkansas Ozarks.[35] But I disguised the name that I had invented for my town in *Lightning Bug* as "Stick Around" in *Some Other Place. The Right Place.*, although I slipped the expression *stay more* into a passage here and there.

BW: What were your goals for *Architecture*?

DH: I knew that this would be the history of Stay More, from the beginning, from its first founders. I had already named them, in *Lightning Bug*. "Jacob and Noah Ingledew had come so many miles from Tennessee to establish the community . . . " So I already had that. I simply had to make up the story of how they got there and what happened to them after they got there.

Of course, it's the funniest of my books in many ways. I had originally ended each chapter with a list of twelve questions for the student of architecture. Most of these questions were brilliant, but they were mostly facetious, and eventually, Louie Howland, who loved the book even more than he did *Some Other Place.*, questioned just how necessary those questions were, and I decided to take them all out. But I had only written maybe a hundred pages, four chapters, when I stopped making up the questions.

BW: Did you alter your approach for this very different novel, which is even illustrated by the author?

DH: I just wrote it chapter by chapter, generation by generation, building by building, trying to cover my imagination's view of what the architecture of the Ozarks looked like. Many of those illustrations in the book are based on real buildings in Drakes Creek: the mill, Jacob Ingledew's house, the general store. Those were based on real Drakes Creek buildings. But many of them were just fabrications: Virdy Boatwright's cat-wagon, Fanshaw's double-hut. Many of the buildings were just made up, and I mostly did the illustrations as I went along. Although the one of Jacob Ingledew's house, I did that one before any of the others.

The book took pretty much the form I intended for it to, except what I pointed out in the acknowledgments: "In its original form, this novel was much more sexually explicit than it is now, replete with such language as 'joist,' 'beam,' 'stud,' 'timber,' 'pole,' 'erection,' 'rear elevation,' 'door,' 'gable,' 'sill,' 'rail,' and 'jamb.' I am very grateful to my editor, Llewellyn Howland III, for persuading me to leave such things to the reader's imagination, and I trust that the reader's imagination has succeeded. My editor was the first person to hear of this project, the first person to encourage it, and the first person to see it when it was finished. In addition to removing certain passages, he made two other sweeping changes of an important nature." I don't even remember what those were. But he did use the blue pencil in several places where I had been too sexually explicit. He wanted me to tone it down a bit, and I was glad to comply.

BW: What is the relationship between buildings and human bodies?

DH: Not human bodies so much as human personalities. I have always felt, in teaching architecture, that any building has a personality. I used to take my students on field trips; we'd go down the street and look at various houses and try to guess—not anything about the inhabitants, not anything physically about the house in relation to people—but what personality did the house have. In fact, in the survey History of Art, I still show the Palazzo Medici in Florence and ask the students to come up with ideas for its personality: What kind of car does he drive, or she, as the case might be? Does he take a bath or shower? What magazines does he subscribe to? What other things you can tell me about him? Does he drink wine or beer? Etc., etc., etc. I've always encouraged my students to look at buildings as having personalities, so I thought of each of the twenty buildings in *Architecture* as having a distinct personality beginning with the primitive, savage, uncivilized character of Fanshaw's hut and culminating with the obscure but sophisticated double-sphere of Vernon Ingledew.

BW: How would you describe your home's personality?[36]

DH: It's deceptive. On the exterior, it attempts to fit in with all of the other houses of the neighborhood, more or less, except we have done enormous amounts of landscaping around the exterior that distinguish the house from its neighbors and make it seem more rural. But I've always been influenced by a famous quotation from Flaubert that William Styron told me about. Flaubert wrote to this young woman who was a protégée of his and told her to always live your life as an ordinary, inconspicuous bourgeois so that you can be wild and extravagant in your work. And I wanted my house, at least on the exterior, to be conventional like all of the other houses in the neighborhood. But on the interior—this is Kim's world, not mine—the interior has a very distinctive, original personality.

BW: What is the relationship between *Architecture of the Arkansas Ozarks* and Gabriel García Márquez's *One Hundred Years of Solitude?*

DH: Just as *Ekaterina* was based upon the idea of *Lolita* and followed the book, more or less, and *Cockroaches of Stay More* was based upon Thomas Hardy's *Tess of the d'Urbervilles*, perhaps even more so, *Architecture* was inspired by *One Hundred Years of Solitude*. It covers generations of the Ingledew family in the same way that *One Hundred Years* covered generations of the Buendía family. It has a traveling salesman like Eli Willard who reappears recurrently year after year. Someone could write a dissertation for a college English department on the similarities between *One Hundred Years of Solitude* and *Architecture of the Arkansas Ozarks*. It's safe to say that I could never have written *Architecture of the Arkansas Ozarks* if I had not read *One Hundred Years of Solitude*.

BW: What's left of Eli Willard?[37]

DH: In *Farther Along*, which was never published, he was taken up onto the mountain where the hero had lived and given a proper burial. So what's left of Eli Willard is what's left of anyone who had been buried in the ground. Probably the worms got him over the years, but he had just been embalmed in the showcase and then taken and given a proper burial. [To Kim] You remember *Farther Along?* He was buried in that book. *Farther Along* may be published farther along.

Let Us Build

BW: Why did you go so long without publishing a book after *The Architecture of the Arkansas Ozarks?*

DH: After the publication of *The Architecture of the Arkansas Ozarks*, there was a kind of dark ages in my history. Eleven years separated the publication of that book and my next book. During those eleven years, my personal life was filled with large and small calamities—and with death. My father died. My marriage died. The college where I had been teaching for a number of years died, collapsing because of mismanagement and lack of enrollment.[38] I was practically killing myself with booze. My life was just a complete mess. And, of course, I just went into the doldrums because of the lack of any commercial success for *Architecture of the Arkansas Ozarks*. My editor, Louie Howland, quit Little, Brown mostly because of his disappointment at the way the book collapsed. So, all of these factors kept me from writing for a long period of time. I started several versions of a novel called *Farther Along* and was not able to finish any of them. Well, I finally got one finished after several years, and it was considered unpublishable. So, for a period of eleven years, I was in a kind of hiatus of recovery from all of those losses and deaths and disturbances that characterized my life at the time. That fact that I did survive that whole period of time is further evidence of what a stoic I am.

BW: How severe was the drinking problem?

DH: Very severe. Also, I was having what was diagnosed as hypomania, which is just beneath being manic. I wasn't aware of being manic at all, but my first wife told me that I was manic. Looking for a job, I finally found one teaching not my subject of art history, but creative writing at the University of Pittsburgh, which would come back later as a useful experience in the writing of my novel *Ekaterina*. I taught just one semester at Pittsburgh, mostly drunk all the time, and I was not asked to continue beyond that one semester. I went out to Rolla, Missouri, to stay with my friends at the University of Missouri–Rolla. I spent the summer with them, and at the last moment, I found a job teaching in South Dakota—at South Dakota State University. I would be teaching art history there. So, I spent a year in South Dakota, and during that period, I corresponded with this fan that I had taken to dinner years before in Little Rock named Kim McClish. And I gradually decided that, if this was the end of the line for me, I would rather spend it in Arkansas.

But getting back to Arkansas wasn't going to be all that easy either, because my car died too. Among all of the other things—publisher, editor, college, marriage, all of these things that died—my poor Chevrolet Blazer died. The engine cracked because I had neglected to put anti-freeze in during the severe South Dakota winter. I bought a cheap second-hand car for two hundred fifty dollars, an old Nash Ambassador, and dumped all of my stuff in it and drove back to Arkansas and spent most of the summer at a friend's shack out on Beaver Lake. During this period, Kim came from her home in Memphis to visit me. We met for the first time and fell in love, or at least I did. And she decided she was going to start an epic correspondence with me. Throughout the whole autumn, we wrote to each other.

BW: What would have happened to you if Kim had never written you? How would the books you have written in the years since have been different if you had never met her?

DH: The books I've written in the years since would not exist, because I would not have written them. I was able to recover from that eleven-year hiatus by writing *Let Us Build Us a City* with her help. If Kim had not come into my life at that particular time, I simply would not have written that book, I would not have written any other books—I would probably have ceased to exist somewhere along about . . . nineteen hundred and eighty. I would probably have killed myself by 1980—I mean, not consciously, not literally—but just from bad habits and lousy living.

There is a place reserved for me in the Wesley Cemetery, which is the closest cemetery to Drake's Creek, and that's where most of my relatives have been buried. I would be inhabiting a plot with a nice green carpet over my head if Kim had not written to me. She literally saved my life, in other words.

BW: But apart from their actual existence, how did Kim affect the actual substance of the books?

DH: Well, I recognized very early that life follows art. Kim was my creation Diana,[39] whom I had already created in *Some Other Place. The Right Place.* before I ever knew her. And she was my own, personal Diana. So, I wrote *Let Us Build Us a City* as a love story of *our* relationship, exploring those towns all over Arkansas. And then when I went back to a novel and tried *The Cockroaches of Stay More*, I was able to have a sense of humor, because I was in a good mood. I was married to Kim, and I was able to have a love story between Sam and Tish.[40] There's a little bit of Kim in Tish, not that she looks anything like Tish. There's a little bit of Kim in Ekaterina; there's a lot of Kim in Viridis Monday.[41] I could go down through all of my books and liken the heroine to Kim. Just like the artist Rembrandt would use his wife to pose for Bathsheba, and nobody thought that Rembrandt's great painting of Bathsheba was Mrs. Rembrandt. And all of these novels that I've written were using Kim as a model, but I've never written anything about her life in my novels, never actually depicted her in my novels.

BW: Is Kim in *With*'s Robin? How?

DH: Oh, yes. I can show you a photograph that I found in a magazine of a little girl that was Robin's age when she was kidnapped. It looks exactly like Kim would have at that age. I had a lot of fun pretending that Robin was Kim, that she was going through all of these experiences as she grew up. Yes, I think there's probably more of Robin in Kim than most of my other heroines.

KH: I think you mean "more Kim in Robin," not "Robin in Kim."

BW: What was your first meeting with Kim like? What surprised you about her in person after getting to know her from her letters?

DH: We had not had that many letters when I first got to know her, just a few. And the letters were a little bit schoolteacherish. She was a school teacher. The letters were just a little bit prim. They were not really warm or funny or attractive letters. They were mostly matter-of-fact and — what's the word I'm looking for — diffident, in the sense that she knew I was a famous author and she was nobody in the sticks of Arkansas. So there was a sense of diffidence that held her back in the letters. So I was surprised to see in person that she was really so warm and engaging. We had agreed to meet in Little Rock; I was visiting my mother and was staying with her. And Beebe, Kim's hometown, is only about thirty miles from Little Rock. She would drive into town, and we would meet at a restaurant called Cajun's Wharf, which was on the Arkansas River and specializes in seafood. And I walked into the foyer, and she was standing there in this beautiful green dress — she recently found it in the attic, that beautiful green dress. She looked so slender, and her hair was done so beautifully. I would say that it was love at first sight, except that's corny. I was immensely drawn to her at first sight and, as soon as we got seated and ordered a bottle of wine, I started talking nonsense, and she couldn't get me to shut up — didn't try to get me to shut up. And we had a perfectly delightful date, the best date I ever had in my life. That was the autumn of 1977, and I didn't see her again until summer of '81.

BW: What is the story of the post-office-box headboard on your bed?

DH: Our whole romance was conducted courtesy of the United States Post Office. For a long, long time when I was here in Fayetteville and she was in Memphis, we exchanged dozens and dozens and dozens of letters. Love letters, if you will. So the post office played an important part in our romance. Kim went to the Memphis post office to see if, in her box, which she had taken especially for the purpose, there was any mail from her lover. So, about a year after she had come to Fayetteville and we had taken up life together, we happened to see, in an antique store down on Dickson Street, this array of post-office boxes. We did not know at the time that they came from . . . Limestone, which is in southern Newton County, Arkansas. Those post-office boxes were the Limestone, Arkansas post office boxes for maybe a hundred years, who knows? We bought the boxes. And a man across the street—who, not long after, was stabbed to death by his girlfriend—was a jack-of-all-trades carpenter who built the pedestal for the post-office boxes to go on. The pedestal also serves as a headboard and storage for pillows and blankets and so forth, and that sets the thing up as you see it. And we've stuffed the post-office boxes with various cards, letters, mementoes.

BW: How did your collaboration on *Let Us Build Us a City* get started?

DH: I made an error a little while back, but you can edit this. Kim, whom I had met at Cajun's Wharf in Little Rock several years previously, came to Fayetteville and spent the weekend with me. And thereafter, we started a monumental correspondence, writing each other practically every day, until eventually, it was determined that she would—with her husband's permission—come and spend the summer in Fayetteville with me.

During that summer, I came up with the idea of doing a book on lost towns of Arkansas. I'd always been fascinated with lost towns. I had investigated several of them in Vermont. In *Some Other Place. The Right Place.*, I had written about three real lost towns and one imaginary lost town, in Arkansas. So, I decided to investigate *actual* lost towns in Arkansas and to write a book about them with Kim's help.

As the book would have it, I was still in South Dakota when I got this first fan letter from Kim, and I suggested to her the idea of investigating these lost towns, and she went around to all of them by herself with a tape recorder interviewing people, making notes, taking photographs. That wasn't actually the way it happened. We went together to each of these towns. I came to think of it as a nonfiction novel with Kim as the heroine. For the sake of the narrative, I made it look like she was by herself visiting these eleven lost towns in Arkansas. I actually went with her; we did not go to all of them at once. We would go to one, come back home to Fayetteville, go to another one, come back home. Finally, Kim left her husband and moved to Fayetteville to live with me, and we continued driving to all of these lost towns, investigating them. I began writing the book itself and finished it within a year.

I had this amateur agent in Arkansas. Her name was Anne Courtemanche-Ellis, and I think she sent the book out unsuccessfully to several people. I don't remember the record of rejections for it. Anyway, I had already written the first two hundred pages when, out of the blue, I decided to send a fan letter to the great editor Helen Wolff, who was an independent publisher with her husband, Kurt Wolff. They had both been publishers in Germany with quite a reputation before Kurt Wolff died. Helen Wolff came to America and connected with Harcourt Brace Jovanovich as her publisher for her imprint. I had seen an article about her in the *New Yorker*,[42] which I admire very much, and that inspired me to send her a letter. She was kind enough to answer and say that she wanted to see what I had written. At that point, I swore off agents, because I had never had any luck at all with agents promoting my books. So I was able to get her to look at the first three or four chapters, which she considered much too autobiographical. I didn't know at the time that I was writing a novel; I thought I was writing an autobiography, and I was telling too much about myself and not enough about the towns. Helen Wolff talked me out of that. Eventually, I thought of the idea of having this story of Kim and Harrigan meeting up on the road in the process of discovery.

I bought a second-hand camera, a Canon with a wide-angle lens, and we took that with us to all of these towns. And I took the photographs. I intended for it to be a novel illustrated with photographs with the heroine just appearing slightly in two of the photographs.

When I finished the book, I sent it off to Helen Wolff. She put her blue pencil to it and made fabulous corrections and changes; even though she was in her eighties, she turned out to be the best editor I'd ever had. Then she published it under her own imprint in a very handsome edition, which probably sold better than any of my novels had done, but it unfortunately did not make the *New York Times* bestseller list. In fact, it had a large first printing of something like twenty-five thousand copies, and it did not even sell out that large printing. And so, when Helen Wolff retired, she was no longer involved in the decision, and her successor wouldn't consider my next book, *The Cockroaches of Stay More*. From their point of view, *Let Us Build* was not successful.

BW: Apart from your relationship with Kim, who or what inspired *Let Us Build Us a City*?

DH: I've always been an admirer of James Agee, in particular, James Agee's *Let Us Now Praise Famous Men*, in which he collaborated with

Walker Evans, a photographer, to produce a study of Alabama share-croppers. I collaborated with my wife, Kim, to interview the remaining inhabitants of eleven lost towns in Arkansas, all of which aspired to become cities and put the word *city* into their official name. But not one of them ever actually became a city. Some of them today are ghost towns, some of them are just tiny little communities that all had aspirations to become cities. So I took the title of the book from Genesis, the passage that says, "And the whole earth was of one language and of one speech. And it came to pass as they journeyed from the east, that they found a plain in the land of Shinar, and they dwelt there, and they said to one another, 'O true, let us make brick and burn them thoroughly.' And they had brick for stone, and slime had they for mortar. And they said, 'Go to, let us build us a city and a tower whose top may reach unto heaven; and let us make us a name, lest we be scattered abroad upon the face of the whole earth.'"[43]

That was the first recorded instance of mankind's vainglory, the aspiration to build a tower that would reach all the way to heaven. The cities, as we know them, don't reach all the way to heaven, although the World Trade Center got pretty close to it, before somebody put it down. But all of these aspirations to heaven are reflected in the aspirations of the people who founded these little places in Arkansas and called them cities. Actually, the original title was from another passage of the Bible, I forget which one it was, but it had the words, "No need of the sun."[44] And the original concept was that these little towns did not need any sunshine to exist; they could thrive and flourish without sun. That was the working title for quite a while of the book that eventually became *Let Us Build Us a City.*

But eventually, I hit upon that quotation from Genesis, which was perfect in several respects, not only because it had the concept of wanting to do something that was impossible — building a town to heaven — but wanting to do something that *was* possible: *to make us a name* as a people in these little communities. And they at least thought, "Even if we don't become a huge metropolis, at least when people see on the map 'Sulphur *City*,' they will think, 'Well, it must be something special.'" In fact, Sulphur City was the first of the cities that I had any familiarity with because it's the closest to Drakes Creek, where I grew up, and I had often looked at maps of the area around Drakes Creek and between Drakes Creek and Fayetteville, and I had often seen Sulphur City on the map off the main highway, off the secondary roads, all by itself out there in the middle of nowhere, and I wondered why it was called "city." I never got a chance to visit it, but I kept it in the back of my mind. And I've always been, of course, fascinated with ghost towns, just like Day Whittacker and Diana Stoving in *Some Other Place. The Right Place.* So I decided eventually to write a book about Arkansas ghost towns.

BW: How about the marvelously despairing South Dakota foreword? How much of that was based on real life?

DH: Except for two things, they are mostly identical. I actually did live in an apartment, a walk-up apartment, over a furniture store on Main Street. And I actually did teach art history at South Dakota State University. And yes, every evening, the "real" Harrigan would drink a lot and begin what he called his "meditation upon ruins"—primarily the ruin of himself. He, too, was a washed-up writer.[45] But I did not jump in my Blazer on a cold winter's day and take off for Sauk Centre, Minnesota, to see Sinclair Lewis's Main Street hometown—I never did that.[46] And I never received a fan letter from Kim Gunn in Arkansas—I made that up. I had *already* received a fan letter from her several years before, and she did not write me in South Dakota.

So really, it's all fiction. I invented the idea that this person named Harrigan, who was one of my numerous alter egos, was living in a desolate apartment over a furniture store in downtown Brooking, South Dakota, when he got a fine letter from Arkansas, from a high school English teacher named Kim. Kim was not only a great admirer of his work, but she also proposed to him the idea that they collaborate on a book about Arkansas ghost towns, which, of course, he was happy to do. But, of course, he had to finish out the term. So, while he was doing that, Kim got into her Nissan Zephyr . . . Or was it a Datsun? No, it was a Nissan.[47]

Anyway, she got into her car and took off by herself to travel around in these towns with the agreement that, somewhere along the road, Harrigan would catch up with her. But he didn't manage to catch up with her until she was down to the next-to-last town, Bear City. Then they went on to the last city, Y City, together, and then eventually wrote the book. All of those dozens and dozens of tapes that Kim recorded with the citizens of those towns still exist in Special Collections at the University of Arkansas in Fayetteville. I would not have been able to make those tapes, because I'm deaf. She actually made those tapes and transcribed them for me, and I used them to put together the book.

BW: So the book that resulted was a true collaborative effort?

DH: I, of course, took the photographs in the book of the actual places in each of those eleven lost cities. The pictures I took, but Kim did all of the hard work, the interviewing, which was the main challenge, and the even more grueling challenge of having to transcribe out into longhand what the tapes said. It took her many hours of work to do that.

For that reason, a lot of people thought that Kim ought to be listed as the coauthor of the book. But Kim did not actually write a word of the book itself, so, in that respect, she's not coauthor. But the new edition, which Toby Press will bring out in October of this year, is dedicated to Kim, so she gets some credit in that respect, and it will have a double photograph of Kim and me in full color on the back cover of the edition. And it will have a new afterword written by Fred Chappell, taken from his essay which appeared in *Southern Quarterly*,[48] in which he points out that *Let Us Build Us a City* seems to be a travelogue; in fact, most public libraries who don't know what else to do with it have filed it away as a travel book, but as Chappell astutely points out, *Let Us Build Us a City* is very much a novel.

BW: What is a nonfiction novel? How does a nonfiction novel differ from an unqualified novel?

DH: The term, I think, originated with Truman Capote's *In Cold Blood*, in which Capote went out to Kansas to interview the two men who where on trial for having murdered a farm family and then were eventually executed. At least two movies have been made about that situation. Capote interviewed all of these people and then took all of the interviews and put them together and wrote it as if he were writing a novel, with the same sense of plot tension and suspense and building up to a climax and so forth. But the story he happened to be telling was a true story, therefore nonfiction, but nonfiction written in novelistic form. I can't say that *Let Us Build Us a City* was written in nonfiction form because there's no other book like it in terms of its form. It does not imitate Agee's *Let Us Now Praise Famous Men*, except in the first two words of the title. It has its own structure and its own pace and its own characterization, plot development, all the other features. But it does fabricate and to the extent that it fabricates or fictionalizes, that is a novelistic quality. It differs from what you call an "unqualified" novel by being about real places and real people. I think it was Marianne Moore, the poet, who said that a poem should be about imaginary gardens with real toads in them—

is that the way it goes?[49] *Let Us Build Us a City* is about real towns with real people in them, but written with a considerable degree of imagination.

Let me give you a better example. A famous American novel, Melville's *Moby-Dick*, is supposed to be about an obsessed whaling captain named Ahab who is searching for a white whale. That's the story, but the book is entirely interlarded with nonfictional information about the whaling industry and about all kinds of nonfictional things. But it's still called a novel. In fact, the preface to it is about a retired customs official from Salem, Massachusetts, who finally became the territorial governor of a godforsaken place out in the Midwest called Arkansas. And in fact, Miller County, Arkansas, where we found Garland City of *Let Us Build Us a City*, was named after that customs official, Miller, who appears in the preface of Melville's *Moby-Dick*.

BW: Why does it matter to you that *LUB* be classified as a novel? How does it connect to your other novels?

DH: It differs from all my other novels primarily in the sense that it's not about Stay More—it's about the whole state of Arkansas. But you could say that my other novels are not about Stay More but lost places in the heart, so *Let Us Build Us a City* fits in completely with that concept. I recently had the experience for the first time in many years of rereading the novel myself. I had it in mind to write my own preface to it, or my own afterword, even though it occurred to me eventually that Fred Chappell could do a much better job than I could. Still, to write that afterword myself, I had to reread it, and I was surprised in rereading how very novelistic it is. In fact, one of these days—maybe when the Toby edition comes out—I might even be able to persuade Kim to read it.

It is not only a novel; it's a love story between this character named Harrigan and this character named Kim, and it even has a structure and a plot like a novel. Parts of it are fabricated, fictionalized, made up like a novel. So Toby Press is going to be marketing it in the same format as the other fourteen Toby Harington books—the same kind of lettering on the cover, the same kind of illustration by Wendell Minor on the cover. And I hope that, eventually, it will be come to be considered one of my novels rather than just a travel book.

BW: What distinguishes a "lost" town from a ghost town?

DH: A ghost town has no population at all; it is supposedly completely devoid of population. I don't think there is a single ghost town in *Let*

Us Build Us a City, is there? I think every one of those towns—like Drakes Creek—had at least one person living in it! And all of those towns had one or two or three people living in it. A lost town is one that's not on the way to anywhere; it's certainly not on the way to becoming a city. It's hard to get to, it's off the beaten path, it's out of the ordinary, it's inaccessible . . . lost.

BW: Why did you decide to tell the story of the sinking of the Sultana in *Let Us Build*?

DH: Okay, here's a case-in-point for the nonfiction novel. The matter of the sinking of the Sultana, the Titanic of the Mississippi—all of that actually happened, right after the Civil War, and with a loss of more lives than the Titanic itself. It's the greatest maritime disaster in American history, and it sank right off the shore of Mound City, one of the cities in *Let Us Build Us a City*.

It was a steamboat, a troop ship. It was taking released Confederate prisoners—Union soldiers—away from prison in Mississippi when it sank, north of Memphis and killed so many people on board. What I did was to pick an actual East Tennessee hillbilly by the name of Sam Dunlap and have him as a prisoner in this god-awful Confederate prison in Alabama somewhere. He escaped from that terrible prison and made his way to the place where he got on the Sultana steamboat. He was trying to make his way home. And when the ship goes down, he saves the life of a woman who was one of the passengers on the steamboat, an excursion passenger. He saves her life, and they become romantically involved, but she eventually drowns. It's a long and very gripping, romantic story—and all of that is made up. The same Sam Dunlap eventually finds his way to Sulphur City, Arkansas, and that also is made up.

BW: Should James Cameron, the director of *Titanic*, be paying royalties to you?

DH: I'm sure that James Cameron never read *Let Us Build Us a City*, and in any case, the *Titanic* was its own disaster. The idea of putting a romance into *Titanic*—I don't think he stole that idea from me. Who knows?[50]

BW: Which of the lost towns have you ever gone back to visit, and which would you most like to revisit now?

DH: When I made the decision to reread the book, one of my motives was that perhaps Kim and I could go around and visit all of these towns, twenty-five years later, and compare the way they are now with the

way they were back then, and I could put in a whole new chapter on
that. But the more I thought about it, the more I realized that would be
tampering with history—or tampering with fiction.

I have not revisited any of them. Did we drive through Sulphur City
one time?

KH: Maybe.

DH: We might have driven through it real fast. I would never revisit any
of these cities. I think I probably realized that we would find them in
worse condition now than they were twenty-five years ago, and that
would be distressing. Dogpatch, which is near Marble City, went out
of business many years ago; it has just faded into a ghost town itself.
Thank God; I wouldn't care to see it, because it was fake to begin with.
And the places that do have any possible habitation are probably pretty
run down.

BW: What's the backstory for *The Cockroaches of Stay More*, your improbable comeback novel about cockroaches? How did you come up with
the idea for it?

DH: I'm afraid I can't tell you just how the idea originated. I was writing my first novel in eleven years, after having finished a supposedly
nonfiction book. I wanted to return to the idea of the novel, tightly
plotted, with characterization. And so, I thought it might be easier to
start off with a kind of fable, cockroaches instead of human beings. But,
of course, there would be no cockroaches without human beings; they
need people to leave crumbs on the floor for them to have for supper.
And so, I thought of the outrageous title *The Cockroaches of Stay More*.

We were living on Shady Lane in Fayetteville. All of these years,
Stay More—which I had created in *Lightning Bug* and expanded considerably in *Architecture* and *Some Other Place.*—it was mostly mori-
bund. No one was living there, except Latha's granddaughter Sharon,
who moved into the house that had been Latha's store and post office,
and her boyfriend from Chicago, Larry Brace, soon followed her and
moved into the house that had been Jacob Ingledew's. He was a drunk,
working on a book on the poetry of Daniel Lyam Montross. But in
his drunkenness in a house infested with cockroaches, he got himself
a six-shooter and started filling the house full of holes, trying to shoot
the cockroaches. That was the basic comic idea behind the book that
came to be known as *The Cockroaches of Stay More.*

It tells how the cockroaches who lived in Stay More worshipped
humankind so much that they had modeled themselves upon humans.

They even learned the Ozark dialect and got involved in some of the same adventures that humans were involved in. Their primary belief was that man—and there was only one of them, the drunken man that inhabited that house—was God. They worshipped Him, and they believed that when He shot any of them, it was a form of rapture; it was to be desired to be executed by Man. They hadn't quite learned that Man had a Woman living over in another house in Stay More. But at one point, Man, in His drunkenness shooting the cockroaches, shoots Himself in the foot and becomes seriously injured; His foot becomes infected. The cockroaches get their own Doc Swain—Doc Swain cockroach—and he doesn't know what to do about the foot infection. All they can do is to somehow alert the Woman, let the Woman know that the Man needs help. So, they formed themselves into a sign, a banner, that said, "Help," went over to the Woman's house and attracted Her attention so that She could come and save the Man and take Him to the hospital.

These cockroaches would be just like the human inhabitants of Stay More, especially in speaking the same Ozark dialect. Of course, in the Ozarks nobody would ever, ever say "cock"—that's a taboo word. In fact, that is how the word *rooster* originated, to get around referring to the cock as a cock. So, strictly speaking, the book should have been called *The Roosterroaches of Stay More*, but then a lot of people wouldn't have known just what it meant. So, I took a deep breath and decided to call it *The Cockroaches of Stay More*.

I don't know if I mentioned it in my previous interview, but all of my books have acronyms or abbreviations—usually acronyms. For example, the acronym for *Let Us Build Us a City* was simply the first three letters, L-U-B, which spells *LUB*. I think of *Let Us Build Us a City* not just as a nonfiction novel but as a *love* story, so *LUB* comes in handy as the acronym for that book. *Cockroaches* had an accidental acronym, just as *Architecture of the Arkansas Ozarks* did; my brother pointed out to me that it made the acronym "TAOTAO," or double-Tao. Tao is a Chinese philosophy, a Chinese way of life, and in a sense, the Ozarks—or at least the Ingledews—are natural Taoists. So, TAOTAO makes a nice double acronym for *Architecture of the Arkansas Ozarks*. In the case of *Cockroaches of Stay More*, only later did I discover that the title makes the perfect acronym "COSM." The cockroaches of Stay More are a *micro*cosm of humanity and of the whole world, in which I could poke fun at religion, education, politics, all kinds of human frailty.

Particularly religion. At the time of the book, there was a lot of discussion in America—I think it's gone out of fashion today—of what they called "rapture," which was what the fundamentalist sects called the experience of dying and being taken into the arms of our Lord Jesus. So, these cockroaches happened to be inhabiting what they called the Holy House, where the lone human inhabitant was a drunken literature scholar trying to write his thesis on a poet who had died in Stay More. The cockroaches didn't know that, of course, but they knew there was this man, living alone there in the house, who hated the cockroaches, though they didn't know he hated them. They thought he was God because he was the only human being they could see. But when he was drunk, he would take his six-shooter and shoot at them. Sometimes—not often—sometimes, he hit one, and if you happened to be shot by one of Man's bullets, then you were "raptured"—that was the best way to go. His shooting left holes in all the walls and ceiling; that's why they called it "Holy House."

There was only one other building in town. The building that had been Latha Bourne's store was now inhabited by her granddaughter, Sharon. Back in Chicago, she had known Larry, who inhabited Holy House. The cockroaches didn't know that either, but a few cockroaches, they called her house "Parthenon," which is the name of another town; they called her house "Parthenon" because it was like a sacred Greek temple. Only the Ingledew cockroaches wandered out to inhabit Parthenon.

Well, anyway, the whole story is very closely modeled upon Thomas Hardy's *Tess of the d'Urbervilles*; it even begins in pretty much the same fashion that *Tess* begins. The heroine, the primary cockroach, was named not Tess, but Tish, and the main cockroach hero is named Sam, which is short for Gregor Samsa Ingledew,[51] the son of Hank Ingledew and the main cockroach inhabitant of Parthenon. Sam becomes the lover of Tish. Unfortunately, because he lives in a clock, and the clock chimes every hour, it has driven him deaf, unlike other cockroaches, who have very good hearing. Anyway, Sam can't hear, so he and Tish have to invent a kind of sign language based upon the movement of their hands.

As I said, I don't remember how the idea first popped into my head, but after I came up with the title, one of the challenges was that I did not know a thing about cockroaches, and at the time, I probably had most people's aversion toward them. One reason I had chosen them as the central characters in the book is that a lot of people look down, literally and figuratively, on cockroaches the same way they look down on hillbillies. Hillbillies are the outcasts of mountain society. I wanted my hillbillies as cockroaches to be outcasts.

But I knew nothing about cockroaches. I didn't know how they reproduced or *with what* they reproduced. So I had to do extremely thorough research on cockroaches. I got all of the books from the entomology section of the library on cockroaches. There were quite a few of them, and I read them all. Then I got a round glass goldfish bowl and put a few cockroaches in it. Cockroaches can't climb glass very well, so I didn't have to have a lid on top of it. I put them in there and gave them a slice of banana now and then to eat. I also kept throwing other things into the bowl for them to play with or eat. In the course of time, they reproduced, and they permitted me to watch them mating, and they permitted me to watch them giving birth, and they permitted me to watch them raising their children. For a long, long time, I kept that bowl full of cockroaches on my desk and used it throughout the writing of the book. I think I can say that everything I wrote about cockroaches is the truth, particularly the fact that, of all God's creatures, they are the *cleanest*. They are obsessively fastidious; they obsessively clean themselves, even cleaning each one of their sniffwhips each day. I call them "sniffwhips" because they use the antenna to sniff with and detect communication signals in the pheromones of the air. But to do that, the antennae, or sniffwhips, have to be kept meticulously clean. And with my magnifying glass, I would watch the process of a cockroach each day, or several times each day, very carefully cleaning his sniffwhips all the way down. And I came to the conclusion that not only were cockroaches fastidiously clean, but they are not carriers of any germs, any viruses, any bacteria, because of their cleanliness. Mankind has no reason for its revulsion against cockroaches except that they are ugly and they scurry around all over the place and tempt you to stomp on one of them. People just don't like them. I sympathize with some of the apartment renters in cities who have real infestations of cockroaches. But except for the sight of them, those people are not in any danger from the cockroaches themselves. In fact, the German name for cockroach means "kitchen cleaner."[52] The cockroaches come out at night after you have gone to bed and clean up the crumbs that you left on the kitchen floor. They perform a little service for mankind.

There are so many plots and subplots in the novel that I won't even attempt to mention all of them. It was meant primarily as a comic novel that is also a fable, also an allegory, and it helped me get back into the world of writing fiction. Of course, Helen Wolff herself did not publish fiction, and even if she did, she might not have been interested in publishing a book with that title. So she handed it along to her deputy editor, whose name was Drenka Willen, and Drenka Willen thought it was a terrible book. She lived in an apartment in New York City that had cockroaches all over the place, and she thought it was a completely repulsive book. She stopped short of calling it "prurient," the adjective that was held in reserve by another New York editor for a later book of mine,[53] but she thought it was repulsive and would not publish it.

I appealed to Helen Wolff to intercede, and she sought out a deputy assistant junior sub-editor, who was a big fan of science fiction and had edited a few science fiction books. He took over the editing of *Cockroaches of Stay More* and more or less decided to publish it in the form in which it was written. I had a lot of help in editing the book from my close friend Jack Butler, an Arkansas novelist, one of the best Arkansas novelists, who also made a good editor. He did a great job editing *Cockroaches*. I also kept the original manuscript, in which Drenka Willen had simply taken a red pencil and marked a slash mark across the entire page of any page which supposedly needed change or bothered her, and the whole manuscript consisted of these red slash marks. I'm sure there's a metaphor in there somewhere, but it escapes me right at the moment.

Harcourt Brace brought it out, and it was very well received. We were brought to New York for the coming-out party and put up in a nice Park Avenue hotel, and *Publishers Weekly* sent in a nice young reporter to interview me. Mark Harris, who later became a distinguished critic and writer,[54] did the interview, and the book got pretty good publicity. It sold pretty well and was picked up by Vintage as an American Original Vintage paperback. It didn't become famous, but it got better attention than most of my earlier books.

BW: What, from a human standpoint, would be the greatest benefits of cockroach sex?

DH: Well, as I point out in the book, once the male has inserted himself, the female clamps onto him and keeps him for a long, long time. In a sense, dogs do that too. When dogs mate, the female has a sphincter which imprisons the dog inside her to guarantee that all of his semen winds up in her womb. The cockroaches not only do something similar with their clamps, but they have really long, extended tantric sex,

Kama Sutra. The sex descriptions in *Cockroaches of Stay More* are really fabulous; they're almost enough to make a human being horny.

BW: What would be the biggest drawback of cockroach sex?

DH: Well, probably the fact that the male is just a tool, figuratively speaking; he has no control over himself. The female secretes, from a gland in her back, a pheromone that I call *affy-dizzy*.[55] He has to come and lap it up; he is spellbound by it, and he can't help himself—he has to mate, that's his function in life. And he has to be imprisoned in the act of sex for hours; he has no control over himself. Presumably, he's enjoying it, but we don't know. No scientist was ever able to ask a cockroach if he was enjoying himself, and no scientist was able to hook up a·"love probe"[56] that showed whether he was even having an orgasm or not. So, in a sense, the male is just used by the female for the purposes of reproduction:

> The intricate anatomy of the mechanisms of reproduction is astonishing: there are not one but two phallomeres, and it is the right one which first probes the female.
>
> "Sam!" she cried out, and then attempted to spell it, "S-A-A-M-!-!" but he could not see her; their bodies were already turning into the opposed position, end to end at 180 degrees.
>
> The second clamp, whose function is titillation as well as coupling, clinched a second latch and began tickling and was tickled in return. The third clamp grabbed the third latch.[57]

I just realized that the fact that the male cockroach has two phallomeres—that's a penis—that he has two phallomeres is a forerunner of the bigeminality of *Butterfly Weed*, in which Russ has a double penis.[58] I also realize that, in an earlier part of the interview, I was misspeaking when I said that the female secretes the affy-dizzy. The male secretes it, and he does it on purpose, so he's not just her tool. They both are enjoying the hell out of themselves.

BW: What surprised you in the course of writing *COSM*? What that you couldn't have anticipated at the beginning ended up happening in the end?[59]

DH: It's been so long since I read the book that I cannot honestly recall any surprises that occurred. I don't think that when I started out writing it that I intended to have Sharon—a woman who reappears in several of my other novels and who is the narrator of *Enduring*, the novel that I'm writing now—so prominent in it.[60] I don't think I anticipated that she would rescue Sam and Tish from the water of the toilet bowl; she probably would've flushed them down, but she decides to take a piece of paper and put it down for them to grab onto and be rescued from drowning. That may have been a surprise.

I think it may have been a surprise that the so-called Mockroach writes "The Mockroach's Song," which is the conclusion of the book. The Mockroach was thought of as a kind of mysterious demon. I don't think I intended for the Mockroach to turn out to be a good guy, but by the end of the book, he's really a kind of *über*-roach.[61] He's the best roach of them all, even above Sam. And, of course, the Mockroach is the persona of Dawny, the author, who has appeared in one form or another in all of the other books. He appears as the mock-roach in this book.

BW: What is the mock-roach? Can you read or sing its song for the camera?

DH: [*Chuckling*] It doesn't have a tune to it that I know of, but I would be happy to read the Mockroach's song.[62] To answer your question, the Mockroach is the super roach, the supreme roach, the roach above all roaches. He is the architect, or TAOGU, the architect of the grand universe of Stay More.[63]

BW: What does *COSM* contribute to the story of Stay More? How does its perspective on and treatment of Stay More differ from those of your other novels?

DH: Essentially, it does not really differ except, by becoming a comic fable, it gives you an entirely different perspective on the behavior of Stay Morons. The similarities between the way the cockroaches behave and the way people behave is instructive, shall we say? The part that I just read about cockroach sex—although it's completely unlike human sex—is yet rhapsodic. So many writers are rhapsodic, or try to be rhapsodic, about human sex, or they idolize it, they worship it, they make it into movies and books and poems and pictures. I think *COSM* makes a picture out of human behavior as it's performed by insects. It tries to make a bond between human life and insect life. It tries to show, at least in that song at the end, how the destinies of mankind and all other creatures are bound together, how—if man succeeds in killing himself off—he will kill off everything else too. He's not like the dinosaur in that respect.

I'm just at the point in writing *Enduring* where I'm getting around to some of the citizens that come to Latha's store and post office, and I forgot what their names are, so I have to look in *COSM* to be reminded of the names that I gave them. I might even put Chidiock Tichborne into human form,[64] although that's the name of an actual Elizabethan poet. I don't know if the human beings, Larry and Sharon, eventually actually marry, but they do spend most of their lives together. He moves out of Holy House, and they both live in the building that we call Parthenon in the book, which is Latha's store. And some of the other human beings who appear toward the end transport Larry to the hospital after he's wounded himself, they are real people from Stay More. And then, of course, one of my favorite Stay More characters, Doc Swain, is Doc Swain, the roosterroach doctor, who takes care of all of the cockroaches when they get sick or injured.

Another note about *COSM*. I have not read very many fables; the only one I can remember having read was *Watership Down*, about rabbits, and there may be some influence of *Watership Down* on *Cockroaches*. But I wrote *Cockroaches* to be a fable, the first of an ambitious project consisting of five genres that I intended to attempt. The second after the fable was prison novel. The third was a Nabokov novel; the fourth was a doctor novel, and the fifth was a war novel. I thought maybe if any one of those five really took off commercially, I might stick to it, but as it turned out, all five of them were just experiments.

BW: How did your next novel, the prison story *The Choiring of the Trees*, come about?

DH: The original working title of the book I was working on while I was waiting for *The Cockroaches of Stay More* to come out was "Shades of Green." I liked that as a title because it's a very green book, full of green; it has an epigraph from Andrew Marvell about a green thought in a green shade and one from Eugene Delacroix's journals about the different greens that can be used by the painter on a canvas.[65] So, just as García Márquez, throughout *One Hundred Years of Solitude*, puts in those words, "one hundred years of solitude" as a kind of catchphrase, I put "shades of green" throughout the book as a catchphrase, and many of those are still there.

It was turned down by the woman who had been the editor of *Cockroaches*. It was turned down by several other editors at Harcourt Brace. I don't remember just how I got my eventual editor; I think I appealed to Helen Wolff, even though she was retired. I told her about my problems getting this masterpiece published, of finding a publisher for it, and she persuaded someone at Harcourt Brace to give it to some young editor named . . . John Radziewicz, and he became the editor. The first thing he did was to tell me that *Shades of Green* was a very bland title. He didn't think it would sell very well if it was called *Shades of Green*. He called attention to one place in the novel where I use the expression "the choiring of the trees" and suggested that that be the title. Whether that was good or bad, I don't know, but I accepted it reluctantly just to get the book published. Radziewicz also extensively edited the book itself. He had probably the best copy editor that I ever worked with, a young man named Douglas Woodyard, who unfortunately died not long after the book was published. He did a bang-up good job of correcting everything that could be corrected in terms of sense and substance and grammar and punctuation.

So it was not an easy book to get into print. It, too, was rejected by Harcourt at least twice before John Radziewicz was persuaded to take it on and publish it. Then when it got published, it had a major review in *Entertainment Weekly*, calling me "America's Greatest Unknown Novelist," and with a full-color photograph and everything. That made the initial reception of the book a pretty good one; it did not make the bestseller list, but it did pretty well compared with my earlier books.

BW: How did you come up with the idea for it?

DH: I got the original idea when I was a judge for the essay contest of the Pulaski County Historical Association, and one entry—by a woman named Marcia Kemp—was about a courageous Arkansas woman who sought to rescue an Ozarks mountaineer condemned to the electric chair who was sent to die not once, but three times, and escaped with the help of a minor Little Rock novelist by the name of Bernie Babcock. She wrote *The Soul of Ann Rutledge*, Abraham Lincoln's wife—that was probably her best known work. She was not a very distinguished novelist.[66] So, I converted her into a newspaper woman and just took the idea of a convict who went to the electric chair three times and survived all three of them. But he survived by various different means that I invented; his character and his circumstances were nothing like the man in the essay-story I read. That essay simply formed the nucleus for the idea of the story.

I made a big mistake putting that in the front of the book because some reviewers—notably William Vollmann of the *New York Times*— jumped on that and said that this was just a nonfiction book or fictionalized story of an Ozark mountaineer who went to the electric chair three times. There is absolutely nothing about the book which is based upon actual facts other than the fact he *was* an Ozark man and he *did* go to the electric chair three times. That's all—no other similarity. But that essay misled some reviewers, notably Vollmann. He raised the question of just how much it was a biographical, nonfiction novel, even though it's all an invention. But as far as the *New York Times* was concerned, Vollmann's review killed whatever chances the poor book had. So while *The Choiring of the Trees* did attract some good critical attention, it was not enough to sell out its printing.

BW: How did you come up with the dual protagonists for *Choiring*, Viridis Monday and Nail Chism, perhaps the most successful romantic pairing in the Stay More canon?

DH: I decided to make my woman a newspaper illustrator in a time when, early in the century, newspapers were frequently illustrated with black-and-white line drawings and lithographs instead of photographs. Viridis Monday was a reporter for the *Arkansas Gazette*, an actual newspaper, and she was sent to the state prison to attend the execution of a convict by the name of Nail Chism—Nail Chism was a Stay Moron. Inspired, of course, by *Lightning Bug*, where the makers of Chism's Dew are the Chism family of Stay More; Luther Chism of *Lightning Bug* is Nail Chism's younger brother. Nail is just a shepherd, in line with the idea of writing a pastoral novel that would contrast with the prison, drawing the contrast between pastoral and prison. He was a nice guy who helped his brothers and his father distill moonshine whiskey but spent most of his time taking care of his flock of sheep. And he gets railroaded by a series of circumstances into taking the rap for a girl who was supposedly raped at the age of thirteen, and he is convicted and sent to prison for that crime and sentenced to be electrocuted.

I should mention that *The Choiring of the Trees* begins and ends in Stay More. It is, in a sense, the most Stay More-ish of all of my novels. It starts out to tell the story of Nail Chism in prison and of this woman who had been sent to make a drawing of him for the newspaper who takes an interest in him and tries to rescue him from the prison. But in the course of events, she travels to Stay More, investigates his home setting, his background, the town of Stay More itself. As several critics have pointed out, it's the most realistic, the least comical, of my novels, possibly because I discovered with *Cockroaches* that comedy is unpopular. So, *The Choiring of the Trees* is a straight novel, a straight Stay More novel.

BW: Apart from the setting, does it have anything notably in common with *COSM*?

DH: Just as *COSM* was a study of the scientific characteristics of the insect cockroach, I wanted *Choiring of the Trees* to be a scientific study of the inhumane American habit of electrocution as execution and of conditions in the Arkansas prisons at the time, early in the twentieth century. Those conditions were terrible.

BW: Could you elaborate, please? What did you discover in the course of writing *Choiring* about the experience of death row or prison?

DH: As I said, it's a pretty horrible place. Actually, I think the lead-up to the execution is more of a cruel and unusual punishment than the execution itself. The execution is supposed to be over in a matter of minutes, but death row can sometimes last for years before the person is actually executed. I did as much research as possible and found a manuscript in Special Collections of the University of Arkansas library that had been written by an inmate of the Walls, as the Arkansas prison was called in Little Rock. He describes in detail what the food is like, how horrible the guards are, how unsanitary the conditions are. I took practically my entire description of the prison and its conditions right out of his autograph manuscript.

BW: How else does *Choiring* connect or compare with the Stay More novels that preceded it?

DH: The novel is narrated by Latha Bourne, who was our heroine in *Lightning Bug* and who is going to be our heroine in *Enduring*.[67] She narrated the story, which happened at the time she was just reaching puberty herself. She tells the story of how the woman attempts to rescue Nail Chism and how her efforts fail; she finally has to resort to subterfuge to get him out of being electrocuted.

It's a very gripping, fast-paced novel, some people say the most realistic of all of my novels. There's very little magic realism in it as my other novels have. As the blurb on the jacket said, "Nail Chism, strangest and most solitary of the Chism clan that populates all of Donald Harington's acclaimed novels about Stay More, Arkansas, appears doomed to execution until his innocence is championed by the staff artist of the state's leading newspaper. Viridis Monday could have become a painter in Paris during the era of Cubism and the Fauves"—and, by the way, being an art historian, I had to research Cubism, Fauvism, and the famous people like Picasso and Apollinaire that she knows in

Paris during a whole chapter devoted to her Paris year; she could have become a famous painter, but instead, she returned home to Little Rock — "Will she succeed in saving Nail, or will the singing, or choiring, of the trees that Nail hears while strapped into the chair be the last earthly sound he will ever hear?" Nail, from the beginning, supposedly is able to hear trees singing. That is the one element of magic realism that occurs several times in the book.

BW: As a longtime professor of art history, how would you describe Viridis's art, her portraits of Nail in particular? Which factual artist's work might they invoke?

DH: The portrait of Nail that she did for the newspaper was as naturalistic as possible — what laymen would call realistic. In art-historical terms, realism means any attempt to make real, while naturalism means an attempt to make something look exactly as it is. Her portraits of Nail are naturalistic, but the paintings she did in Paris came under the sway of Marguerite Thompson, who was her best friend in Paris, and was the wife eventually of the American artist William Zorach.[68] Viridis's Parisian art was sort of modern. It wasn't modern like Picasso and Braque were doing at the time, but it wasn't old-fashioned art; it was bold, colorful, experimental. But she didn't do a portrait of Nail in oil. Most of her drawings of Nail had been done when he was in prison, and the only artist's work that they would invoke would be — though I hesitate to say it — Andrew Wyeth, who's a very naturalistic pencil drawer. There are any number of artists in pencil whose naturalistic work is like Viridis's.

BW: How would you describe the prison-novel genre? What is *Choiring*'s relationship to the traditional prison novel?

DH: I'm not sure that there is such a thing as a *traditional* prison novel, but there are hundreds and thousands of prison novels. In fact, *Choiring* came out just before Stephen King's *Shawshank Redemption*, which was made into a great movie with Tim Robbins and Morgan Freeman, one of my all-time favorite movies.[69] But that did not influence the book, because my book came out first. I can think of several other prison novels I have read or prison novels that I have seen made into movies. It's a pretty commonplace genre. But I would not think that my novel is like any of the others because the cast of characters is so different. One thing it does have in common with some other prison novels is the brutality of the guards and the warden; that seems to be a very common theme in prison novels. Another great one that I think Stephen King did is *The Green Mile*, but Stephen King has had more than one prison novel to his credit. Come to think of it, I think *Shawshank Redemption* was not a novel but a short story.

But it was enough for me to do one prison novel; I don't think I would want to do another one. Because the prison is in Little Rock, it reflects this long-seated antipathy toward my birthplace that I reflected in *The Cherry Pit* and some of my other novels. I don't know just why it is, but I just don't like Little Rock, and that is reflected in the fact that the horrible prison and the prison characters and the prison staff are all associated with Little Rock. And then, of course, when I get to *Enduring*—as is already mentioned in *Lightning Bug*—Latha is in prison in the Arkansas state lunatic asylum, which is also in Little Rock, so there is another reflection and a kind of parallel, perhaps, between Latha's imprisonment and Nail Chism's imprisonment. As a matter of fact, when Nail has escaped and is hiding out in a cave in Stay More, Latha herself comes to his rescue. Because he has terrible malaria, which gives him horrible shakes, she gets into bed with him to keep him warm, and one thing leads to another. They don't actually have sex, but they have a kind of sex with clothes on, that is, for a girl of her age, pretty bold, pretty daring. That's a coincidence that the two of them, the two people who had been . . . the one *to be* in prison, the other has escaped from the prison.

BW: What does the young Latha's experience of Nail's story contribute to her sense of herself, Stay More, and the world at large in this, her only first-person narrative?

DH: Her only first-person narrative except for her stories she tells to Dawny. The entire book of *Choiring of the Trees* is narrated in her intelligent, unobtrusive voice. She very rarely refers to herself in the first person, and in only one place does she refer to me, the author. She refers to me as "you," getting a kind of revenge for my calling her "you" throughout *Lightning Bug*. It was a very meaningful story because the girl that Nail Chism was convicted of raping—which he did not do—was Rindy Witter, Latha's best friend as a child. I get into that extensively in *Enduring*. Rindy taught her a lot about sex, and a lot of what she knows about human relationships, she picked up from her friend Rindy.

Nail's story did make a big impact on Latha. It brought out her sense of youthful compassion. She's still a girl, practically, when she tells Nail where to go when he escapes. She tells him about the hidden cave up on the mountain and how to get to it. She's responsible for his being there, and that cove of the lost waterfall is destined to reappear significantly in both *When Angels Rest* and *With*. Lots of authors take considerable pleasure in taking a character from one of their novels and putting her in another novel, just as I do. But for me, place has always been more important than people, and so I've taken more thrill from taking certain places such as that glen of the waterfall that I have in *Choiring of the Trees* and using that place in two other novels.

BW: How does Nail's homecoming to Stay More resemble or differ from the returns that other characters make? Like Diana in *Some Other Place.* or Latha in *Lightning Bug* and *Enduring*?

DH: Diana did not return to Stay More; she came into Stay More from the outside. That was not a return. Latha comes back after ten years in exile in the company, as you will find out, of Daniel Lyam Montross, who rescued her in Tennessee, where she had been living for years as a maid.

When Nail returns to Stay More — except for his dramatic encounter with Latha in the cave and Viridis's subsequently moving into the cave with him — Nail is not returning to Stay More. He is returning to the remote wilderness north of Stay More. He doesn't see the town for quite some time. So, I don't know how I could describe his homecoming to Stay More.

BW: Next up was your "Nabokov novel"?

DH: Before I had finished *Choiring*, before it was published — and it took a while to get it published — I had started *Ekaterina*, my homage to Nabokov, inspired, of course, by Nabokov's *Lolita*. But I inverted it so that it's not about an old lecher and a young girl, but about a successful, middle-aged woman novelist — not middle-aged, she's still young — a young Russian novelist and boys at the age of puberty.

Ekaterina is a good Russian woman's name, often spelled with a Y at the beginning. It's the Russian form of Katherine, a common American name. The book was done in homage to Nabokov, so I wanted a title that was the heroine's name and came up with the name *Ekaterina*. For many years, I had thought about doing a kind of Americanized version of Humbert Humbert. Then I decided to just reverse it, shift it around, and have the protagonist as a female and her lovers as young men, twelve years old or less, mostly twelve. I had been thinking of that idea for years, and I had already decided that — just as Nabokov took over a floor of a hotel in Montreux, Switzerland — my heroine would take over the floor of an actual hotel in Arkansas known as the Crescent, a name I disguised as the Halfmoon throughout the book.[70]

BW: How challenging was the research for *Ekaterina*?

DH: I did just as much research for *KAT* as for any other book. When I started, I wanted my heroine to be from the hill country of Russia, but most of Russia is very flat, except for the Urals, so I decided to have her come from the Ural Mountains. And I started off doing a whole lot of research on the Urals and then decided I didn't like the Urals, although I had never been there. So, then I decided she did not have to be from Russia itself but from one of the Russian-speaking countries associated with Russia, such as Georgia. And one northern, hillbilly part of Georgia is known as Svanetia. So, once I had settled on a home for Ekaterina, I had to do extensive research on Svanetia, the names of the places, the countryside, the speech — I even got a dictionary of the Svanetian language. The plant life too; I had a whole book I got from interlibrary loan on the plant life in Svanetia.

There was a fortuitous coincidence. I discovered that a princess in Svanetia had been known as Ekaterina Dadeshkeliani, and so I literally used her name intact as my heroine's name, but pointed out that she was just a niece of the actual Dadeshkeliani. And I wanted her, somehow, to make contact with myself in the disguise of a professor of creative writing at the University of Pittsburgh. But I had decided to use disguises. Although Ekaterina Dadeshkeliani was an actual name, everybody else had to be disguised. So, for myself — since I called myself G. in *Some Other Place*, and G. is one letter ahead of my actual initial, H — I chose one letter *after* my actual initial, which is I. and which, of course, makes a useful first-person reference for my protagonist. I. was a teacher at University of Pittsburgh, which was never identified as such by name, but you would have to be pretty stupid not to recognize it as Pittsburgh.

So it was also inspired by my experiences in Pittsburgh. It opens with Ekaterina arriving in Pittsburgh, or wherever it is, to teach her field, which is mycology, or mushrooms, just as Nabokov's hobby was butterflies. Actually, I don't know if University of Pittsburgh even offers courses in mycology. Anyway, at her rooming house, a Fifth Avenue mansion in Pittsburgh, she meets the aforementioned professor of creative writing known simply as Professor I. In disguise, she begins to sit in on some of his classes to study creative writing and learn how to write a novel based upon her own experiences, which were rather extensive, in the Serbsky Institute of Russia, which was a mental hospital; that, of course, ties in with Latha in *Lightning Bug* and in *Enduring*. Although she is a mycologist, she wants to tell the story of her experiences in Soviet psychiatric hospitals. She and Professor I. develop a friendship.[71]

At the end of the semester, when he is dismissed from the university, just as I had been dismissed from the University of Pittsburgh, she decides to accompany him to his homeland of Stick Around in the Bodark (instead of the Ozark) Mountains of Arkansas. He takes her out there and introduces her to some of his friends, then leaves her, goes on his way. She stays there and begins writing a novel, which will become known as *Georgie Boy*. She eventually finishes it but has a lot of trouble finding a publisher. She makes friends with Sharon Ingledew, who had last appeared as the woman in *Cockroaches of Stay More*, and they move in together and live together while Ekaterina struggles to find a publisher. There's quite a lot in the book about the publishing world, the inside information about what's wrong with agents and publishers and all of that.

Eventually, the novel is picked up and becomes, unlike any of my novels, a runaway bestseller, thanks to a great review written in *New York Review of Books*, which appears in its entirety in the novel, a five-thousand-word book review. Ekaterina becomes phenomenally rich, just as Nabokov did after *Lolita*. She takes over the top floor of a hotel in—I call it "Arcata Springs"—but it's Eureka Springs, Arkansas. The Crescent Hotel is disguised as the Halfmoon Hotel. She takes over the top floor and lives in luxury among some of her young boyfriends that she accumulates, particularly one known as Travis Coe, who comes originally from Stay More.

BW: Is *Lolita* the only Nabokov novel you allude to in *Ekaterina*?

DH: No, of course not. Just as, throughout *Pale Fire*, the hero is being stalked by Gradus, a menacing man who is out to kill our hero, throughout *my* novel, Ekaterina is being stalked by one of the doctors from the Serbsky Institute. I wanted very much to name him Vollmann after the guy who did badly on his review of *Choiring of the Trees*, but Radziewicz persuaded me that the lawyers at Harcourt Brace simply would not permit that to happen. So, I called him Bolshakov, which, in Russian, means "the big one." It doesn't really have anything to do with Vollmann.

Bolshakov tracks down Ekaterina in her hotel and plans to assassinate her, but I don't want to give away the ending of the book.[72] All we know is that Clive Henry, the same critic for the *New York Review of Books*, writes an epilogue to the book, which is an imitation of Nabokov's epilogue to *Lolita*. In addition to the *New York Review of Books* review of her novel, it has a fake *Paris Review* interview with her, interview number fifty-eight, complete. They have a habit of showing a manuscript page of the author's work, so there is even a page of Ekaterina's last manuscript, her autobiography, which is done supposedly in Ekaterina's handwriting with a number of corrections. It was actually done in Kim's handwriting to look like Ekaterina's. Just as Nabokov called his memoirs *Speak, Memory*, she calls hers *Louder, Engram!*, a play on the actual name of I., which is Ingraham. So again, the book is, in many ways, about publishing and publishers and the whole business of getting published and the craft of writing and about Stay More, of course, disguised once again as Stick Around.

My editor at Harcourt Brace, John Radziewicz, had majored in Russian literature in college, so I thought that was one of those fate things. I did not have a lot of trouble getting Harcourt to publish the book, but I did have a lot of trouble with Ekaterina's Svanetian. She speaks a lot of Svanetian in the book that I carefully checked out in my dictionary of Svanetian grammar and languages. I forget just how I did it, but I found a man in Nova Scotia who spoke Svanetian and agreed to read the manuscript and check those expressions for authenticity. I sent the manuscript off to him, but I never heard from him again. To this day, I'm curious whether he found it offensive that I use a lot of dirty language or if he simply thought it was so bad, such a misrendering of the Svanetian language, that it wasn't worth commenting on. But I never heard from him, so the Svanetian as it stands in the book has to stand on its own; I can't guarantee you that her expressions are authentic.

Anyway, *Ekaterina* did not set the world on fire as I had hoped, and it did not allow me to take over one of the floors of the Crescent Hotel the way Nabokov took over the hotel in Montreux. Still, it was a lot of fun to write and to pay homage to Nabokov in the process, and when Toby got around to hiring my customary artist to do the cover for the book, Wendell Minor chose a very famous painting by Edward Hopper, the American artist, which depicts a beautiful nude woman sitting in a chair, looking out the window of her room or apartment. He showed the room, the chair, the window, but where she would be is just a single red rose. I thought that was a very clever interpretation on his part of that famous Hopper painting.

BW: Do Latha and Ekaterina ever commiserate over their experiences in mental-health institutions?

DH: I can't find it for you now, but there's a paragraph or two to that effect in the book. Latha and Ekaterina become the best of friends. Ekaterina refers to Latha's yard, which has always been filled with cats, because Latha loves cats, as "a cat arena," which is a play on her own name. And they commiserate at length about their experiences in mental-health institutions.

BW: And in *Enduring?*

DH: I haven't gotten that far yet. That will be in the latter part in *Enduring* when she meets Ekaterina and they talk specifically about their experiences. But this is in Ekaterina's first-person voice, from her memoirs. "Of all the many things that Lara" — that was Latha's pseudonym for the purposes of the book—

and I had in common, this is the most noteworthy. She, too, in her early twenties, spent three years in a psychiatric hospital, specifically the state asylum for the insane. Unlike me, she was not confined for political motives, and I will not pretend that our incarcerations were identical, beyond the fact that neither of us was certifiably mad: She was diagnosed as having "aphasic catalepsy" (whereas in truth she was simply so angry at those who were trying to steal her baby that she would not speak to anyone), and I was diagnosed by Bolshakov, as we have seen, as having "creeping schizophrenia," the Serbsky's convenient catch-all category for nonconformists. But both Lara and I had spent three years exposed to genuinely sick minds, among the doctors as well as the patients, and we could spend many an hour swapping memories of the dazzling flights of the truly possessed. More, even, than our repertoire of ghost stories, wherein we were constantly delighted to discover the kinship of the Bodarkian spook and the Svanetian *lanchal*, these tales of bughouse behavior cemented a bond between us. There are, come to think of it, many affinities between the *lanchal* and the lunatic: both have left this sorry world behind.

Neither Lara nor I entertained Danny with tales of loonies, but we practically competed with each other in telling him ghost stories.

BW: Apart from Wendell Minor's Hopper tribute for Toby, how would you describe the other covers for *Ekaterina*?

DH: The original hardback edition had a matryoshka doll on the cover, which I thought was very clever. The idea of the matryoshka doll is that you take the head off, and there's another matryoshka doll inside, you take the head off of that, there's another matryoshka doll inside of that, and so on—like Chinese boxes. I thought that was very appropriate for the content of the book, but I doubt if one person out of a hundred in visiting bookstores recognized the significance of the matryoshka doll on the cover. The Harvest edition paperback showed the nude backside of a very handsome young boy of the age probably that Ekaterina liked to seduce. But again, it's almost difficult for the average viewer to tell that that is a male; it might just as well be a female.

BW: How would you describe *KAT*'s relationship to *Lolita* and yours to Nabokov in general?

DH: Her relationship to Lolita is completely inverted, because Lolita is supposedly the victim of Humbert Humbert.[73] Ekaterina is the seducer of the young boys; Ekaterina is not a nymphet by any means. She picks up the male equivalent of nymphets. Do I give them a name in the book? If a nymph creates a "nymphet," what does a satyr give birth to?

BW: "Faunlets"?

DH: Do I use that word in the book? I don't think so.[74]

My relationship to Nabokov is simply that I extravagantly admire and envy the man. I've read everything he's written, including all of his short stories. I gave permission for the first five chapters of *Ekaterina* to appear on the Nabokov website that was set up at the University of Pennsylvania. As far as I know, they are still on that website, and you can find references to Nabokov and to *Lolita* throughout the book.

BW: Why make this novel a full first-person narrative—that is, the only one in which the narrator is the primary character in the plot?

DH: Is the narrator the primary character? Is Ekaterina the narrator?

BW: Part of the time.

DH: She narrates in the first person only her autobiography, which is called—like Nabokov's *Speak, Memory*—*Louder, Engram!* Ingraham is supposedly the name that I. is short for, and she's telling him not to speak, but to speak louder. And she narrates that in the first person, that part of her autobiography, but most of the first part of the book is told in the third person. Isn't there a part in the second person? Yes, the whole first part about her time in Pittsburgh is narrated in the second person by Daniel Lyam Montross, and he addresses her as "you." He starts off, "Ekaterina you were, and you were not at all. You were from a land far away, once upon a time and upon no time at all, where stories always begin, 'There was, and there was not at all . . . ,' as if to confute truth or affirm invention, in celebration of the imagination's freedom to transcend the stubborn facts of 'reality' . . . " That voice is Daniel Lyam Montross, and it continues throughout Part One of the book, and then Ekaterina's voice takes over for the parts that come from her autobiography.

BW: Did writing *KAT* rid you of your need to write a "Nabokov novel"?

DH: When I said I had a need to write a "Nabokov novel," I did not mean that as a genre like the other books that I was imitating — prison novels and war novels and so forth. I would not say that this is an example of a "Nabokov genre" so much as an homage to Nabokov. I would dearly love to know what Nabokov would have thought of the book if he had lived to read it himself, but he would not have recognized any imitation of his own style. It does not seek to imitate his style. It has, for example, in the confrontation between I. and Bolshakov, the crazy Russian psychiatrist, toward the end a distinct echo of a confrontation between Humbert Humbert and Quilty. There are a lot of things borrowed from Nabokov, but I would not say his style is borrowed from Nabokov.[75] And yes, I have no desire now to do another imitation of Nabokov. Unless I can come up with a good idea for *Pale Fire*, and it would take too long to write the poem. And in a sense I've already done that but in the poetry section of *Some Other Place. The Right Place.*, which was very strongly inspired by the poetry section of the *Pale Fire*.[76]

BW: How would you describe the relationship between Ekaterina and I.?

DH: Well, of course, I. has the hots for her, but she only has the hots for twelve-year-old boys, so I. is much too old for her to get in bed with him. There's a moment where they have to stop at a hotel and spend the night sharing the bed, but they resort to the Ozark custom of what's called "ride and tie." When two men were going on a journey, and they only had one horse, one man would get on the horse and ride it for so many miles and get off and tie it to a tree while the other man walked.

And the other man walking would come along and get on the horse and ride until he caught up and passed the first guy. So Ekaterina and I. do share a bed, but only in the sense of "ride and tie." He's awake while she's asleep and vice versa. There is no romantic relationship between them, although there certainly would've been if she had permitted it.

Anyway, in the book, Ekaterina wants to sit in on I.'s classes in fiction writing without him knowing it, so she disguises herself, and her disguise is described in considerable detail in the book. In fact, on our thirteenth anniversary, my sweet wife, Kim, went to considerable pains to disguise herself as Ekaterina and came to my evening class. She sat in on the class and left me up there lecturing, wondering who is this mysterious dame who has walked in and is sitting in on my class? After the class, she came up and handed me the first of several written notes that she'd prepared—as if she knew that I couldn't hear her, so I would have to read the notes. I've still got all the notes somewhere. I thought she was some great fan of mine who was coming to seduce me, and it took me the longest time to figure out that it was Kim herself. Which wasn't a nice thing for you to do, but it was a very clever thing for you to do.

BW: Can we get her version now?

KH: It's my turn to tell the story. I need to sit there, so get up. I'm going to sit where you're sitting.

DH: You can sit where I'm sitting.

KH: I'm not sure where this idea came from, but it occurred to me one day, not long before our anniversary, that I could do something special. I didn't know what to do. Don would be in class that night, so . . . I don't know how I dreamed it up, I really don't.

BW: What day is your anniversary?

KH: October 8.

BW: And the thirteenth would've been what year?

KH: Don said that it was our thirteenth anniversary; I don't remember that it was the thirteenth. He may very well be right. If that's true, then it would have been 1996. So, I thought about it for days and secretly assembled what I would need. I knew that I needed to wear clothes that Don would not remember, maybe something that I had in a trunk somewhere. So I found an old dress and a lacy cover up that I knew he wouldn't recognize. The wig of long, red hair—very long, red hair—came from a shop here in Fayetteville, a costume shop. It was a very cheap wig, and I rented it for five dollars for the evening. It wasn't real hair; it was almost plastic in the way that it felt, but it was really fun to wear. I became almost a different person when I put it on. I knew that I had to exaggerate everything, so I wore — like Ekaterina wore — tacky, loud jewelry, and I exaggerated my eye makeup and my lipstick and everything, huge earrings, plastic, ugly, something I must've had back in the sixties or seventies. I borrowed a hat from a friend. I hitched a ride to campus so that my car would not be on campus. I didn't come into Don's class at the start; I waited until there were thirty to forty minutes left in the class.

BW: So if you hitched a ride from somebody else to campus, that means someone else was in on the joke — is that right?

KH: That's right, someone else knew.

BW: A close friend?

KH: Yes, and here's another aspect to it. There was also a woman in the class who was a close friend of mine, and I did tell her that I was thinking about this. She was waiting as she sat there listening to Don's lecture, and she must've known that I would come into class sooner or later. I came in the back door, and I took a seat at the end of a row, so I was probably five seats behind my friend. Those seats were empty. She turned to look at me and, literally, had to stifle a laugh. I think she put her hand over her mouth, and her shoulders began to shake violently in laughter; I knew we would talk later. Don certainly noticed my presence; he watched me come in.

I didn't know how long I could keep up the act. I didn't know at what point he would recognize me, but I knew he wouldn't recognize me from that distance. I was very nervous. I was nervous in costume. I was nervous about his reaction. I was not planning to speak at all, and I was armed with note cards and, I think, purple ink pens. Didn't Ekaterina always use purple ink?

I watched Don to see what reaction my presence would have — or this strange woman's presence would have. Our stories differ; Don says that he was unruffled and continued to lecture as if nothing had happened and no one had entered the classroom — that he just smoothly went on. That's not the case. He stumbled, he forgot things, he gestured in that way that people do when they can't quite get the right word, he paced around, he wasn't at all comfortable with my presence. Who knows what he was thinking? After class, I followed him to his office. I had no idea, again, how long it would take him to recognize me, but I handed him some cards. I don't remember what I wrote on them;

I was nervous, not knowing exactly where this would take us. I *think* that he recognized me while we were in his office, and then I think that he must've decided to play along with it. He didn't say, "Kim, what are you doing?" He just went with the flow of it. I have a feeling that he does not remember exactly when he really did recognize me. I was playing it up, with sheer exaggeration, and I loved it, really, because the wig was fun. I'd always wanted long hair but had never had it, so I got my chance to toss around this beautiful fake hair—emphasis on fake—and the sunglasses hid my eyes.

I guess that's the anniversary that is most memorable.

BW: How does the novel *KAT* embody the "ride and tie" metaphor?

DH: Well it literally does it in the sense that I. and Ekaterina ride and tie that one night that they had to spend together in the hotel. If you're talking about how the novel itself is "ride and tie," I'm afraid we'll have to leave that to guys who are writing their dissertation fifty years from now. I really can't conceive how the novel itself is a matter of riding and tying.

BW: Play Hollywood casting agent: whom would you cast for Ekaterina?

DH: Nicole Kidman. [To Kim] Whom would you cast for Ekaterina?

KH: Let me think a little bit. Maybe Nicole Kidman . . . let's see. What's the name of Ingrid Bergman's daughter?

BW: Isabella Rossellini.

DH: I would go along with that.

BW: And for other characters in *Ekaterina*—Kenny, Travis, Bolshakov, and Ingraham?

DH: Donald Sutherland to play I.

KH: I knew you would say Donald Sutherland.

BW: How did you know he would say Donald Sutherland?

KH: Don's always loved Donald Sutherland and he fancies himself looking like Donald Sutherland. Maybe there is some sort of resemblance.

BW: Any particular movies of his that Don really likes?

KH: I can't answer that.

DH: I'm not too familiar with available actors of the age of twelve to play Kenny and Travis.

BW: They can be from any time. If you can think of a child actor from forty years ago whom you would've put in this role, that's fine.

DH: If that's permissible, I would have Mickey Rooney play Travis—the same who was in *A Midsummer Night's Dream*.[77] Or who's the kid who did *Home Alone*? Macaulay Culkin. We could have him do Kenny.

KH: He has a little brother who acts too, but don't forget that Leo DiCaprio was acting at a young age, too. And River Phoenix.

DH: For Bolshakov, Robert De Niro. Maybe Robert De Niro is not quite comic enough. Who played Quilty in the original movie of *Lolita*?

BW: Peter Sellers.

DH: Peter Sellers, oh yes. So let's get Oliver Platt to play Bolshakov instead of De Niro. Who played Quilty in the later movie?

BW: Frank Langella.

DH: Oh, yes. He wasn't the greatest for that movie.

BW: Why mushrooms for Ekaterina's counterpart to Nabokov's butterflies?

DH: Well, for Nabokov, butterflies were primarily a hobby, and for Ekaterina, I wanted them to be a profession. And, of course, there is a not very closely veiled allusion—I think it is even mentioned in the book a couple of times—to the similarity of the shape and size of the mushroom to the young boy's penis. That might've had something to do with it, but as I recall, Kim and I were riding out to Kingston, I can remember where we were in the car when *she* suggested that Ekaterina be a collector of mushrooms.

BW: Where is Ekaterina now?

DH: I wish you hadn't asked me that. Supposedly, during the time of *Thirteen Albatrosses*, she is still the principal inhabitant of the Jacob Ingledew mansion in Stay More. But by the time of *Enduring*, she no longer lives there. I'm going to have to think about what to do to get her out of Stay More and put that in some future novel, but I can assume she would probably suffer homesickness for Svanetia, and now that Svanetia is no longer under Soviet rule, she would be free to go back home, and she would be the princess of Svanetia, or if Svanetia had become a republic, she could run for president of Svanetia, I don't know. But I don't think she would be content, even though Sharon was such a dear friend of hers and Ekaterina has moved into Holy House after Sharon's husband, Larry, has moved out. I don't think she would be content to have no other friends except Sharon, and the only boys that might be available to her are the sons of characters like the son of Day Whittacker and Diana Stoving, and I. tells Ekaterina to stay away from him, to not bother him. I don't know where Ekaterina would find any sexual satisfaction if she stayed in Stay More.

BW: It was around this time of *Ekaterina*'s publication that you were diagnosed with cancer, wasn't it?

DH: I knew that I had something wrong with my throat. And I had been referred to the doctor in Little Rock. The ENT already knew it was cancer; it had been biopsied here, and he knew it was already cancer. That was in the clinic, here in Fayetteville, likely. The ENT, Dr. Crocker, had biopsied a suspicious lump in my throat and discovered that it was malignant. And then he sent me to Little Rock to see Dr. Stern, who's one of the best specialists in the state, if not this part of the world. He confirmed the diagnosis and told me the prognosis, that I would need to have radiation for a certain amount of time. Chemotherapy first, for a certain amount of time, then radiation, and if those two together did not succeed, I would have to have surgery. And that was exactly the progression. I came back home and went to North Arkansas Radiation Institute for daily treatments for three, four weeks, and they reduced the cancer. The chemotherapy caused me to become bald, as is customary, and greatly weakened me. This semester was still on, so I had very great difficulty teaching my classes and going for chemotherapy, which was administered daily. Chemo and radiation greatly reduced the tumor but did not eradicate it. So Dr. Stern felt that surgery would be necessary.

I went to Little Rock to the University of Arkansas Medical Center, and Dr. Stern himself performed the surgery, warning me in advance that I was in danger of losing my larynx and not being able to speak. I said, "Could you tell me upon coming out of the ether or have someone give a thumbs-up or a thumbs-down to let me know if my larynx had been spared?" And I remember coming out of the ether and getting the thumbs-up.

My larynx was spared, but my ability to eat was lost. I could not swallow, and I went through a very lengthy and painful process of trying to learn how to eat again. For a long time, in fact, I could eat nothing but baby food. We had a pantry full of Gerber's. And then, step by step, there was this special technique I recall. It's called the cough-swallow technique. I would swallow something and then cough. Take another bite, cough. Take another bite, cough. It would drive anyone crazy who was in my presence. So, I had to do all of my eating in private. But after several months, as Dr. Stern had promised, "One of these days you'll be eating fried chicken again." And after several months, 1 was able to eat fried chicken.

BW: What was your favorite Gerber's flavor?

DH: Very imaginative question. [To Kim] Do you remember the one you bought the most of? I think it was probably spinach, because I had the idea that, like Popeye getting strong, if I ate my Gerber's spinach, I would get strong. I don't remember when the Gerber's treatment stopped.

BW: So the Fate Thing had synchronized your doctor novel with your illness?

DH: Doctor novels and doctor TV programs and doctor stories are just about the most popular genre of American entertainment. So I thought sure that *Butterfly Weed* would really catch on with everyone. Also, I already had my doctor and had been promising him a novel of his own ever since the time of *Lightning Bug*: Doc Colvin Swain. That's another reason, after *Ekaterina*, I wrote *Butterfly Weed*, the life story of Doc Swain, who had first appeared significantly in *Lightning Bug* and reappeared significantly in *The Choiring of the Trees*. It was time for his story.

BW: How would *Butterfly Weed* be different if you had not had cancer yourself?

DH: I came down with cancer about the time I was writing the part at which Tenny comes down with tuberculosis, but I'm not sure I could honestly answer that question. In fact, the surgery occurred just at the point where Tenny discovers that she has tuberculosis. So, the whole experience of my illness could be tied in with Tenny's illness.

KH: "Hug Tenny. She definitely has TB."

DH: I wrote that down after having discovered that I had cancer. Someday, probably, someone will write a dissertation on the effect of Harington's cancer on *Butterfly Weed* and point out the correlation between the dates of my recovery and the dates when I gradually finished the novel. By the time I was through with the novel, my recovery from the cancer was pretty much complete.

So there is a kind of connection, possibly, but I don't think you could say that *Butterfly Weed* would be different if I had not had cancer. Well, it certainly gave me a new appreciation—maybe not a new appreciation, but a new understanding—of hospitals and nurses that I had, in a sense, prefigured in the early part of *Butterfly Weed* when discussing the Saint Louis hospitals and nurses that Doc Swain encounters.

BW: Why cast Vance Randolph as the narrator?

DH: I wanted to pay homage to our great collector of Ozark folktales, Ozark folklore. I would not have been able to write any of my books without Vance Randolph, so I put Vance into the book with flashbacks.

At the time of the book, he was living in a horrible nursing home called Sunrise Manor in Fayetteville, with his wife, Mary Celestia Parler, and supposedly, he was visited by Harington. In fact, I actually did visit him a couple of times. The joke is that Harington is deaf and cannot hear him, and therefore, Randolph is free to tell whatever stories he wants to tell. So, conceivably, he fabricates Doc Swain's story, basing it upon Greek mythology. Possibly. As far as I know, Vance Randolph wasn't interested in Greek mythology. In his collections of folk stories and folktales, I can't think of a single one that is traced back to Greek mythology.

Anyway, I hit upon the idea of having an encounter between Vance Randolph and Doc Swain taking place in Stay More. During this encounter, Vance Randolph learns Doc Swain's story and, perhaps, stretches it a little bit with his own knowledge of mythology and folklore. We never know for sure in *Butterfly Weed* just what is definitely happening in reality and what is just a *re*-presentation of mythology or folklore. *Butterfly Weed* is essentially the story of Doc Swain as recounted and reinterpreted by Vance Randolph.

BW: How much did you know about the Newton County Academy before you sent Doc Swain to teach there?

DH: That's another thing I can thank Kim for, like the way she inspired me with the idea of the mushrooms in *Ekaterina*. We had driven out to Murray, which is the Stay More of Newton County, and we stopped by the quaint little village of Parthenon, which is mentioned in so many of my books as the only principal hamlet anywhere near Stay More. On that trip, we discovered, for the first time, the remains of Newton County Academy. There was such a place that had a main building, a gymnasium—it was a thriving academy back in the teens and twenties. There was nothing left of it at that time, except the stone administration building, which had a beautiful view of Parthenon Valley.[78] Kim remarked, "Wouldn't this be a great setting for a novel?" That was the seed of *Butterfly Weed*.

From that point on, I had to think up a novel that I could put at Newton County Academy. So we, in fact, did some interviews for it too. We located some women who had graduated from Newton County Academy and were living in Springdale. We went and Kim interviewed them, just as she had interviewed the people in *Let Us Build Us a City*. And I provided a lot of information about the actual academy. I found a yearbook of the academy and was able to get information out of that, and so I completely fabricated this academy where Doc Colvin Swain met this lovely young student of his whose name was Tennessee Tennyson, a distant descendant of Alfred Lord Tennyson. Everybody called her "Tenny."

BW: How would you describe *Butterfly Weed*'s relationship to mythology?

DH: I decided to populate the book with the Greek myths: the myth of Venus, the myth of Mars, the myth of Eros. And Tenny is, in a way, the personification of Psyche, so Wendell Minor, in his cover, shows Tenny as an angel. The angel could also be a butterfly, the usual personification of Psyche. And Psyche is the girlfriend, in Greek mythology, of Eros, the son of Venus herself. Eros's name is converted simply to "Russ" in the book, and his mother, Venus, is simply called Venda. They are actual characters; Venda is a music teacher at Newton County Academy, and Russ is a fellow student of Tenny's who, despite being diphallic (that is, he has two penises), falls in love with Tenny. Meanwhile, his mother, Venda, has the hots for Doc Swain and tries to seduce him with the help of some mysterious aphrodisiac.

But his heart still belongs to Tenny. The problem is Tenny comes down with tuberculosis, and even though Doc Swain is capable of curing any disease known to man, he cannot cure Tenny's TB. So Tenny has to be shipped off to the Arkansas Tuberculosis Sanitarium. I hadn't thought of it, but there is one more prison; much like Latha is in the nuthouse and Nail Chism in the state prison, Tenny is incarcerated at the TB sanitarium. There must be something in the fact that I have three of those. Anyway, she's practically a prisoner, so Colvin takes his team of horses and wagon down to rescue her from that sanitarium. Vance Randolph tells this whole complicated story to me, and I tell it to the reader, and somewhere along the line, it gets lost in translation and turns out to be a fabulous novel of magic realism.

BW: Which is more important, the magic or the realism?

DH: Why separate them? The major Greek myths come together in the subplots and the stories in the book, but it also tells the story of how Doc Swain got his so-called medical degree as an apprentice to a backwoods country doctor who, in turn, had got his knowledge from a backwoods country doctor. None of them had diplomas. When Arkansas passes a law that you have to have a medical degree to get a license, Doc Swain—although he is a thoroughly capable doctor who happens not to have a diploma—notices that Doc Plowright, who lives across the road in Stay More, has a certificate on the wall from the Royal

Academy of Physicians and Surgeons, giving him a doctor's degree. He asks Doc Plowright how he got it, and Doc Plowright says he ordered it by mail from Saint Louis. So Doc Swain sends off his money, and he waits and waits and never gets his diploma or any reply. He decides he has to go to Saint Louis and confront those people to get his diploma, but when he gets to Saint Louis, he discovers that it's just a diploma mill, a print shop that churns out diplomas. They offer to churn one out for him on the spot. But he thinks as long as he's in Saint Louis, he might as well find out what all of this doctoring business is about. So, he visits the hospital and sees the nurses and the physicians, and . . . well, it's one of the funniest passages I ever wrote.

BW: You've said you prefer comedy in your work; why did you choose such a non-comedic ending for *Butterfly Weed*?

DH: I often need critics and readers to tell me what I am doing or to explain to me what I'm doing, and I could not honestly tell you why I chose that ending except that it is so dramatic and cathartic. So many great tragedies end with tragedy, because tragedy is supposed to be just as powerful as comedy. This is a point that Lee Smith makes when she talks about my use of tense changes. Like all of my other books, *Butterfly Weed* starts out in the past tense, then shifts to the present tense, and then finally shifts to the future tense. So, let's return to Tenny and Colvin. Together at last so tragically, so briefly, before the end. He's sucking her breasts, and the "exquisiteness of the sensation will be something that she will never be able to take with her, wherever it is that she is soon going, that Other Place perhaps. In the past tense, 'He sucked her breasts,' and regardless of how well he did it, it was done, and all she had left was the memory of it. In the present tense, 'He sucks her breasts,' and it is driving her wild, for the whole duration of the present moment, but the moment does not last. In the future tense, 'He will suck her breasts,' and it will be a feeling that she will be able to have any time she will want it. For eternity." In the same way, as they approach Stay More, "'Thank you for bringing me home,' she will say to him."

"'Thank ye for coming home,' he will say, and then, in the future tense, 'We will soon be there.'"

"And in the future tense, they will always soon be there."

And Lee Smith says, "I have to say: this kills me. I read it again and again. There is something so much more poignant, to my mind, about imminence, about always *almost* being there, than about being there.

May these novels never end, both individually and in their entirety. At the end of *When Angels Rest,* Harington promises something of the sort, telling us that his 'promise' will be 'to find *all* the stories of Stay More.' I hope so. I'm hooked. I agree with the narrator of *Butterfly Weed,* who says, 'Stay More is not simply remote and hard to get to, if not inaccessible, but . . . it's harder to *escape* than it is to *find.*' I'm there. And I *will be* there. Listening. Waiting." That's a beautiful passage by Lee Smith; she puts her finger on the poignance of *Butterfly Weed's* ending, which is so moving. It would not be nearly so moving if they lived happily ever after. That's all I can say about that question.

BW: What is the dream cure, and have you ever tried it on yourself?

DH: Doc Colvin Swain, like all the other figures in the book, is based on Greek mythology. Doc Swain is patterned after Asclepius, the founder of modern medicine. All doctors know who Asclepius is. And Asclepius supposedly found a way to cure his patients in their dreams, if they would permit him into their dreams. So, Doc Swain—until he discovers that you really can't bill a patient for such a service—starts appearing in the dreams of his patients and curing them. Thus it's known as the "dream cure." And no, I've never tried the dream cure on myself, and I'm not sure the dream cure has ever worked, even for Asclepius. Remember that Asclepius was a mythological creature, but like mythological creatures, he contained a lot of truth.

BW: How would you explain the Asclepius epigraph?

DH: There are three epigraphs in *Butterfly Weed.* One is from Vance Randolph himself, the narrator of the story, in which he was commenting on his reaction after he had read my novel *The Architecture of the Arkansas Ozarks.* He wrote in his bibliography of Ozark literature, "All lies and fantasy, but true as God's gospel." And in her review of *Lightning Bug* for *Time* magazine, Martha Duffy said, "To him the men of Stay More are still gods." That, of course, is an allusion to my use of Greek mythology in *Butterfly Weed.* The third is the last words of Socrates, recorded by his disciple Plato. He said, "Give a cock to Asclepius."

Now, that can be taken two ways. It was a custom, when you were ill in ancient Greece, to give a rooster to Asclepius, who was the greatest of all doctors, and it would bring you good health. So Socrates was simply asking his disciples to make a token of giving the rooster to Asclepius for the sake of everyone's health; those were his last words. But to give a *cock* to Asclepius means, literally, to put a penis on the guy! And that's what the book does—it puts a penis on Asclepius in the form of Doc Colvin Swain. Thank you. I had forgotten about that—important epigraph.

BW: What do you think now of *Butterfly Weed*?

DH: Next to *Lightning Bug*, I think *Butterfly Weed* is the sweetest of all of my novels. Also, in a way, *Butterfly Weed* probably has more magic realism than any of my other novels. I can't, at this point, stop to name all of the examples of magic realism, but one is that Colvin Swain and Tenny are lovers in their imaginations before they are lovers in reality. That's why Wendell Minor chose to show on the cover the bed in which they made love—it's floating in the air, as if it's only a dream.

And finally, in many places, it's also the funniest of my novels. I read a passage from it when I was invited to attend the Cultural Olympiad in Atlanta, Georgia, that coincided with the physical Olympiad.[79] They invited fifteen great novelists to appear at the Cultural Olympiad, and I read the passage from *Butterfly Weed* about Doc Swain's visit to Saint Louis to see medical schools, and that left them in the aisles. It was also very well-received at the University of the Ozarks in Clarksville, Arkansas.[80]

BW: What did Harcourt Brace think of *Butterfly Weed*?

DH: John Radziewicz was still my editor when I started writing it, but I think by the time I had finished it, he was no longer my editor. Once again, it was a commercial failure. It did not make enough money, and Harcourt was eager to get rid of me, so they declined the next genre novel. It was my last book for Harcourt Brace.

Falling Off the Mountain

BW: How did you get started on *When Angels Rest*, your war novel?

DH: For once, I started off with the acronym *WAR* and made up a title to fit the acronym. I tried several possibilities before I came up with *When Angels Rest*, which is almost perfect, because when angels rest, mankind goes to war. Angels are busy and on the job all the time, but if they get tired and have to rest, mankind does something utterly stupid. Like bombing Hiroshima, so *When Angels Rest* is a story of when angels rested in the history of Stay More, specifically during the second world war, when it's invaded by the U.S. Army on maneuvers. It has a bunch of U.S. Army soldiers who are imitating the Japanese in preparation for the invasion of Japan. The whole thing is told by Dawny of *Lightning*

Bug, who's much older now—I think he's twelve[81]—and running a local newspaper, which he calls the *Stay Morning Star.* It's told mostly from Dawny's point of view, and it's a very lively novel.

BW: With Harcourt Brace having cut you loose, how did you find a publisher for *WAR?*

DH: It was sent around to several different publishers after Harcourt had turned it down. I had a new agent by this time, and she sent it to Counterpoint Press, where Jack Shoemaker was a distinguished independent publisher who had founded Counterpoint in California and eventually brought it to Washington, D.C. They were particularly distinguished for the quality of their printing; their editions were very handsome, so I was very happy to be with Counterpoint. But once again, despite Shoemaker's best efforts, he could not find an audience for *When Angels Rest.*[82]

BW: When you think of *WAR* now, which elements or passages particularly come to mind, and why?

DH: I was just thinking of the passage that Lee Smith quotes from the end of *When Angels Rest.* It was (I promised, in the future tense) to tell all of the stories of Stay More, as I put it. "So this story, this world, if it will exist at all, it will exist only in your mind, for as long as you can hold onto it." Throughout the book the reader is solicited to become a character in the story and is called "Gentle Reader."[83] "That will be your promise. Mine will be to find *all* the stories of Stay More. We will conspire: my secret to you is that you will be, as you have been, the real creator of this world. Your secret to me is that you will have known that all along."

Have you memorized the passage yourself? That's a key passage in the sense that I like to think of the reader as the real creator of each one of my novels, and I like to think the intelligent reader damn well knows that and has known it all along.

BW: Why bring war to Stay More?

DH: Well, America went to the Second World War, and several people of Stay More were taken into the Army. A few of them were killed. Gerald Coe, who first appears in *Lightning Bug* as one of the triplet sons of blacksmith Lawlor Coe—their names were Earl, Burl, and Gerald, and you ought to know that the way they pronounced "Gerald," he rhymes with his brothers—he's drafted into the Marines and fights at Iwo Jima. Today's newspaper coincidentally is filled with the distressing news that the people on Iwo Jima have chosen to rename their island Iwo To, which means exactly the same thing. In Japanese, it means "sulfur island," and "sulfur" has allusions of hell. Iwo Jima was a real hell for the Japanese, as shown in a recent movie.[84] And in my telling of the story, Gerald Coe is a member of the marines who assault Mount Suribachi to plant the flag, but he is killed in the process and declared a war hero.

But the book starts off with the kids of Stay More, in their restlessness, trying to come up with something to do. Gerald Coe decides to run for mayor, or as they would pronounce it, "mare," and that becomes his nickname. Everybody has a nickname, and Gerald Coe was called "Mare Coe," with allusions of his being a female horse. But Mare Coe is running for mayor of Stay More, and the first part of *WAR* is a political novel about his campaign and how he solicits the help of young Dawny, who was seen in *Lightning Bug* as a five-going-on-six-year-old. Dawny is now, at the time of this book, twelve or thirteen, and he has started a neighborhood newspaper, which he calls the *Stay Morning Star.*

BW: An example of your life intruding on—or informing—your art?

DH: Yes, that's based on autobiography. I had a neighborhood newspaper in Little Rock when I was a kid, and so I know most of the business about starting and running a newspaper. And a lot of it is about the news that he reports with the help of Latha, to whom he is still devoted and who acquires the very first radio in Stay More. It's a battery-operated radio, but a real radio nonetheless, on which they could pick up news broadcasts on which Dawny and Latha together first hear that Franklin Delano Roosevelt has died of a cerebral hemorrhage. And not long after that, the great journalist, Ernie Pyle, who is Dawny's hero in terms of journalism, is killed by the Japanese in the Pacific, which is a great distress to Dawny.

BW: When angels rest, death haunts the kids of Stay More?

DH: Yes, there's a lot of death in this book. In one passage, the bullies at the Stay More school have beaten to death a mule named Old Jarhead, which was an allusion to the fact that U.S. Marines are called jarheads. The mule is beaten to death by the bullies, who call themselves the Allies, and they make all of the weaker kids serve as the Axis. Dawny is a member of the Axis, and these struggles between the Allies and the Axis had been going on for years. Miss Jerram, the schoolteacher at Stay More school, makes the students go up on the hill and bury the mule, give him a sacred burial, and sing "Farther Along," the funeral hymn, over him as he's put into the earth. Just as the funeral ceremony comes to an end, the first part of the book comes to an end, and they see an aircraft flying over, the first aircraft that anyone in Stay More has ever seen. Actually, the aircraft is a plane pulling a glider; the plane lets go of the glider and wanders on, and the glider comes down and settles to earth, where the kids of Stay More discover it.

BW: How do the Stay More kids get along with the invading soldiers?

DH: Pretty well, really. In the second part of the book, when the glider unloads its cargo of marines dressed as Japanese, the Japanese take the kids captive, and Dawny makes friends with the lieutenant in charge of the marines. Lt. McPherson is from Vermont, and he's a very nice guy, very good guy, and he becomes Dawny's friend for the rest of the book, in which it's explained that the purpose of the glider was to land behind the enemy lines in training for doing the same thing in Japan. As the war in Japan is coming to a close, America plans to flood the Japanese continent with hundreds of gliders with American soldiers in them who would prevent the atomic bomb from being necessary. But that operation goes awry when the atomic bomb is dropped after all, wiping out hundreds of thousands of innocent people. Dawny witnesses all of this with the knowledge that his friend Mare Coe has been killed on Iwo Jima.

Meanwhile, a romance is growing up between Dawny and one of the Dinsmore girls, known as Ella Jean. She's pretty cute, somewhat homespun, one of thirteen kids of Selena Dinsmore. Meanwhile, in alternate passages, these soldiers who've landed in the glider are setting up a bivouac to wage war games against the tank corps that are being sent from Saint Louis. Several battalions of tanks with expert tank drivers and tanksmen are going to fight against the guerrillas who landed in the glider.

BW: So you had to become an expert on army maneuvers and other aspects of the military to tell this story?

DH: Well, I had to research not only the particular type of glider that was used and learn its structure thoroughly, but also how the army conducted war-time maneuvers. Our cameraman, on his way from Saint Louis, has passed repeatedly through Fort Leonard Wood in Missouri. I had to contact the army historian at Ft. Leonard Wood to find out how the army conducted maneuvers during their preparation for the second World War in Missouri to make the whole thing seem authentic. Stay More becomes completely populated with soldiers for the duration of the maneuvers. The business is good for Latha's general store, and the business is good for her husband Every, who runs an automobile repair shop. Everybody's getting rich, making money, and Dawny's friend McPherson and his "Japanese" soldiers are engaging the real Allies in mock-combat, winning a few, losing a few. Because of the huge population of soldiers in Stay More, there is not an awful lot of law and order and justice, and the crucial plot of the story hangs upon the fact that Dawny's amorous relationship with his girlfriend Ella Jean has reached a point where they have agreed to meet at the creek and make love to each other in the water, but at the time Dawny arrives there to meet her, he can't find her, only her body. There are several possible suspects for having killed Ella Jean. The army interviews all of them, but they never find out who kills Ella Jean. You talk about the sad ending of *Butterfly Weed*; I've heard even more complaints from readers about how they hated to see Ella Jean die at the end of *When Angels Rest*. Maybe I got in the habit of killing off my heroine in *Butterfly Weed*, and I couldn't get out of the habit in time for *When Angels Rest*. But I wanted to make the point that war is hell! And who do we blame for the innocent people who get killed? Can we put our finger on a culprit? Is there a number-one suspect? We never know who has killed Ella Jean.

Eventually all of the soldiers leave. Dawny keeps in touch with McPherson after McPherson himself goes to Japan. He speaks fluent Japanese and plays an important part in the rehabilitation of the Japanese after the war. The book is extremely sympathetic to the Japanese and uses a number of expressions in Japanese which I bothered to verify with the help of the internet. By this time, all of us authors are using Google, the internet. It's a lot easier for us to do research and to verify things like the Japanese expressions that I used in the book.

BW: What do biographers need to steer clear of in comparing Dawny to his author?

DH: Not only in this book, in all of my books. Probably the best rule of thumb is, as I said about *Architecture of the Arkansas Ozarks*, that there's an inverse relationship between how likely something was to actually have happened and whether it really happened or not. So that the most unlikely things—such as the Battle of Whiteley's Mill, in which hundreds of soldiers shot at each other for hours and not one was killed— that's incredible, but it's true.

The incredible things that happen in *When Angels Rest* are not true. I never lived with Latha or anyone like her. I never ran a newspaper in Stay More, though I did in Little Rock. I never had a girlfriend like

Ella Jean who was killed by soldiers on maneuvers; well, we don't know if soldiers on maneuvers killed her. It could even have been Sugrue Alan, who lived in Stay More and could have killed her, we don't know. But we should know that most of the things that happen to Dawny did not actually happen to me, and biographers need to steer clear of that stuff. Dawny loses his hearing because, when he discovers Ella Jean's corpse, he begins screaming at the top of his lungs and keeps on screaming until he has literally deafened himself. I lost my hearing because I had meningococcal meningitis at the age of twelve. I was the same age as Dawny when we lost our hearing, but not under the same circumstances.

BW: How is it that your war novel is also your children's novel, that is, focusing on and told from the perspective of the child's war? What's the relationship between the two, war and childhood?

DH: Again, see my epigraphs for Part One. First, by Novalis: "Where children are, there is the golden age." And from Johan Huizinga's *Homo Ludens*, or "Playful Man," "In all the wild imaginings of mythology, a fanciful spirit is playing on the borderline between jest and earnest." That's the epigraph referring primarily to children, and there is, I think, another epigraph for the second part of the novel from the same author, Johan Huizinga: "War and everything to do with it remains fast in the daemonic and magical bonds of play. Only by transcending that pitiable friend-foe relationship will mankind ever enter into the dignity of man's estate." I think that he's trying to say, with those two inscriptions, that children play war games. There's something about the idea of war, of the friend-and-foe relationship in war that's behind children's games and, for that matter, on through life and football and baseball and other games. Games are a sense of warfare; there always has to be a winner and a loser, and that concept becomes entrenched in childhood. So, to tell the best war novel, you also, in the process, have to be telling a children's story—until you reach the dividing line between what is just done in play—the war games, the bivouac, the maneuvers—and what is done in reality—the bombing of Hiroshima, the killing of Ella Jean. I think there's a very close connection between children's stories and war stories.

BW: What are your own memories of World War II? Did you participate in the war effort, the drives, etc.?

DH: First question first. I wanted to mention, by the way, if my biographers want to be on alert, that the character Dawny is two years older than myself. I had decided that *Lightning Bug* would take place in 1939, but in 1939, the real Dawny was only three, going on four, which would not have been enough, by any means. In fact, people think that five, going on six, was not enough for Dawny to be sleeping with Latha. But, anyway, Dawny has always been two years older than me, so in *When Angels Rest*, at the time of the war when he's already twelve, I'm only ten.

But I do remember, during the war, the war drives, stomping on tin cans to flatten them out, make them into scrap steel, saving up and using bacon grease. Gas rationing. Food rationing. All the hardships of the Second World War. I was old enough—I was six when the war broke out and ten, going on eleven, when it was over. So I was old enough to know what was going on. I used to follow the progress of the war in Europe with all of those arrows. On a map of Europe, the arrows would show, here are the Allies, here are the Nazis, and our side kept encroaching on the Nazis. I used to—first thing in the morning—get the paper to see who's winning that war in Europe. That was very important. I also remember the death of FDR. But I don't remember the death of Ernie Pyle; I probably didn't even know who Ernie Pyle was at the time.

BW: What does Dawny learn in writing the story of Mare Coe's death?

DH: As I point out at the end of Chapter Six, "If Ernie Pyle had met Mare Coe, what would he have written about what happened to him? Of course, to tell Mare's story, Ernie would have had to know Mare as well as I did. So what if Ernie and I had collaborated on Mare's story? We would have needed a little help from you"—the Gentle Reader, who had been telling all of my stories. That Gentle Reader, with his intelligence, is now about to tell Mare Coe's story in the Gentle Reader's own voice and intelligence, but from Dawny's point of view as a friend of Mare and with Ernie Pyle's style. It's Pyle's style filtered through Dawny and told by the Gentle Reader. That's what happened in the short, little passage that tells the story of Mare's death on Iwo Jima.

BW: What's the story behind the story of the killing of Old Jarhead?

DH: The Allies, the gang of bad guys that call themselves the Allies, have tried to kidnap Gypsy, and Daniel Lyam Montross has thwarted their attempt to kidnap her. "The onrush of that history thundered into our own little world of make-believe warfare and snatched us up"—what was happening in Europe. "Whatever angels had been watching over our play decided they needed a vacation, a break from the chore of

guardianship, and they went to sleep." The angels rested. "The Allies—
the bad guys—so-called, taking revenge upon Gypsy for their failure
to kidnap her, kidnapped instead her mule, Old Jarhead, and drove
it into the woods, and cornered it, and speared it, and beat it until it
died." So that's the play of the children becoming very serious. The
next chapter begins, "When the rustling, the trapping, the stabbing,
and the brutal cudgeling of Old Jarhead were reported to us by Sammy,
he was in a state of shock himself and had decided to quit the Allies
forever." He joins the Axis side, because Sammy doesn't want anything
to do with them anymore. And the leader of those Allies who beat the
mule to death, I should point out, is Sugrue Alan, who will later join
the state police and become the killer of Daniel Lyam Montross and
still later become the kidnapper of Robin in the novel called *With*.

BW: Last one. Who is responsible for Ella Jean's death?

DH: In this case, the author himself does not know, and if he knew, he
would not tell. So, since the author maintains that the whole book has
been told by the Gentle Reader as part of a pact between the author
and the Gentle Reader, the Gentle Reader is in a better position to
answer that question than the author himself would be. There are
many suspects.

BW: What's the story behind the original title for your next novel?

DH: For the fourth genre novel, my political novel, the working title was
Falling Off the Mountain, based upon Vance Randolph's quotation:
"Some of the backwoods farms in the Ozarks are pretty steep, and
steep also are the stories that the natives tell about them. Many of the
wildest of these tales are true, at that. The old gag about the farmer
falling out of his cornfield sounds like a tall tale, but people who live in
the Ozarks know that such accidents are not uncommon." I intended
with that title to tell the story of Vernon Ingledew, whom we left in the
last chapter of *The Architecture of the Arkansas Ozarks* as supposedly
the last of the Ingledews. He has grown into middle age, made a fortune from his pig farm, selling ham, and he decides to run for governor
of Arkansas. This is the story of his campaign. With all of his money,
he can afford to hire media experts, the best campaign manager (who
was Al Gore's campaign manager in the last election) and all of these
experts to help him get elected. It's essentially a comic novel, but it was
also intended to be my political novel, although I had treated politics
extensively in *When Angels Rest*. In fact, it was meant to be a kind of *All
the King's Men*, which I have great admiration for as a novel. It's a very
ambitious book, but it did not quite achieve its ambition.

BW: Did you try it first at Counterpoint?

DH: Yes, that's what left me without a publisher. When the guy at Counterpoint, whatever his name was—Shoemaker—he read the first few chapters and said he was sorry, but he did not like it at all and just didn't want anything more to do with me. And my agent, who had been my agent for several years, she said, "Well, if he feels that way about it, then I don't want anything to do with you either." So, I was without an agent, without a publisher, and pretty discouraged. Once again, the real truth was that Shoemaker was concerned that *When Angels Rest* had not made any money; therefore, nothing of mine could make money.

So, after he turned it down, I had to shop for a new publisher. My old editor Louie Howland suggested that I try Henry Holt because they had an editor who was an old friend of his; the man was actually the publisher more than the editor. He didn't have time to read the book himself, but he gave it to his young assistant editor, Tom Bissell, who was only twenty-three years old, to see what he thought of it. And he read it and said he liked it, but I would have to make changes, starting with the title; he didn't think that *Falling Off the Mountain* was a good title, which he decided should refer to the thirteen "albatrosses" that Vernon had, the reasons—according to his opponent—that he could not be elected. I was reluctant to change the title in view of my experience with changing the title of *Shades of Green* to *The Choiring of the Trees*, but I agreed to do so, and *Thirteen Albatrosses* turned out to be the conclusive title with Tom Bissell as the editor. He was actually a big help to me, thought a lot of me, did a good job on the book; he did not make very many changes.

So it wasn't his fault that the book flopped. The publicity that Holt put into it was very tiny. In fact, probably of all my novels, it had the least publicity and the least advertising. Therefore, of course, it did not do well in the marketplace, although the paperback rights were picked up by the paperback wing of Henry Holt, known as Picador. Picador brought out a paperback edition with a really goofy cover. We have some extra copies.

BW: Is that the one that shows the cast of characters as comic caricatures?

DH: Yes, unfortunately. The Holt paperback shows all of the main characters of the book. The central character, who is running for governor of Arkansas, is Vernon Ingledew, as I mentioned. We last saw him primarily when he was still a very young man at the end of *Architecture of the Arkansas Ozarks*; he is the last of the male Ingledews because the woman he is in love with, his first cousin, could not have any more children, so he will be the final Ingledew. He got very wealthy raising pigs and processing ham and other hog products and byproducts. He accumulated quite a lot of money and used that money to hire the best possible campaign staff, including the person who had been campaign manager for Al Gore. The assistant campaign manager was an actual person, Arch Schaffer, vice president of Tyson Foods, and he's called by name, his actual name. The media expert, press secretary, and various other members of his staff are also shown, including the so-called "oppo" research director, whose job was to dig up dirt on the opponent and was very skilled at it. They were very good at their jobs.

BW: How about that guy "Donald Harington," the author who shows up in it—how good is he at his job?

DH: [*Chuckling*] Yes, it not only has real people in it, like Arch Schaffer; it also has the author in it, identified by name and telling parts of the story. I wanted him there so the characters themselves could be aware of the novel as it is being written. He makes references to the fact that you haven't read Chapter Five yet, so you don't know what's going to happen. The whole postmodern concept of involvement in the novel is taken to an extreme in *Thirteen Albatrosses*.

BW: Why is there no pseudonym for the author in this book?

DH: It's because I use the actual names of just about everyone, like Arch Schaffer. I made up the name of the campaign director because he was stolen away from Proctor and Gamble where he was head of publicity after leaving the Al Gore campaign; I don't use his actual name. But everybody else, including the publicity director, has their actual names. So, I figured if I did that, I might as well give an actual name to myself. I give an actual name to Vernon Ingledew, to Jelena, his wife, and to the Osage girl. What's her name—Juliana?[85] Everybody has real names in the book.

BW: Speaking of her, who is Juliana Heartstays, and why did you bring her into the Stay More pantheon at this point?

DH: She is Vernon's cousin, a member of the Osage tribe, and a direct descendant of Fanshaw's wife, who had been impregnated by Jacob Ingledew, the first of the Ingledews.[86] She's a direct descendant of that woman and therefore a cousin of Vernon, and she's very wealthy in her own right from oil rights in Oklahoma. She joins the campaign, and Vernon falls in love with her. Although, he's got a deep attachment to his own first cousin. So, things are getting more and more complicated and scandalous.

BW: Your interest in the Osage Nation's roots in this region long predates this book, doesn't it?

DH: Well, I have not deeply explored it myself, but I've read the book called *Wah'Kon-tah*, which is a study of Osage beliefs in God, Osage folklore, Osage life.[87] So, to the extent that I've read that book, I'm fully familiar with the Osages. They were the tallest of all American Indian tribes. A lot of people think they must not have been directly related to the Cherokees and the Choctaw, and they were the early settlers of the Ozarks. So, I've had a deep interest in the Osage above all others. And, of course, that interest figures into the novel, not only in the character of Juliana, but her bodyguard, who is also her relative and is a huge, tall, strapping Osage Indian brave who happens to be homosexual and who accounts for a lot of humor in the book. I can't even remember what his name was.

BW: Does it have "Bear" in it?

DH: Bending Bear. Of course, during their intercourse, he has to bend over. But that's just one of those Indian names I gave him. But those Indian characters in the book are based upon my knowledge of the Indians. While researching the book, I drove over to the center of Osage Culture in Oklahoma—what's the name of that town, Tahlequah?

BW: Sounds right.

DH: I went to the Center of Osage Culture and researched as much of it as I possibly could and tried to familiarize myself with the country that Juliana had come from.

BW: Would you call *Thirteen Albatrosses* a love story?

DH: Well, to the extent that all of my books are "love stories," sure, but it's really about Vernon's adventures in politics. Nobody gives Vernon a chance in the election. Everybody's trying to talk him out of it, but he persists. And he manages somehow to get himself elected, by a lot of intrigues that the book is concerned with. As the book jacket puts it, "Despite all of these albatrosses, the fact that he's opposed to guns, he's in favor of very strict gun control, and he's against tobacco in any form. He's against schools, prisons, hospitals. He wants to wipe out all of these things. But his candidacy quickly attracts the heavy political hitters, who are challenged not only by Vernon's extensive and dazzling liabilities but also by various kidnappings, adulterous liaisons within their own camp, and the unrelenting evildoing of their detested adversary, Governor Shoat Bradfield. *Thirteen Albatrosses* knowingly chronicles the dizzying display of nonsense and idealism that is contemporary politics." *Kirkus* said it was wild, weird, and wonderful, but once again, it did not attract very many reviews.

BW: How improbable is Vernon's election?

DH: As his opponents are quick to point out, and as I just read, Vernon has a lot of things against him. In addition to being an Ozark hillbilly, he's living out of wedlock with a woman who is his first cousin. He doesn't believe in God; like all Ingledews, he's an atheist. And he has several other, in fact, he has thirteen albatrosses around his neck to prevent him from becoming governor. The book is essentially a story of he and his crew attempting to overcome these albatrosses.

BW: How did the research for *TA-FOM* compare to the research you did for your other novels?

DH: As you might guess, I did quite a bit of research into politics. One of Vernon's biggest drawbacks is that he is enormously intelligent. He spent his life getting the equivalent of a PhD in about twenty different fields of human knowledge. He knows everything, and nobody likes a know-it-all. So that's another strike against him. But his opponent happens to be a real . . . piece of shit — that's the best way to put it. He's a creepy caricature of some of the worst politicians that Arkansas or the United States has ever had. And step by step, Vernon tries to defeat his opposition with the help of his group.

BW: What is your definition of "politics" in the political novel?

DH: Well, as a character in the book points out, the word *politics* comes from the Greek, meaning "many biting insects," and politics consists of many biting insects. But, of course, that's not the original, intended meaning of *politics.* The only reason Vernon is doing that is that he's been going systematically through the alphabet, thoroughly immersing himself into a field of study that begins with each letter of the alphabet. And now he gets to the Ps, and the only thing he can think of under P is politics. So he reads everything on the subject he can find. That's the only reason he's running, to immerse himself into politics. But the political novel — American literature is filled with them, not only things like *All the King's Men*, the authentic example, but I think I end the book itself with a list of a dozen political novels that Vernon reads, books about people running for senator, for president, for governor. What was the one about colors?

BW: *Primary Colors?*

DH: That's it — *Primary Colors*, about Clinton's presidency. There are many political novels.

BW: What would "oppo man" Harry Wolfe dredge up on you?

DH: The oppo man, as he's called, the so-called opposition research director. His job was to dig up the dirt on all of the opponents. If I were running for office—which I would be very foolish to do—the oppo man would discover all kinds of liabilities to keep me from running for office, starting with the fact that I'm deaf, and nobody deaf would even consider political office. He'd discover that I've been married twice, and my present wife's been married three times. The oppo man would find all kinds of shady dealings in my past. I dread to think what all the oppo man would find on me. That's why I'm not running for any office; I could not afford an oppo man to start investigating me.

BW: Where would Vernon choose to spend eternity?

DH: Since he doesn't believe in God, he can't believe in heaven. But he has studied enough about religions and beliefs and science and life that he realizes very strongly that there is a kind of survival after death. I've gone into this before, about my own personal belief that everyone after death retains a certain degree of awareness even though they no longer breathe or eat or drink or have any physical manifestation. They still have awareness. And I'm sure Vernon will be able to entertain himself throughout eternity by observing what continues to happen among the politicians on Earth as well as the scientists and everyone else.

Of course, if you wanted to be sarcastic, you could just say that he'll spend eternity on the remainder table. *Thirteen Albatrosses* had a very poor reception commercially and critically, so I had about bottomed out as far as my reputation was concerned.

BW: What kind of governor would Vernon have been?

DH: Well, presumably, if all of this is true, Vernon is still the governor of Arkansas. And in *Enduring*, his sister Sharon, who narrates the book, refers to her brother as the governor. When their father dies, he comes from Little Rock, from the governor's mansion, in a state trooper's car to attend his father's funeral in Stay More. But his administration was unprecedented in the history of American governors. In fact, he was so successful at making life healthier and better for everyone—reforming the school system, eliminating the prison system, eliminating the hospital system, for God's sake—that people wanted him to run for president. But he refused on two grounds. One, he had had enough of politics, being governor; he didn't want any more of it. And two, Arkansas had already sent one of its governors to the White House. That was enough.

BW: How does Vernon in *Thirteen Albatrosses* evoke the figure of Don Quixote?

DH: Don Quixote had to fight against the windmills, and Vernon has to fight against his albatrosses. But Don Quixote was a ludicrous figure, and Vernon, in a sense, is the only *non*-ludicrous figure in *Thirteen Albatrosses*. Everybody else is a little bit goofy, except for Vernon, so he has no windmills that he's fighting against. I don't remember exactly how he evokes Don Quixote in the book.

BW: It's in there, but it would take me awhile to find it. His factotum, who is his best friend . . .

DH: His best friend's Day Whittacker.

BW: No, the short one, kind of fat. The book says he's like Sancho Panza, Don Quixote's sidekick, and his name is . . .

DH: Do you mean George Dinsmore? He's not Vernon's best friend, and he's not a little guy like Sancho. He doesn't have any of the physical attributes, but I guess he could serve as the equivalent to Vernon's Don Quixote. You could probably draw all kinds of parallels between the two, but I wasn't thinking of *Don Quixote* when I wrote the book.[88]

BW: Do you feel up to telling the remarkably complex story behind your next novel, *With*?

DH: [*Chuckling*] The cameraman will have to disqualify himself from operating the camera for our discussion of this book, because this book is dedicated to the cameraman. It's a long story.[89] Like most of my books, I started writing it before the previous book was published. I was already hard at work on *With* before *Thirteen Albatrosses* came out. *With* was a story that had been germinating in my mind for quite some time, since a young Arkansas girl was kidnapped from a ballfield in Alma, Arkansas. It was a sensational news story at the time because nobody could find any trace of who her kidnapper was or whatever happened to her. We still don't know fifteen years later.

But when the story came out, I began to imagine that her kidnapper might have been someone like Sugrue Alan, who appears in my previous books, working for the Arkansas State police. And he decides, being a pedophile, that he wants a girl of his own. And he goes to elaborate means to get everything ready for kidnapping the girl, the little girl of his dreams. He equips a remote house on a mountaintop with all the provisions that he would possibly need to live for years in the arms of this little girl. And once he has the house thoroughly equipped, all he needs is the little girl.

So, he happens to spy the girl on a street in Harrison, Arkansas, a real place, where she's living with her mother, separated from her father. And he arranges to kidnap her from a roller-skating rink while she goes skating. Kidnaps her, spirits her off to the place that he has prepared for her to live in along with a dog, a female dog that the kidnapper calls "Bitch." That's the name he gives her. But like all other dogs, she names herself after the sound that she makes when she barks. And that sound is "hreapha," so she is simply called Hreapha throughout the book. And the population of that house on the mountaintop consists of the kidnapper, the little girl, and Hreapha.

Hreapha devotes herself to the kidnapper as any dog does to its master, but she's also devoted to the little girl and senses that the kidnapper may be up to evil as far as the little girl is concerned. At one point, Hreapha attacks the kidnapper to keep him from molesting her. The kidnapper keeps trying, but he comes down with a mysterious malady, and eventually—despite everything—he turns out to be not such a bad guy after all.

Meantime, Robin remains stuck up there on the mountain top. Even though she's only seven years old at the start, she has to learn how to cook. All she has for reading is the Holy Bible and an old copy of a farm wife's one-volume encyclopedia, which includes instructions of how to cook, take care of the place, and do all kinds of chores connected with farm life. She manages to shoot a razorback hog, but she doesn't know how to butcher it, so she is aided in that endeavor by the discovery that there are voices, or there is a voice, of a young boy, her own age, who is somewhere around the premises, although she can never see him. She can only hear him and converse with him. He gives her lots of advice on how to live in this situation, how to butcher the hog and salt it away, how to do all kinds of things.

As explained to the reader, that voice she hears is of the in-habit of Adam Madewell, who had been the son of the last occupants of that house. An in-habit is something that you leave behind in a place that you loved very much and cannot bear to part with. Your in-habit will remain there forever even after you're gone. And so, after Adam Madewell's family had taken him to California, like everyone else going to California, his in-habit remains behind as a companion for Robin.

And eventually, there is a kind of romantic entanglement between Robin and her in-habit; even though she can't see him, she can certainly imagine him. And she can certainly pretend that she feels him.

There's eventually a shift in the book's narration to California where we find Adam Madewell growing up, getting his education, going to work in a winery, Inglenook Winery in California, where eventually he becomes a wine master and is befriended by an actual wine maker. His name is an actual name, but I can't remember it.[90] It's been so long since I actually read it. But Adam is aware that he left his in-habit back in Stay More, and he's determined to go back there.

In the meantime, month by month, year by year, Robin has been getting, on her birthday, a new creature, a new cow, raccoons, a snake, many other animals—frankly, everything except an elephant. And now, for her eighteenth birthday, she tells her menagerie that the gift she wants is a real live man. And the animals of the menagerie conspire to attract Adam to the mountaintop. They don't know that he is the in-habit, but he comes back to the mountaintop, and at that moment, he crosses a certain line separating the real world from the world of the in-habit.

BW: What was the risk of using animals as narrators? Which one ended up as your favorite? Which one was the most difficult?

DH: Well, as I took pains to point out to some of the publishers who rejected it for that very reason, there are no animal narrators in the book! There's nobody in the book who narrates, except the omniscient author. Several animals receive some of the action from the animal's point of view, but that's not at all animal narration. Of course, Hreapha, whom I start out with, is my favorite; we end up with Hreapha as one of the final points of view for the book.

Possibly my second favorite is the bobcat Robert, who is a really glib and a really horny bobcat. And he narrates with much gusto in the story. He doesn't narrate—we see from his point of view with much gusto the way the animals conspire to lure the grown man Adam Madewell up to the mountaintop. I had a lot of fun with all of those animals, but none of the animals ever used the first person as the narrative.

BW: How does your Robin connect to Defoe's Crusoe?

DH: The connection between Robin and Robinson Crusoe is deliberate. There are several parallels between *Robinson Crusoe* and *With*. The idea of living in the wilderness, for example. There are also many parallels between this and W. H. Hudson's *Green Mansions*, the story of Rima the Bird Girl living in the wilderness and meeting up with an

actual man. That book ends tragically; my book has the happiest ending, in a sense, of all my books.

BW: How does Robin's education in Stay More compare to the one that
Daniel Lyam Montross had planned to give Diana Stoving?

DH: Well, there is a big difference, of course. Montross was not limited
to only the Bible like Robin was, the Bible and that farmer's almanac.
But she got a lot of education from the woods and from the animals.
I'm glad you mentioned that because I should mention that, in the
part of *Enduring* in which Daniel Lyam Montross tries to educate his
daughter. So, there are a lot of connections and similarities between the
two educations but a big difference in that Robin's reading was limited
entirely to those two books.

BW: What kinds of stories does Robin tell with her cut-out dolls?

DH: As one of her primary forms self-entertainment, she makes paper
dolls and paper houses and recreates the entire village of Stay More
and all of its inhabitants, which she has never seen, and invents the stories of who they are and what happened to them. We don't know what
stories she told. We don't hear them. We just know that she is playing
with her paper dolls, her paper cut-outs, and telling stories about them
to her animals, to herself, and to her fellow paper dolls. She is telling
the story, supposedly, the entire story of Stay More, although she has
never been to Stay More.

BW: Where is Sog Alan's place in the pantheon of Stay More characters?

DH: Well, it begins when he is a young member of the bullying gang of
Allies in *When Angels Rest*. He's just a kid when that happens, and he
kills Old Jarhead the mule by beating it to death. He later, when he's
somewhat older and a member of the state police hunting for Daniel
Lyam Montross, who has kidnapped his own daughter, shoots and kills
Daniel Lyam Montross, and that's mentioned in *Some Other Place. The
Right Place*. And then he appears in *With* as a kidnapper of Robin. So,
he figures very large in the pantheon of Stay More characters.

BW: Will Robin's visit to Latha show up in *Enduring*?

DH: Oh, yes, of course. *Enduring* is the story of Latha's entire life from
the very beginning and everything that happens to her, everyone she
meets, including Robin.

BW: How would you cast the main characters in a Hollywood film of
With? Whom would you cast as Robin, as Sog, and as Adam?

DH: Kim has already suggested that, for Robin, we have Dakota Fanning
in the main part and Dakota's younger sister Elle playing Robin at the

very beginning. Then Dakota Fanning could play her at the age of thirteen or fourteen, whatever.

KH: How about John C. Reilly?

DH: Who? John C. Reilly as the grownup Robin? Oh, you're talking about Sog! No, I was thinking of Robin, the grownup Robin. John C. Reilly would be great for Sog Alan. Young Adam would be just a voice. For the mature Adam, Hugh Grant.

KH: What?

DH: Hugh Grant, as the grownup Adam.

KH: No. That's very badly cast.

DH: [Laughs]

KH: No way.

DH: Who would you cast as the grownup Adam? Knowing Hollywood, they'd probably cast Sean Penn.

KH: No, that would be horrible.

⚡⚡⚡

BW: You're dressed rather differently today — why?

DH: This is the summer solstice, June 22, 2007, and so I'm wearing a short-sleeve shirt as I wore long-sleeve shirts in all the other interviews. I'm also refreshed at the beginning of the day. I did a bad job on *With* last night, for several reasons. One, it was late in the evening after a long day, and I was very tired, and my memory was not functioning. And it's a very complex book, which is very difficult to talk about, let alone to synopsize. So I've thought of several things to add about *With*. I should've written them down, because they've slipped my mind.

First, I don't think I did a very good job of depicting the in-habit. In-habits are very hard to depict because they're invisible, but I don't think I convinced the viewer, the way the book convinces the reader, that in-habits are legitimate, that they're not just flights of fancy, that they actually exist and that the in-habit was not just a product of Robin's imagination.

Second, I was not able to describe the various episodes involving all of Robin's animals. Each one of them has a significant name; each one of them becomes involved in some kind of episode. I think, instead of making a movie out of *With*, they ought to make an HBO series to cover the whole thing, all of the animals involved, the whole length of the book.

BW: How many in-habits do you have? Where are they?

DH: I have only one in-habit, and as the biographical information at the end of *With* points out, my in-habit resides permanently in Stay More, Arkansas. Everyone is permitted only one in-habit. Even if you lived ten years in Paris and ten years in London and loved both of them equally, I'm sorry, but you could not leave your in-habit in both towns; you would have to decide between them. You can have only one in-habit just like you can have only one soul. My in-habit is permanently in Stay More, which, of course, exists only in the mind of the reader, so my in-habit resides permanently and perpetually in the mind of the reader.

BW: This happiest of all endings didn't make it any easier to get *With* published, right?

DH: That's an understatement. Because of the possibility of sex and the mention of Sugrue's being a pedophile and Robin being a desirable young girl and so forth, my editor . . .

So it's time now for the other *With* story. Someone should have told me that if I had submitted *Moby-Dick* to Holt as my next novel, it would have been rejected, or *Gone with the Wind*—it would have been rejected based upon my sales record. Nobody told me that, so I had hopes that my next novel would find a good home—I hoped it would be Henry Holt & Company. But Tom Bissell, who had published *Thirteen Albatrosses*, defected from Holt, to . . . Well, he had a girlfriend, and he was just twenty-three years old, and so he left Holt and turned me over to another editor named George Hodgeman.

I had thought maybe if I shortened my titles, that might help, so I shortened the title to simply the preposition "with." It's a big novel. It's a very exciting novel—a very good novel. But George thought it was prurient because of the very idea of a pedophile kidnapping a young girl—it was just too much for George. And I suggested that he might show it to some of the other editors at Holt, like Jennifer Barth, who was a very distinguished editor. And I think about three editors at Holt read the book, and they all decided that it was prurient, unpublishable. Of course, their main motive was that *Thirteen Albatrosses* had simply not earned any money for them. So, they rejected it.

I was on my own. My agent that I had had for the last five or six novels kicked me out too, because she thought, "If Holt doesn't want it, I don't think I could find a publisher for it." And it's supposedly a dirty book. I didn't know what to do. So, I sent it to an editor at

Random House, who was a friend of my friend Peter Straub. I'd been good friends with Peter Straub ever since he had written a great review of *Ekaterina* for the *Washington Post*, and Peter hooked me up with his editor at Random House. She kept it a long time, but she rejected it too. So, I just began systematically sending it out to various publishers, telling them who I was, the fact that I had recently won the Robert Penn Warren Award for Fiction from the Fellowship of Southern Writers, a very distinguished award. I sent cover letters out to a dozen publishers, telling them about my various awards and giving them an idea of what *With* was about.

Meanwhile, I was so disappointed in Holt's rejection of the book that I sent a copy of the manuscript to my friend Brian Walter in Saint Louis, and Brian Walter read it and negated everything bad that George had said about it. He showed it to his wife, and she read it and agreed with him that it was not only not prurient, but it was highly publishable.

So with the encouragement of the Walters, I sent it out all over the place. By this time, I had got to the point that I could send not the physical book in manuscript, but an electronic copy of it by e-mail. Publishers were accepting that. And to each place I sent out, I sent out the cover letter pointing out my Robert Penn Warren Award, my list of novels. I waited and waited, and one by one, each of the publishers turned me down. I got up to about forty-five or fifty rejections. I was running out of places to send it. I discovered on the internet a website called *Everybody Who is Anybody in the World of Publishing*, which had a list of all of the agents, all of the publishers, and all of the editors, and each one of the publishing houses. So I could send it directly to all of the ones that I had not already sent it to. So, of course, the number of rejections was able to incrementally go up and up and up. After about the seventy-sixth rejection—and by then, I had broken the record of Malcolm Cowley for rejections of *Under the Volcano* (I've broken several other notorious records for rejections)—after the seventy-sixth publisher, I was just about out of publishers to send it to.

But there was one more on the list, an obscure publisher—in Jerusalem, not in America—known as the Toby Press. I sent it to Toby Press and, meanwhile, I looked around and discovered that they were the publishers of Morris West, who is one of my favorite mid-list novelists. And they had a rather distinguished list of American and European authors. Well, Toby Press kept it for two months, and finally, I had an email from Matthew Miller,[91] saying that they were going to publish it. He was handing it over to his associate editor to get her opinion of it, but he thought they would probably publish it, and he was preparing a contract to send me. He thought the book sagged in the middle, and perhaps I could do something—maybe cut a lot of it—to keep it from sagging in the middle. But his editor, Deborah Meghnagi—who has been my editor ever since and is one of the nicest people on Earth—she said, in effect, that he was full of shit, that the book did not sag in the middle, that that was just his opinion, that she felt it was strong all the way through.

Toby Press not only loved the book and agreed to publish it but also hired Wendell Minor to paint a great cover for it. The book did get good reviews. It sold well. Toby Press brought out a second edition, the first time that any book of mine had ever gone into a second printing. Toby also began, systematically, one-by-one, bringing out each of my previous novels until now, all of my novels are in print as Toby Press books, and I could not be happier with the situation.

BW: Sorry for this question, but could you please explain the book's dedication?

DH: Of course. The dedication reads "To Brian Walter and Lynnea Brumbaugh-Walter,[92] who believed." They not only believed in the book; they believed in all of the magic realism of the book. They believed that the book was worth publishing. I was almost ready to gut the story to try to get it published when they gave me the first encouraging reading.

BW: What would have happened if you hadn't found Toby?

DH: I hate to think about this; I really dread the thought. You know that I've spoken frequently of the Fate Thing, and I have utmost confidence that the Fate Thing found Toby for me. I dread the thought that the Fate Thing would not have found Toby for me. So, I can't tell you what I would have done if I hadn't found Toby, because I know I was *destined*—I was destined to find Toby.

BW: How did you get going on your next book, *The Pitcher Shower?*[93]

DH: After all the work that I put into *With*, especially the work of getting it into print, I needed a breather. So I thought of my next novel, *The Pitcher Shower*, as a breather; it's a relatively thin book compared with *With*. It's a serious book, it's very funny, but it's not a major contribution to the Stay More canon. In fact, it doesn't take place in Stay More at all, except in passing. It's about a native of Stay More who earns his living traveling around the Ozarks showing motion pictures, or "pitch-ers," as it's pronounced in the Ozarks. It was based upon a memory I'd had as a child in Drakes Creek of going to see a traveling picture show. This man had brought western movies to Drakes Creek, or to a suburb of Drakes Creek, where they were shown in a field at night, and I had a pleasant memory of having been able to go to the movies right there in Drakes Creek. So I decided to write this story of a man who not only shows western movies but specializes in movies about Hopalong Cassidy. Since his last name happens to be Boyd—and Hopalong's actual name was William Boyd—he goes to the point of calling him-self Hopalong and he wears a ten-gallon hat, like Hopalong, and travels around the Ozarks from town to town, showing movies. That's why he is a "pitcher shower."

Of course, because of that unusual title, there was quite a lot of difficulty identifying and talking about it. I was even introduced for several readings and interviews as the author of "The Pitcher *Shower*," which has the association of the pitcher filled with some liquid that's being showered over you. I had to explain that, actually, the title means the place where losing pitchers in baseball games go when they've been called out of the game—they go to the showers. So this is the pitcher shower, a shower for losing pitchers.

But it is actually about a show-er, that is pronounced the same way that the Ozarkers pronounced "shore."[94] He has a circuit that he fol-lows of twelve different towns scattered around in the Ozarks. The book opens in one of these towns, where he is extremely popular, enor-mously popular with everyone, because he brings the movies to town. This is in 1937, and most people had not even seen a motion picture before. He puts a bedsheet between two trees, and, in a truck that he had rigged together of his own devising, he has his projection booth in the back end of the truck, and he shows movies and charges people a nickel to get in. That was a lot of money in the Depression, but he was enormously popular. The girls throw themselves at him, but while he is not necessarily shy, he's ethical because he doesn't want any girl to attach herself to him permanently and have to be taken out on the road for the life of the pitcher shower, which can get pretty dull at times. And despite the efforts of many of these girls, and young men, too, to join up with his show, he rejected all until he meets one, a resource-ful, hardworking, handsome young boy named Carl, and he decides to break his scruples and take Carl with him on the tour.

No, I'm sorry, he does not take Carl with him. Carl stows away in the truck, and Hoppy doesn't discover it until he's driving to Clarksville (I put that in, in honor of my cameraman)[95] and by then, it's too late to call the sheriff and have the kid sent back home. So he accepts the kid.

It turns out, in a funny way, that Carl is actually a girl by the name of Sharline in disguise. She's a very pretty girl, but she could pass for a male. So, naturally, a romance blows up between Hoppy and Sharline. Their only obstacle is a secret riding preacher, an evangelist, who believes that pitcher shows are sinful, and he travels around in Hoppy's wake, preaching against pitcher shows. At one point Hoppy discovers that someone has stolen all of his pitcher shows, so he's out of business. But there's one possibility: there are other pitcher showers in the Ozarks, and if Hoppy could hook up with one of them, he might be able to beg, borrow, or steal some other films that could replace those that the preacher had stolen. But they don't have any movies to sell—except one, which consists of twelve reels of a 1935 black-and-white film called *A Midsummer Night's Dream*, by this dude Bill—what's Bill's last name? Shakespeare. Bill Shakespeare wrote this book called *Midsummer Night's Dream*, and a great movie was made of it in 1935 with James Cagney as Puck and Olivia de Havilland and an all-star cast.[96] Still, Hoppy doesn't think it sounds like Hopalong Cassidy, let alone Gene Autry, Roy Rogers, or any of those others. He wonders if it even has a horse in it. I had a lot of fun writing that part, especially the efforts of Hoppy and his girlfriend Sharline and this couple in one of the towns where they're staying to put together the four characters of *A Midsummer Night's Dream*—the four principal young men and women—and have them act out the movie. He has a big problem finding an audience for this movie, which, in a very subtle way, is an autobiographical commentary on my difficulty in finding an audience for my books.

Anyway, the days of that itinerant pitcher shower are failing. Sharline and Hoppy, in the future tense, take over the Buffalo Theater in Jasper, Arkansas, for a number of years, and then they take over, on the outskirts of Jasper, a video store, which they are still running, in the future tense, as life goes on. So, you could say that he finally does find an audience, just as I had found an audience for *With*, the first of my books to go into a second edition. *The Pitcher Shower* hasn't gone into a second edition, or it hasn't yet, but it was given respectable notices.

BW: How was *The Pitcher Shower* received?

DH: It got a good reception, nice reviews. Toby was happy with it. I dedicated it to Matthew Miller, the publisher of Toby. I put an inscrip-
tion under his name, in Hebrew letters; the translation of the Hebrew
is, literally, "For Matthew Miller—who brought me to light." The
Hebrew word for "bring to light" is very similar to Hebrew for "to pub-
licize or to make known." And what I'm really saying in Hebrew is that
Matthew Miller has made me known after all these years of obscurity.
Without Matthew Miller, I would be nobody, so next to Kim, Matthew
is the most important person in my life.

BW: How does *The Pitcher Shower* connect film art to literary art?

DH: That's one of those complicated literary critic questions; I would
have to ponder it for a long time. Probably while I was writing it, I
was very unconsciously aware of the fact that there are many similarities between showing a movie and creating a novel. You could say
things like the pacing of the novel is similar to the pacing of the movie.
There are actual places where the passage of time in the novel mirrors the passage of time in a movie. The movies, of course, were for
country people, who were (many of them) illiterate, not able to read.
The motion picture became an art form for the masses, and the masses
who, even if they could read, they never read literature. Even today,
in our more sophisticated world, I think there's a big gap between the
audience for literature and the audience for film. There's so many films
based upon works of literature, and in fact, I'm waiting on somebody
to pick up the film rights for *Pitcher Shower*, but that would really be a
self-referential, postmodernist film if a filmmaker would make a movie
out of *The Pitcher Shower*.

BW: How does Hoppy's taste in movies compare to yours?

DH: Hoppy was exclusively a fan of Westerns; he didn't care at all for
other genres. He had accidentally been sent *It Happened One Night*,
that fabulous old movie with Cary Grant and Claudette Colbert.[97] He
accidentally saw that one time, and it didn't bother him too much,
but he knew it would not appeal to his customers. He likes to show
Westerns because they appeal to himself as well as to his customers. I
can't remember the last Western I watched. When I was a kid, I'd watch
Westerns in Drakes Creek because there was nothing else to watch.
But my taste in movies has been more toward the fantastic, things like
Pan's Labyrinth, that are completely far removed from realism. I cannot stand slice-of-life, realistic movies which show life, and war, and
dialogue as they are actually are. I find that extremely boring.

BW: Why *A Midsummer Night's Dream* for subtext? Does it lend itself better to Stay More than other Shakespearean comedies?

DH: Well, first keep in mind that this is not Stay More; it's a book outside of the Stay More series, because it takes place in little country towns elsewhere in the Ozarks, although they pass through Stay More. The first reason I chose *A Midsummer Night's Dream* is that Sharline, or Carl before her sex becomes known, believes in fairies, not homosexuals, but the kind of fairies that flutter around in the air and communicate with him or her. I had already started to work on the novel, and I happened to catch on cable TV the 1935 black-and-white production of the movie *A Midsummer Night's Dream*, which had Olivia DeHavilland, Mickey Rooney, James Cagney, and a lot of other famous actors in it. I loved that movie, in black and white, especially the scene in which the fairies come dancing through the landscape. When I saw that fabulous scene, I knew that that is exactly what Carl, or Sharline, was visualizing.

Then, after I'd watched the whole movie, I realized that it had four young people who become entangled with each other. And that could be paralleled to the entanglement of Hoppy and Sharline with the couple that they meet in Deer, Arkansas (although, I don't identify the town by name in the book). But there is considerable parallel between what happens in *A Midsummer Night's Dream* and what happens in the later part of *The Pitcher Shower*.

BW: Where does Emmett Binns fit into the pantheon of Stay More preachers, like Long Jack Stapleton, Every Dill, and Brother Chid?

DH: Well, those preachers were, I was about to say, mostly itinerant, but Every Dill was not an itinerant preacher. I guess the only real answer is that all those guys were good guys, and Emmett Binns is a bad guy. Also, Long Jack Stapleton was the grandfather of our hero, Hoppy Boyd. Long Jack Stapleton had first brought film to Stay More in the form of a preaching style that was so dramatic and eloquent that his audience could see what was happening as if it was on a screen. One of the funniest passages in *Architecture of the Arkansas Ozarks* is when Long Jack Stapleton is preaching about Adam and Eve in paradise about to procreate, and it's so unseemly that the deacons of the church take charcoal and make Xs on the door of the church to indicate that the movies that Long Jack Stapleton shows are forbidden. So Long Jack Stapleton, had he lived, would be completely in favor of movies.

Emmett Binns preaches against movies; he thinks that movies are sinful. We remember that the first movie Latha ever saw was when

Every had rescued her from the state hospital and they were living in a hotel in Nashville. One night, Every took her out to the movies, so the first film that Latha had ever seen was in Every's company. Chidiock Tichborne of *COSM* is somewhat sleazy, if not villainous, like Emmett Binns. As I've mentioned before, I was a Church of Christ preacher myself, when I was a teenager, so I know all of the inside angles of being a preacher. I probably put all four of these preachers into my books for that particular reason.

BW: What does the last line of the book mean?

DH: I'll just read that last line. Hoppy and Sharline are setting up their video store on the outskirts of Jasper. "Sometimes when business will be slow, Sharline will stand out front of the shop and blow an old bugle . . . " That's what Hoppy used to do on the way into each one of the towns he was visiting; he would blow a bugle to announce that the pitcher show has arrived. Sharline learned how to do it, and she still did it when they were running a video store to attract attention. "If you will just slow down as you zip down the highway, you will be able to tell what that bugle is saying: something about pitcher shows and about a man and a woman." Well, you would recognize that if you knew that, the first time Hoppy blows his bugle, a transcription is provided of what that bugle is probably saying: "Folks, here come Hoppy Boyd, the traveling showman, to show you another good 'un." And later on, when Sharline learns to blow it, the words are translated in her own voice to say something about pitcher shows, as the book is saying something about pitcher showers.[98] And they were saying something about a man and a woman, Hoppy and Sharline, as the book did, as her bugle did. The Chinese box within the Chinese box.

BW: Is Hoppy capable of being happy?

DH: Well, he thinks so; he is somewhat morose because of his very solitary life. He is probably kind of lonely. He's very horny for that reason, which is the reason that he has acquired — at one time from his film distributor in Memphis, from under the counter — acquired one reel of film that he called "Assortment" and which consisted entirely of a variety of blue movies. Not just men with women, but women with dogs, and all kinds of perversions and bestiality. When Hoppy has nothing better to do, he shows that to himself in the privacy of his projection booth. In fact, one time when he's had too much to drink, he shows it to Carl, not aware yet that Carl is a female. He would've been terribly embarrassed to have known that Carl was Sharline. But he is happy, yes; Sharline makes him happy. And it's a story of how a sad, lonely, forlorn pitcher shower achieves happiness. That's the main storyline of the book.

BW: The next book is quite different?

DH: Yes, you could say that, though I should thank the people at Toby for their encouragement again: having all of my books reprinted in paperback, getting new awards; all of that really helped inspire me to start another novel. Anyway, I began writing it in the summer of '05 and intended to finish it this summer, but I had an automobile accident that kept me from it. Except, because of the accident, I had to take medical leave from the university, and as a result, I have been able to write almost half of the novel at this point. I'm confident I can probably finish it by next summer.[99]

It's called *Enduring*. Once again, I started with the acronym: *END*, E-N-D. You could think of it as the end of all of my novels or the end of the world, or simply the end of whatever. But I decided, after experimenting with several names, to fit that acronym, I would simply expand it into a longer word, and I came up with the idea of enduring, the working title for the new novel. I'm completely confident that my publisher at Toby will make no effort to change the title and will probably bring it into publication very soon after I finish it next summer. It is the life story of Latha Bourne, who appears in so many of my novels, starting with *Lightning Bug*. She *is* the lightning bug of that novel, and she appears throughout that novel. Mention is made of the fact that she has spent three years of her life at the Arkansas State Hospital for the Insane, but nothing is really elaborated upon about that. So, ever since I wrote *Lighting Bug*, I have been thinking that, eventually, I'm going to have to start at the beginning and tell Latha's whole life story. She never dies, like Garcia Marquez's Pilar Ternera, who lives to be one hundred eighteen in *One Hundred Years of Solitude*.[100] Latha, right now, at this moment, is one hundred six years old; she's still going strong, and I don't plan for her ever to die. So, this book is simply going to tell her life up to the point that I stop writing the book, and I'm going to try to cover the three years that she spent in the asylum, the years she was a very good friend with Ekaterina when they exchanged notes about their experiences in the asylum, and the years that her grandson became governor of the state of Arkansas. All of the missing parts of Latha's life will find their way into *Enduring*.

BW: Will you digress for a moment and tell us what happened in your car accident this past year? Why did it have to happen?

DH: We were having some houseguests that weekend, and the woman especially wanted *petits fours* to go with the champagne that we were going to
open to celebrate the man's good luck in having been accepted by Toby
Press as a novelist. That was Jack Butler, by the way. I was going up to
a local supermarket, Harps, to see if they carried *petits fours*. Frankly,
I don't even know what a *petit four* looks like.[101] But I was going up to
Harp's to see if they might have it, and French-roast coffee. That was
my mission.

To get into Harp's parking lot from the highway, it's a five-lane highway. The center lane is the turning lane. I was in the turning lane,
and traffic down to the red light at the corner was backed up. It was
the beginning of rush hour; all the traffic was backed up. But a glass-
company truck coming the opposite direction decided to stop at the
place where you turn to let me make the left turn there. Very thoughtful of him. It was not his fault that his big truck obscured all the traffic
that was coming in the inside lane. So, as soon as I made the left turn,
someone in the inside lane was slowing down for the traffic in the right
corner. They hit me broad side, and knocked my car into a cement
drainage ditch on its side. And I was more or less trapped in the car. I
remember every detail of it, my car seeming to open up and slide down
that drainage ditch. The drainage ditch was right beside Taco Bell, and
everybody in Taco Bell came running out to see what the noise and
commotion was about. Before long, a huge crowd had gathered. The
first rescuers that were on the scene were from a lube, an automobile
lube place down the street. I had not taken my hearing aid with me,
and I could not converse with any of the people who were inquiring or
even hear their instruction. The first thing I could think of was to have
someone call Kim and tell her about the accident and tell her that I was
alright. I was convinced that I was completely alright, nothing broken,
except I could not get out of that position.

They called the EMS, emergency medical service, and then they
called the fire department, and before long, there were all these men
trying to extricate me from the car. They finally had to tie me to a
rescue board and get me in a standing position. Tie me to that board,
brace my neck in case it was broken, and have a crane lift the board.
They had to break the windshield of the car to create an opening and
lift me out and put me in an ambulance. And my fellow passenger in
the ambulance was the woman who was driving the other car. She
wasn't hurt; I think she had a chipped tooth.

KH: She was hurt, Don.

DH: I don't know what the condition her car was in, but our insurance paid for her car. She got a new car, or her car repaired. Our insurance did not cover my car. So, to this day, I'm still without an automobile.

Anyway, they took me to the hospital, and that began the nine-week period of recuperation that's still going on. As I already said in the last interview, in response to the question, "Why did it have to happen?", it was the Fate Thing's way of getting me some attention for more serious ailments: the fluid retention and the pneumonia.

BW: What could you not have learned or otherwise gained without it?

DH: I would not have known that I had a very serious medical condition that was life-threatening and required immediate attention. During all of this period of recovery, I have spent some time thinking about *Enduring* a lot. And it is my hope that, eventually, the whole experience will have some effect on *Enduring* that would be equivalent to what the cancer had on *Butterfly Weed*. But at this particular point in the book, there are no illnesses or accidents or anything. The accident may have made me appreciate life more, and that love of life may find its way into the book in one way or another. It remains to be seen when I move back to work on *Enduring;* I have not yet done that. As soon as we're done with all of this interview stuff, I plan to go back to work on *Enduring*.

BW: A year after your accident now,[102] how do you look on the changes it has wrought?

DH: Well, the only change that really is of any significance is that I am no longer able to eat or drink, and there are occasions when I get a really nasty craving for a slice of cantaloupe on a summer morning, or for my mother-in-law's chicken and dumplings, or for Kim's chicken and rice, or for a nice steak grilled on the grill. We haven't used the grill once this summer. I have offered to grill for Kim because I vicariously appreciate anything that she consumes, but my inability to eat and drink is the only significant change that has been wrought in me.

There is one other significant change. Right after the accident and for a long time after the accident, I had to nap as often as I possibly could. I couldn't seem to catch up on my sleep, and even though I'm not that way now, I got into the habit last fall, when I was writing *Enduring*, of writing for a while in the morning, taking a nap, and then writing again in the afternoon, because that would be the only time I had to write. It used to be that I did all of my writing in the morning; I was finished by noon or one o'clock. Now, that habit has changed completely so that if I get to work by ten o'clock in the morning, work for two hours, take a nap, work for two more hours in the afternoon, I'm a lot more productive than I have been in the past. So that's a good change. Wouldn't you think, Kim?

KH: We just passed the first year anniversary. Last summer was probably the hardest period of time we've gone through since we've known each other. There were times last summer when he was hospitalized, ill with pneumonia, as well as recovering from the effects of the car accident, the broken ankle. It's more complicated than that, but there were times when he was so sick with pneumonia that he didn't know, he didn't understand, how sick he was. I worried so much about his ability to bounce back, mentally and creatively. I didn't know if he would be able to teach again, and he could, and I didn't know if he'd be able to write again, and he did, and is. After two to three weeks in the hospital—and there were a total of six weeks—he didn't always make sense. He couldn't write anything by hand at that time either. He couldn't retain any information. He was so confused. I wondered if I had lost him that way, lost him mentally. So I spent many sleepless nights thinking, "Will the real Donald Harington come back?" And he did; it just took a while.

Now, since then, we've had a year. I think we're both a little more gentle, and maybe we take life a little more slowly. Our pace is slower; it has to be. Probably, we're all that much more aware of just how fragile life really is; I think that as much as we appreciated each other before last summer, the accident and the illness, we have an even deeper appreciation for each other now. There's something a little sweeter, more gentle. Some sort of deeper understanding of each other has occurred out of all that; it's not something I can explain, but it's something that I've seen evolve in the last year. As he said, Don's writing a book right now called *Enduring*. I'm excited about this book, and he's talking about books *beyond Enduring*. I don't know what ideas he has; he hasn't told me yet, but I think there's more to come; in fact, there might be a lot more to come.

DH: Two other changes, as far as my job is concerned, teaching. I'm no longer able to stand up and lecture for eighty minutes. I get tired out too easily; I have to sit down. I'm no longer able to go out among the students and collect the cards of their questions and answers; they have to bring the cards to me. No big problem involved in that.

But there is one other problem. My study has always been cluttered
with my books and papers and manuscripts all over the place. Now, it's
cluttered not only with that stuff, but with my feeding supplies and my
medical supplies. It's so cluttered that Kim, who hates clutter, will no
longer come into my study.

KH: [*Chuckling*] Not exactly true. I'm in there because I clean in there
and try to tidy up when he's not looking. But now that Don has mentioned the fact that he can't eat or drink anymore, I can say that it's
been enormously sad, really sad, kind of a heavy weight that I carry
within my heart. It hurts to know that someone you love cannot any
longer and will never again enjoy food and drink. It's left me as the
lone eater in the house, and I've had to adjust to, first in a practical
sense, just buying much less food and cooking for just one and again. I
don't really even cook; I kind of snack or get take-out food sometimes.
Things are really different for me like that. We no longer have meals
together; we can't use that time to talk. I'm lonely in that sense, and
there's a lot of emotion surrounding the whole idea of giving up food.
I've often wished that maybe I could talk to someone else who's married to someone who's had to endure the same loss so I would know
how anybody else would cope with that. But I don't think there's too
many people I could find who have gone through anything similar. I
wish so much that his inability to eat . . . that it had just never happened; I wish we could reverse this some way and there's not a way,
there's no medical way.

BW: What are your professional plans now? When will you retire?

DH: Kim and I have decided that the coming school year will be my last
year of teaching. I'm seventy-one years old, and a lot of people retire at
sixty-five. It has been my ambition all my life *not* to teach, but I have
had to teach for a little. I like teaching, so I don't mind, but I've constantly looked forward to a time when it's no longer necessary to teach.
The year after next, it will still be necessary to teach, but we've decided
that, somehow, we can get along without it, and that, of course, will
free me up to write full time for the rest of my life.

BW: Now that you're farther along into it, what else can you tell us about
Enduring?

DH: All I can tell you—I can tell you two things. It has to be finished
before August 20, because that's when the fall semester starts, and I
just cannot work during the semester. I've been working on it for two

years now. As I mentioned before, it's the life story of Latha Bourne from infancy to — I won't say death, because as Dawny promised in *Lightning Bug*, Latha never dies. This will be a feat, to pull off the creation of a character who lives forever. Even in García Márquez's *One Hundred Years of Solitude*, the prostitute who became the old woman who was notorious for living throughout the book; she was one hundred twenty-something when she died. But she did die.[103]

By the time my book is finished, Latha will be one hundred seven, but her life does not come to an end, just as the future tense does not come to an end. A supreme stroke of the use of the future tense will be creating a life for Latha that never has any ending to it. But I have to get busy with it, because I'm just at the point where Every, after so many years, comes back into town. The story that was originally told in *Lightning Bug*, that's as far as I've reached at this point. I've got to tell all the rest of her life in the remainder of this summer in the remainder of the book. But I can't say all the rest of her life, because it's *not* all of the rest; it's to set her up for continuing into the twenty-*second* century.

BW: What final words do you have for the Gentle Reader?

DH: Enjoy your hammock, your easy chair, your patch of grass, wherever you choose to read. Enjoy it. Have fun.

Epilogue: Don interviews Brian; Kim interviews Don

DH: Professor Walter, when did you first meet Donald Harington?

BW: I first met him in the fall of 1996, when he sent me an e-mail in response to something I had posted on NABOKV-L, the Vladimir Nabokov Electronic Discussion Forum. I had signed off as "Brian Walter, Assistant Professor of English, University of the Ozarks," and that sign-off caught his attention because of the Ozarks connection — he's the Ozarks embodied, he's been here so long.

DH: How many times altogether — including the present time — have you met him?

BW: [*Laughing*] That would be impossible to number. He invited us, my wife and myself, to come up to Fayetteville to have lunch with him and his wife for the first time in November of 1996, so that was almost eleven years ago now. It's hard even to estimate the number of times I've been here to their home to enjoy their hospitality — a dozen times or more, I'd guess — and they've been to Saint Louis to see us and came to Clarksville for a couple of readings. We've even met in Florida and in Rolla for other events.

DH: Have you met any other great writers, other than William Gass?

BW: [*Laughing*] No. Actually, I have been fortunate to meet a number of fine poets and other good fiction writers. But certainly, when I think of living writers whom I've been fortunate to meet, the two right at the top of the list would be Donald Harington and Bill Gass. There's also a very good one whom I had a chance to work with a little bit named Charles Baxter, who has had a number of well-received books.

DH: You were a great fan of Nabokov until you encountered Harington, is that right?

BW: [*Surprised and laughing*] Yes. I haven't entirely ceased being a great fan of Nabokov; the wording of that question is characteristically clever on the part of my counterpart. But, it's true that, in some ways, what I thought I would be doing at this point in my scholarly life—devoting it to Nabokov, the subject of my dissertation—I've probably turned now more toward Harington and the Stay More novels.

DH: Have you ever played chess with Mr. Harington?

BW: Not a once. He's tried to entice me into it, but I know what his record is with his computer; it's 151 wins to, I believe, 81 losses and 20 draws. I'm afraid I would need to practice for many months before I could get up to his level.

DH: Have you ever played basketball with Mr. Harington?

BW: [*Laughing*] No, we've not had that good fortune either. One time, however, when we were visiting and took a little walk down the cul-de-sac here, the four of us, someone had set up a short hoop. I think we shot a basket or two, and then I went and got a couple more things to juggle with the basketballs. I thought that would be more appropriate for our court jester of the Ozarks.

DH: When you first met Mr. Harington, he was an inch taller than you, and now he is an inch shorter than you. How do you account for that? Have you grown two inches since you first met him?

BW: [*Laughing*] Only around the waistline. It's a remarkable thing, this process of aging. I look forward to the day when my children rib me about how tall I used to be.

DH: If you had to rank Mr. Harington's novels in order, how would you do it?

BW: With tremendous difficulty I was just talking with Kim about this last night, and as I told her, although there are a couple of them (and I'm not going to tell you which ones) that I would put on a slightly lower rung than the others, it never fails to amaze me how many of them, when I reread them, make me think, "This one has to go right to the top of the list." It's an astonishingly, uniformly powerful, wonderful body of work that he's managed to produce over the decades.

DH: When you gave such a glowing report on *With* and led Mr. Harington to believe that the editor who had called it "prurient" was full of shit, was that a strictly honest opinion, or did you just say that because of your friendship with Mr. Harington?

BW: That was as honest an opinion as I've ever been able to muster in an e-mail. This was, I thought, just a fantastic work of the imagination. What I particularly love about his work in general is distilled in *With* with particular power: his ability to give full rein to the horrors and the tragedies that are visited upon us in this wonderful human condition but to somehow find a way to redeem them, to make them part of something much greater and larger. Robin's ordeal turns into Robin's fantastic education, as improbable as that sounds, and she ends up having the kind of childhood—as impossible as this sounds, given the scenario—that, in many ways, we all would benefit from: something that's close to the earth, something that grounds her in her body in a way that she's always going to incorporate into her sense of herself for the rest of her life. That all of this happens because of the horrible attentions and disgraceful actions of a pedophile just makes it all the more improbable, but that, to me, makes it a work of absolutely permanent art, and those things are all too rare. I think it's a marvelous, marvelous book, and the frightful thing is that I would say that about almost all of his books.

DH: If you did not have to teach for a living, what would you do?

BW: I would sit around and talk to writers whom I like and ask them lots of questions on video. I would take pictures; I would write a little myself, probably not too much fiction. I would hold a glass of water too long in front of the camera before I take a drink. I would, most of all, try to continue on a path toward some sort of wisdom. This is something I've said as I head toward a change of job here in the fall: I don't have professional ambitions as such; what I do have are some philosophical aspirations. Ultimately, what my job is does not matter in the pursuit of those philosophical aspirations; I could pursue them, theoretically, in any position. I could be, theoretically, happy as a janitor somewhere; I could also be miserable as king of the world. Ultimately, the job isn't what matters; it's what we do to connect to something larger and more enduring than our little three-score-years-and-ten. That's where I'm trying to head, and that's where I find the connection with Don and his work so rewarding, because that's what they're all about, finding a way to live inside these mortal shells and to connect them to something larger, what's going to happen, what we have waiting for us farther along and how we can make all of that part of our daily experience.

DH: You're so familiar with Harington's work that, if he were hit by a bus tomorrow and ceased to exist, would you be able to finish *Enduring* for him?

BW: Could I finish *Enduring*? [*Laughing*] Not in the way that it needs to be finished. I have my own ideas of how I would want to end it, and they would be different, I'm afraid, from the way that he's going to end it, thank goodness, and the way he's going to end his future novels. I've certainly thought about what it would be like to try to use my familiarity with his work and with his person to connect to his plots at that level, to make a story the way that he does. I think it would be impossible not to; that's part of what we do as readers, to link our sensibilities and inclinations up with those of the creative imagination that we are spending so much time immersed in. I've thought about what I would do with Latha's end, certainly, but that's never going to be written because we're going to have something much better from the author himself. So, sure, anybody *could* finish the book, but no one could do it quite like this man here is going to do it.

DH: You're going to be leaving shortly for West Plains, Missouri, to meet your son; are you looking forward to that?

BW: Yes, I am. I haven't been able to spend as much time with him this past spring, and it's been an important one. He just turned thirteen in April, and all of the changes that go with that transition are ones that I have not been able to participate in, for a variety of reasons, nearly as much as I would like. It's hard to imagine quite what he's been thinking, what he's going through, because we've been at a remove from each other, so I'm looking forward to spending time and reconnecting with who he is now, because I just haven't had a chance to see that very much in recent months.

DH: Did you know that Daniel Woodrell, the novelist, lives in West Plains?

BW: No, I didn't know that. There are several artistic sorts and a thriving arts community in and around West Plains, as I've learned over the years that our son has lived there, but I didn't know about him. Have you read some of his work?

DH: I reviewed some of his work in the *Atlanta Constitution* and the *Raleigh News and Observer*. His most recent book is called *Winter's Bone*, and I read and reviewed it for a couple of newspapers.

BW: Did you like it?

DH: It's pretty good. It's set in West Plains, and the hillbillies that he presents are a little bit too dark and, maybe I shouldn't say it, dumb. They're real backwoods hicks, not like the kind of hillbillies you would find in Harington. Anyway, I wish you a good trip to West Plains, and if you happen to run across Daniel Woodrell, you can give him my regards.

BW: Has he seen your review?

DH: He wrote and told me how much he liked my review. He used to live in Fayetteville for several years; he lived just down the street from us when we lived on Willow Street. Well, that's all. Did I leave anything out?

BW: No, you're fine. Let me just add one last thing, as long as I've got the camera in front of me. The thing I've often said whenever I've had the chance to teach Don's work—also in articles, reviews, and such—is that it's comedy in the best sense, in the way that Dante wrote a divine comedy several centuries ago. It manages to show how we have to go through hell and maybe even some middling sort of purgatory to reach a vision of heaven. His ability to do all of these things, to make comedy that comprehends tragedy, is what makes him, for me, a permanent artist, someone at the top of a very short list of the best writers of American fiction and American literature, in my estimation. Thank you.

DH: I don't mean this shirt purely in jest, because you will appear in one of the late chapters of *Enduring*.[104]

BW: Oh, my goodness. I don't know how that's going to be.

DH: By the way, did you happen to notice who you pushed out of the way to make room for your camera?

BW: Nabokov. [*Laughing*] There's a coincidence. Do you want to ask him some questions, Kim?

KH: Don, you and I met because I wrote you a fan letter so long ago after I read *Some Other Place. The Right Place.* I never dreamed that we would end up married. Do you think there's any other writer and spouse who have met like that, with one of them having written the other a fan letter?

DH: I've never heard of one, but for that matter, I never heard of a spouse like you. Or a writer like me.

KH: *True.*

DH: We're unique. Babe.

KH: [*Laughing.*] Did you imagine while you were writing *Some Other Place. The Right Place.* that it could lead . . .

DH: I've written all of my books for the Gentle Reader, but I have always fantasized the Gentle Reader as a beautiful blonde who would send me a fan letter someday.

KH: Okay. You used to have a shirt—maybe you still have a shirt—a uniform shirt that we bought in a used clothing store. You took a shine to it, and that shirt said "Solid Waste," right here on a patch . . .

DH: "Fayetteville Solid Waste Company." That's why we . . .

KH: We have a gesture that I use when I think that you are exaggerating or . . .

DH: Full of . . .

KH: Let me finish. When you're exaggerating or not telling the truth exactly; you're embellishing, we have a gesture like this. If I do this [*flicks imaginary waste from shoulder*], it makes reference to that shirt that says "Solid Waste," which could be interpreted with one other word. So, when you tell me these things about writing for the ideal, gentle reader, the "beautiful blonde," it's very sweet of you, but is that. . . ? [*flicking again*]

DH: We never took the trouble to learn sign language other than finger-spelling. But we have, over the years, developed our own system of gestures that are very meaningful to us.

KH: Yeah, there's probably a lot of those. Touching the ear means that your hearing aid is whistling. Again. This means it's thundering so you'll know what's happening. Raining . . .

DH: Kind of like Tish and Sam in *Cockroaches*. They invented their own system of sign language. We do use a lot of orthodox sign language also, like "I love you."

KH: True. But we never learned, and I regret that. I wish that both of us were fluent in sign language, but we just never tried hard enough to learn. And I write down so much for you . . .

DH: Have you ever counted up how many bottle notes?

KH: Over twenty-five notebooks are filled with . . .

DH: Thirty-five?

KH: Over *twenty*-five notebooks are filled with . . .

DH: Oh, twenty-five.

KH: No, no, no, no. It's over forty by now; it's getting close to fifty notebooks by now.

DH: She's filled up fifty notebooks with what she calls "Bottle Notes" because, when you throw a bottle into the sea with a note in it, you don't expect an answer. You're lucky if you get one. So she wrote me all of these long, long notes that I never took the trouble to answer. I just answered in a few words, or whatever. That's why you call them "Bottle Notes," right?

KH: You thought that calling them "bottle notebooks" was a good idea. That's your invention.

ACKNOWLEDGMENTS

If I were to attempt to thank all of the people who have helped this *Guestroom Novelist* to find its way into print, Gentle Reader would run out of patience long before I ran out of thankees. Also, poor gray-haired Mnemosyne—who's taken to squinting through her eyeglasses and hobbling along with a cane these days—would certainly abscond the premises long before she could help me complete such a Herculean task.

So, in the interests of keeping these generic outpourings of humble gratitude to a reasonable length, allow me to reverse their typical order by first thanking all of those family members, friends, colleagues, students, and fellow lovers of Harington's books who have reached out to me over the years or, in a variety of other ways, supported or encouraged the manifold labors that have taken shape in the comparatively humble form of this book. Harington's work overflows with love for his readers, building compelling relationships among characters within the storylines to foster communities around his books and their enduring themes, and it has been my privilege to add to my personal circle of story-lovers with the ardent communities he built up over the decades that continue to celebrate their memories of Harington and their love of Stay More.

Many parties and organizations have also provided more direct support for this *Guestroom Novelist*, and I can't let the moment pass without thanking at least some of them more personally. The Saint Louis College of Pharmacy helped underwrite my work on this book and other Harington-related initiatives with several faculty research awards over the years. Harington's alma mater and final teaching home, the University of Arkansas, proved even more essential to this book's existence; I particularly need to thank Tim Nutt (who lugged boxes and boxes of still-uncataloged Harington materials from storage for my grateful archeological efforts), Geoffery Stark, and their colleagues both in Special Collections and in Mullins Library at large (particularly Norma Johnson) for their expert and generous services. Melissa King reached out to me out of the proverbial blue, helping to establish a great working relationship with Mike Bieker, D. S. Cunningham, Molly Bess Rector, and her other colleagues at the University of Arkansas Press, with whom I look forward to working for some time to come on Harington's literary after-life. Linda Hughes, the dean of Harington scholars, helped to inspire the title essay and has supported the work that produced this final volume in more ways than can be easily enumerated. Susan Rooker Tonymon at the Osher Lifelong Learning Institute; Kris Katrosh, Trey Marley, Randy Dixon, and others at the Pryor Center for Arkansas Oral History; and Harington's colleagues in Art History have all responded generously to my queries and requests over the years.

Let me conclude by singling out three individuals without whom this *Guestroom Novelist* would have been not only impossible, but literally inconceivable, starting with the author's muse herself. Kim Harington deserves more thanks than can easily be offered for cooperation, hospitality, materials, and insights both unique and essential into Harington's life and work. Harington, of course, was the first to speak of Kim as his muse, a real-life character he somehow created or yearned into existence to sustain him in his life just as Latha Bourne, the demigoddess of Stay More, sustained him in his decades of novelist's work. Nicely enough, it doesn't overstate the case to say that he—and their life together—were just as much a creation of hers, quite literally making it possible for him over the last two decades of his life (all while teaching full-time and enduring incapacitating illnesses, injuries, and other physical challenges) to write ten more novels, two works of art scholarship, and numerous other pieces, including the vast majority that comprise this *Guestroom Novelist*. All readers of Harington's books can thank their lucky literary stars that a plucky schoolteacher up and wrote a self-exiled and despairing Arkansawyer author a fan letter out of the blue way back in the mid-seventies, for if she hadn't, all of our bookshelves and our imaginations would almost certainly be much poorer, quite possibly lacking altogether the Nail Chisms and Robin Kerrs and Ekaterina Dadeshkelianis, not to mention the one and only, century-old but ageless Latha Bourne, that Kim's presence in Harington's life helped him to imagine and chronicle.

Next up is *il miglior fabbro* himself. I still marvel to think of the mountain of words that has somehow been built out of the molehill e-mail that Harington sent to a strange young Nabokov scholar in the fall of 1996 with an invitation to lunch in Fayetteville, an encounter that would permanently alter my life as a scholar and teacher of literature. Anyone who has read through my introductions and prologues sprinkled throughout this book has heard enough of my praise for the Nabokovian court jester of the Ozarks, so let me end my effusions with this: Harington's dedication, discipline, and indefatigability as a writer, teacher, and ardently amateur advocate of the life-giving joys of art in so many forms have served (and will always serve) as both a superb and a humbling example for my own dabblings in our mutual vocations and avocations.

Finally, for supporting my fumbling efforts at scholarship in more ways than I can enumerate and, still more, for somehow making it an unaccountable joy to continue at all with this gradual falling off the mountain called life, I have my much better half, Brenda Walter, to thank forever and ever.

Brian Walter

St. Louis, August 21, 2018

NOTES

ESSAYS, ARTICLES, AND SPEECHES

Arkansas's One and Only Hero

1. Harington's article was published simultaneously with a review of Walter Lee Brown's biography, *A Life of Albert Pike*.

Accepting the *Oxford American* Award

1. Archie Schaffer III, former Executive VP of Corporate Affairs for Tyson Foods, a dear friend and former student of Don's, and a character in *Thirteen Albatrosses, or Falling off the Mountain*.

INTERVIEWS

1. This is not to say that the Stay More novels lack all reference to race or racism, but rather that black characters show up in far fewer of them than might be expected from an author of Harington's personal background. The Civil War chapters of *The Architecture of the Arkansas Ozarks* ironize white hillbilly racism for comic effect, with Stay More patriarch Jacob Ingledew nearly getting lynched when he alone opposes Arkansas's secession from the Union. And black characters do play supporting roles in Harington's 1991 prison novel, *The Choiring of the Trees*, but Harington's responses in these interviews easily represent his most extended formal comments on the horrifying American traditions of racism.

2. A description once offered by Harington's fellow novelist and friend, Fred Chappell.

The Linda Hughes and Larry Vonalt Interviews: *The Cherry Pit*, Part 1

1. Harington's first published novel was brought out by Random House in 1965.

2. This ellipsis appears in Harington's original file, and its purpose isn't clear. It might simply indicate a pause in speech, but it seems just as likely that Harington planned to go back and expand on this idea about the indifference of old friends and never got back to it, (If the sentiment had needed no further explanation, he could easily have replaced the ellipsis with "or.")

3. This Descartes quotation and the next one by Shakespeare appear as epigraphs in Harington's second published novel, *Lightning Bug* (1970).

4. Dr. Michael Patrick was a colleague of Hughes's and Vonalt's in the University of Missouri–Rolla's (UMR) English Department at the time; he was also, according to Hughes, the one who first invited Harington to Rolla.

5. In a much later interview, Harington would attribute this particular insight to Hughes. (See p. 175.)

6. Although Harington had completed a version of *Farther Along* at the time of this interview in 1979, the novel describing Clifford Stone's reclusive adventures in the Ozark Mountains near Stay More was not finally published until 2008, when Toby Press brought it out the year before the author's death.

The Architecture of the Arkansas Ozarks, Part I

1. Johann Wolfgang von Goethe (1749–1832), German novelist, dramatist, poet, inter alia, probably most famous for the Romantic epic *Faust*.

2. James R. Frakes (1924–2001) was a professor of English literature at Lehigh from 1958–2001.

3. An apparent slip for "Jake" or "Jacob."

4. The intended meaning here is unclear. The author is "most like Stapleton of my characters that are simply flattering"? (Tall, mysterious, and magically compelling but possibly impotent himself, Stapleton does indeed make a flattering avatar for an author, for the most part.)

The Architecture of the Arkansas Ozarks, Part II

1. When carnival worker Cancetto "Spaghetti" Farmica was killed in a fight in 1911, his father paid ten dollars to have his body embalmed and promised to return to pay for his burial, but never did. The body of "Spaghetti" hung in the embalming room of the McDougald Funeral Home (and other places) in Laurinburg, North Carolina, and became a tourist attraction until a fellow Italian from New York paid to have it buried more than sixty years later, in 1972. See https://www.roadsideamerica.com/tip/7849.

2. See Chapter 22 of Harington's next-to-last published novel, *Farther Along* (2008).

3. Likely a reference to George William Featherstonhaugh (1780–1866), the first US government geologist, who was dispatched by the War Department in 1834 to make a geological survey of Arkansas. See http://www.encyclopedia ofarkansas.net/encyclopedia/entry-detail.aspx?entryID=2410.

The Stay More Interviews

1. In this count, Harington was apparently including both his 1987 "nonfiction novel" *Let Us Build Us a City* and his then-unpublished novel *Farther*

Along, which Toby Press did publish a couple of years later, in 2008. (For more
on *LUB* as a nonfiction novel, see pp. 210–211.)

2. Katsushika Hokusai (1760–1849) was the "first Japanese artist to be interna-
tionally recognized" (http://www.mfa.org/exhibitions/hokusai). The Museum
of Fine Art (MFA) in Boston, where Harington studied art history, maintains
one of the finest Hokusai collections in the world.

3. In June 2006, Harington was involved in a serious car accident that broke
his ankle and left him hospitalized for weeks with complications from pneumonia. (See "Falling Off the Mountain," pp. 270–273.)

4. *Orlando furioso* is a fanciful epic by Italian poet Ludovico Ariosto, first published in full in 1532.

5. A famously enigmatic painting by Italian master Giorgio Barbarelli da
Castelfranco (1477/8–1510) depicting a nursing woman seated in the lower-right
corner opposite a young man (possibly a soldier) standing in the lower left holding a pike. Among many other details, a bolt of lightning appears in the cloudy
sky of the distant background. Harington invokes it several times in his 1973
novel *Some Other Place. The Right Place.*

6. Thomas Hart Benton (1889–1975), American painter and muralist associated with the Regionalist art movement and known especially for his paintings
of the American Midwest.

7. George Caleb Bingham (1811–79), an American artist famous for his lively
depictions of American frontier life in the Missouri Valley.

8. Jose Antonio Parra Menchon (1896–1960), also known as Ginés Parra, was
a Spanish painter whose work was often exhibited alongside that of his contemporary, Picasso. Known for his relatively simple but powerful style, Menchon's
artistic subjects ranged from the nude to architecture to religion. (https://
es.wikipedia.org/wiki/Ginés_Parra)

9. Uruguayan Antonio Frasconi (1919–2013) was declared America's fore-
most artist of the woodcut by *Time* in 1953. Preferring social engagement to
pure aesthetics and known for a playful satiric bent, Frasconi illustrated more
than one hundred books and had his work exhibited in many of America's
most prominent museums, including the Museum of Modern Art, the
National Gallery of Art, and the Smithsonian. (http://www.nytimes.com
/2013/01/22/arts/design/antonio-frasconi-woodcut-master-dies-at-93.html?
_r=0)

10. Author's slip for *Dolph* Rivett; see below for his correction.

11. Academy Award-winning and native Arkansawyer actress Mary
Steenburgen (b. 1953) optioned *Lightning Bug*'s film rights with the intention
of playing protagonist and Stay More demigoddess Latha Bourne in a feature
film. The Porter Prize for Literary Excellence is given annually to Arkansas's
best writer; Harington won it in 1987.

12. Tom Bissell was the Holt editor for Harington's 2002 novel, *Thirteen Albatrosses (or, Falling Off the Mountain)*.

13. Quoted verbatim: "[P]erform in bed in order to father her children."

14. Philosopher Adam Krug is the protagonist of *Bend Sinister* (1947), the first novel that Russian-American novelist Vladimir Nabokov wrote entirely in the United States.

15. Albert Pike (1809–1891) was a schoolteacher and poet from Boston Massachusetts who would go on to become a journalist, attorney, Civil War general, and Grand High Priest of the Masonic Lodge in Arkansas. He is the only Confederate officer to have a monument erected to him in Washington, D.C. http://www.encyclopediaofarkansas.net/encyclopedia/entry-detail.aspx?entryid=1737

16. Toby Press did publish *Farther Along* in 2008, a year before Harington's death, largely in the form in which Harington had last revised it.

17. *With* was optioned by Esperanza Productions but has not yet been adapted for a feature film.

18. Harington seems to switch here from the noun *cachet* (literally, bearing a special mark) to the adjective *cachée* to set up the description that cleverly (if rather ambiguously) combines both senses of the term. The last word of this sentence—here transcribed as "shed"—is not clear in the recording; it could also be "shape," "share," or "seen" (or something else).

19. G. is a narrator of and character within *Some Other Place. The Right Place.* He is hired by Burt Stoving's father in Little Rock to find out what happened to his daughter Diana after she has disappeared; G. eventually tracks Diana and her companion, Day Whittacker, to Stick Around, that novel's disguise for Stay More.

20. Dawny debuts as a prominent character in *Lightning Bug*, the first Stay More novel, in which he is five years old and hopelessly in love with Latha Bourne, the town's postmistress. He is also the protagonist of *When Angels Rest*, where he begins the novel "thoroughly eleven, going on twelve." "Dawny" was Harington's own nickname growing up in Drakes Creek. (See pp. 287–288.)

21. Cormac McCarthy won the William Faulkner Foundation Award for notable first novel in 1966 for *The Orchard Keeper*. Harington's *The Cherry Pit* had also been nominated.

22. In Little Rock.

23. Harington attended the University of Arkansas in Fayetteville as an undergraduate and MFA student before moving to Massachusetts to study at Boston University and, eventually, for a single year, Harvard. (See pp. 168–169.)

24. Harington was an instructor of Art History at Bennett College in Millbrook, New York, from 1960 to 1962.

25. *Set This House on Fire* was published by Random House in 1960.

26. A typescript of the novel is available (with permission) in the University of Arkansas Libraries' Special Collections.

27. In *Requiem for a Nun*, his 1951 sequel to *Sanctuary*, Faulkner wrote, "The past is never dead. It's not even past."

28. The intended meaning here is unclear. Perhaps the Harper & Row editor was reconsidering *A Work of Fiction* for publication but died before he could change his mind back and once again accept it?

29. Or possibly "Georgia or Callico"? (The recording is very hard to decipher here; Drakes Creek's Wesley Cemetery does inter two people with the last name Callico, but none with the surname Georgia. http://freepages .genealogy.rootsweb.ancestry.com/~jdrake71053/arcemetery_drakescreek -3.html.)

30. Harington's fellow American novelist was born in Exeter, New Hampshire, in 1942; Irving's books include (among many others) *The World According to Garp* (1978) and *A Prayer for Owen Meany* (1989).

31. Kim tells her version of this story in the documentary *Farther Along: The World of Donald Harington, Pt. 2* (University of Arkansas Press, 2015).

32. For Day Whittacker, one of the novel's three main characters, to serve as the medium of the long-dead Daniel Lyam Montross (a second main character), he must be hypnotized, first by his high school English teacher P. D. Sedgely, and then (repeatedly and with increasingly unsettling ease for Day) by the novel's heroine, Diana Stoving.

33. Clare is not this counselor's real name.

34. G. is the nickname for the author's avatar (a nearly deaf Arkansawyer writer turned detective) in *Some Other Place*.

35. Diana Stoving and Day Whittacker spend most of the first three parts of *Some Other Place* exploring ghost towns in and around Vermont and Connecticut, the region where Harington had been living for more than a decade while teaching at Windham College in Putney, Vermont. But in the novel's fourth part, their pursuit of Diana's grandfather, Daniel Lyam Montross, takes them to Stick Around in the Ozarks, where Arkansas's own G. finally, eventually, and perhaps symbolically catches up with them after hunting for them throughout the wilds of New England.

36. After living for many years in an Ozark bungalow less than a mile from the old town square in Fayetteville, Don and Kim Harington moved in early 1994 to a house they had had built in a quiet, cul-de-sacked subdivision further north and east (still within the city limits).

37. Traveling salesman Eli Willard returns annually to Stay More for decades before a long hiatus and a final, mysterious appearance as a circus worker who bequeaths a watch that eventually is handed down to Vernon, the last Ingledew. In the meantime, his body has been embalmed and preserved in various Stay More buildings long after his death; Vernon's father, John Henry, eventually goes looking for it.

38. Windham College in Putney, Vermont.

39. Diana Stoving, the dancer heroine of *Some Other Place. The Right Place.*, Kim's favorite Harington novel.

40. Gregor Samsa (Sam) Ingledew and Tish Dingletoon, the "roosterroach" protagonists of *The Cockroaches of Stay More* (1989).

41. The heroines of *Ekaterina* (1993) and *The Choiring of the Trees* (1991), respectively.

42. Probably the extended profile by Herbert Mitgang, which appeared in the August 2, 1982, issue.

43. Genesis 11:1–4 (King James Version).

44. Revelation 22:5: "And there shall be no night there; and they need no candle, neither light of the sun; for the Lord God giveth them light: and they shall reign for ever and ever."

45. During this segment of the live interviews, Harington actually struggled to remember the name of the emblematic tune that Harrigan hears every evening, "Meditation Upon Ruins," so he asked the real-life Kim to help him find the passage in which the book's Kim "passes through Eros" and begins to hear the theme herself—the writer's life and his art once again blending together inextricably.

46. This early episode in *LUB* may be entirely made up, but it perfectly embodies the theme of creative loneliness and the desire for lifegiving connection with a spiritual mate: "When [Harrigan] got to Sauk Centre he discovered that it looked exactly like Brookings. There were even walk-ups over the Main Street furniture store, and he almost knocked at the door of one that looked like his own. Instead he drank a half-pint at the grave of Sinclair Lewis and returned the way he had come. Driving back to South Dakota, he felt a pang of conscience for not having knocked at that door, behind which someone was probably waiting for a knock."

47. At this point in the actual June 2007 interview, Kim pointed out that Zephyra was a 280Z, but her hearing- and memory-challenged collaborator apparently didn't register her clarification and just sent her off in the next sentence in her "car." According to *Let Us Build Us a City*, it was a "sporty Datsun that she named Zephyra after the west wind"; in another place, the book refers to "Zephyra, that saucy Nissan Datsun 280–zx," the author again appearing to hedge his bets on the proper name.

48. The Spring 2002 issue (vol. 40, no. 2) of *Southern Quarterly* was a special issue devoted to Harington and his work.

49. In her 1919 poem "Poetry," Marianne Moore famously plumps for poets to become "'literalists of the imagination' who can present "imaginary gardens with real toads in them" (full poem available at https://www.poets.org/poetsorg/poem/poetry).

50. *Let Us Build Us a City* was published in 1987, almost a decade before Cameron's *Titanic* broke domestic and international box office records. In

Cameron's version, it is the man who dies and the woman who survives (the opposite of Harington's scenario, which eventually makes Sam Dunlap wonder if, in fact, the woman he fell in love with ever actually existed, adding another layer of subtle metafictional possibility to the story).

51. Gregor Samsa is also (uncoincidentally) the name for the protagonist of Franz Kafka's immortal tale "The Metamorphosis," in which Gregor wakes up one morning as a dung beetle (according to the translation of the insistent Vladimir Nabokov, Harington's favorite writer) and who subsequently struggles to continue to live with his human family.

52. Harington's source for this definition is unclear. Word Hippo in fact lists *küchenschabe* as the third of four possible terms for our "cockroach" (http://www.wordhippo.com/what-is/the/german-word-for-cockroach.html), but a more accurate English translation for this term would be "kitchen-louse." In *Insects: Their Ways and Means of Living* (Smithsonian, 1930), Robert Evans Snodgrass characterizes *küchenschabe* as disrespectful (http://www.archive.org /stream/39088001578236/39088001578236_djvu.txt, p. 78).

53. A reference to Tom Bissell, the editor at Holt who published *Thirteen Albatrosses*. (See p. 251.)

54. Mark Harris went on to become the executive editor of *Entertainment Weekly*, author of (among other books) *Pictures at a Revolution: Five Movies and the Birth of the New Hollywood* (2008), and husband of award-winning playwright Tony Kushner.

55. A fun mistake that Harington corrected a little later in the interview. (See p. 218.) The female cockroach's pheromone figures crucially in several passages, but it does not have a separate name in *COSM*.

56. The term Harington uses here is not completely clear in the recording.

57. Donald Harington, *The Nearly Complete Works of Donald Harington*, Volume 1, AmazonEncore. Kindle Edition, locations 20048–20051.

58. Russ Breedlove, the later novel's Ozark counterpart to Eros, is the son of Venda Breedlove, *BUT*'s counterpart to the goddess of love, Aphrodite/Venus; incidentally, Venda imprisons Doc Colvin Swain with an aphrodisiac that forces him to make love to her for weeks, effectively chained to her bed.

59. Harington's response to these questions includes at least one important plot-spoiler.

60. Sharon Brace Ingledew is Latha Bourne's granddaughter; apart from *COSM*, she appears most prominently in *Ekaterina* (as the title character's best friend) and *Enduring*, most of which she narrates. She was also to be the heroine of a novel called *Rose of Sharon* (or *ROS*) which Harington had planned to write after *Enduring*.

61. Harington's phrase here is not clear in the audio recording.

62. The author's reading of the poem is featured in the documentary *Farther Along: The World of Donald Harington, Pt. 2* (University of Arkansas Press, 2015).

63. A reference to the Stay More chapter of the Freemasons, whose origins are described in *The Architecture of the Arkansas Ozarks*. "TGAOTU" is a standard masonic abbreviation for "The Grand Architect of the Universe," but the Stay Morons prefer to have it stand for "The Grinning and Ogling Tipplers' Union."

64. Brother Chidiock "Chid" Tichborne is the Crustian preacher who, among other things, offers up to Man a memorable "abject entreaty": "'Lord, if it be Thy will,' he prayed, 'piss upon me!'"

65. The mind, that ocean where each kind
Does straight its own resemblance find;
Yet it creates, transcending these,
Far other worlds, and other seas,
Annihilating all that's made
To a green thought in a green shade.
— Andrew Marvell, "The Garden," stanza 6

Constable said that the superiority of the green he uses for his landscapes derives from the fact that it is composed of a multitude of different greens. What causes the lack of intensity and of life in verdure as it is painted by the common run of landscapists is that they ordinarily do it with a uniform tint. What he said about the green of the meadows can be applied to all the other shades. — Eugène Delacroix, *Journals*

66. Literary historians may consider Julia Burnelle Smade "Bernie" Babcock (1868–1962) a "minor" novelist, but she was a major figure in Arkansas and American literary culture for much of the twentieth century and enjoyed successes that subsequent novelists could well envy. Her first book, *The Daughter of the Republican* (1900), was a "temperance novel" that sold 100,000 copies in six months; among her subsequent novels was 1919's *The Soul of Ann Rutledge*, about the love affair of Abraham Lincoln and Miss Rutledge; it won an international audience, going through fourteen printings and translations into several other languages. After founding, managing, and even painting murals for Arkansas's Museum of Natural History, Babcock eventually retired to a "small house on top of Petit Jean Mountain" to paint and, still more eventually, publish a volume of poetry called *The Marble Woman*. She was found dead at home in the summer of 1962, apparently with a manuscript in her hand. (From *The Encyclopedia of Arkansas History & Culture*.)

67. The novel Harington was working on at the time of the interviews in 2006 and 2007. It was eventually published in September of 2009, the last one to appear in print before his passing in November of 2009.

68. Marguerite Thompson Zorach (1887–1968) was an American Fauvist painter, textile artist, and graphic designer and an early exponent of modernism in America who won the Logan Medal of the Arts in 1920. William Zorach (1887–1966) was a Lithuanian-born American sculptor, painter, printmaker, and writer who also won the Logan Medal of the Arts.

69. The coincidence seems a bit more wishful than literal. *Choiring* was published in April, 1991, some three-and-a-half years before the author's favorite movie hit the screens in October of 1994 (and more than a year after Harington's next novel, *Ekaterina*, was published, in fact).

70. Nabokov and his wife, Vera, moved into the Montreux Palace Hotel in 1961, taking over a suite of rooms in the Cygne Wing on the sixth floor; although they originally thought it was a temporary move (to be near their opera-singer son Dmitri in Milan), they ended up spending the rest of their lives there (Vladimir passed in 1977 and Vera in 1991, a year after she had finally moved out of the hotel to Vevey).

The Crescent Hotel and Spa, founded in 1886, remains to this day a popular site for wedding parties, literary festivals, and ghost tours in Eureka Springs.

71. An extremely complicated "friendship," at best. Ekaterina needs I. to become a writer, but she has to both fend off his sexual advances and pretend she doesn't know anything about the star student in his course—who is, of course, Ekaterina herself in disguise.

72. In the actual interview, Harington proceeded, more or less, to give away the climax of the book at this point.

73. It's not clear if Harington intentionally altered the question so that it was asking about the relationship between the title characters instead of the relationship between the books themselves.

74. He does use the word in the book, albeit tentatively: "[H]e seemed to possess Dzhordzha's quality—aura or emanation—of *makap*, precocious sexuality, of being what your fellow writer and near-compatriot, Nabokov (a very real name, of whom you had not yet heard), called (coined and minted) a faunlet: the male equivalent, if there is one, of his immortal nymphet." Harington, Donald (2012–11–20). *The Nearly Complete Works of Donald Harington*, Volume 2 (Kindle Locations 296–298). AmazonEncore. Kindle Edition.

75. It is not clear whom the term "his style" is supposed to refer to—perhaps Harington slipping back into the book's I. to refer to the author who who wanted to write a "Nabokov novel"?

76. Another curious and highly suggestive remark. The 'poetry section' of *SOP.TRP.* comprises the collected verse of Daniel Lyam Montross, one of the three protagonists for that novel as well as the "tutelary spirit" of the Stay More novels as a whole (as Harington refers to him; see p. [183]); Harington also says that the chief inspiration for Montross's verse was Theodore Roethke, on whom Montross's poetry was modeled. To complicate matters further, the 'poetry section' of *Pale Fire* is, at least theoretically, the primary text of Nabokov's novel, the 999-line poem in four cantos by the avuncular New England poet John Shade that offers pretext for Charles Kinbote's overgrown, pseudo-scholarly apparatus. So, to carry out the author's comparison, who in *SOP. TRP.* plays Kinbote to Montross's Shade?

294 Notes

77. Mickey Rooney played Puck, the impish fairy who hopes that he and his fellow shadows have not offended, in Max Reinhardt's classic 1935 film of Shakespeare's beloved comedy. (This film version of *A Midsummer Night's Dream* figures prominently in Harington's 2006 novel, *The Pitcher Shower*; see p. 267.)

78. It's not clear when they took this drive, but it seems likely to have been in the early to mid-1990s.

79. In 1996.

80. Harington was invited by *Falstaff*, the student literary magazine of the University of the Ozarks, to give a reading from his work on February 15, 1997. During the Q and A after the reading from *Butterfly Weed*, Harington corrected future Henry Holt author Brad McLelland, telling him he shouldn't write about his own life because his own life was boring.

81. For much of the novel, Dawny would, indeed, be twelve, but not at the very beginning: "When I was thoroughly eleven, working on twelve, I first met you."

82. When the topic of *WAR*'s publication came up in a session recorded many months later, the author expressed very different sentiments about his one-off publisher: "I had no trouble at all publishing it. Well, in fact, I had already been dismissed from Harcourt Brace, because of lack of sales, and my agent tried to fix me up with several different publishers, without any luck. Until she discovered Counterpoint—who was the boss of Counterpoint? It doesn't really matter, but the bastard, well, I'm not calling him by his name, because I'm blotting him out of my memory, I'm so angry at him for his treatment of me. But he published *When Angels Rest*."

83. Capitalized throughout the text, like the other characters' proper names.

84. Presumably *Letters from Iwo Jima*, a 2006 film directed by Clint Eastwood.

85. Juliana Heartstays, whose last name tantalizes the author in the book for its possible connections to the origins of "Stay More" as a name.

86. In the opening chapter of *The Architecture of the Arkansas Ozarks*.

87. John Joseph Mathews (1895–1979) published his first novel, *Wah'Kon-tah: The Osage and the White Man's Road*, in 1932 with the University of Oklahoma Press. It became a Book of the Month Club selection, reportedly the first ever university press title so honored. (Oklahoma Historical Society: http://www.okhistory.org/publications/enc/entry.php?entry=MA037.)

88. Despite the author's disclaimers during this interview, *Thirteen Albatrosses* does, in fact, directly invoke the first modern European novel in several passages, first when Bolin Pharis, Vernon's future campaign manager, wonders in an early chapter, "'If George is Sancho Panza,' he said to the empty house, and not just rhetorically, 'then who, or what, am I? One of the windmills?'"

89. In the actual interviews, Harington went on to rehash the plot of *With* in unusually thorough detail, more so than he had with any other book. What

follows substantially condenses his summary, omitting or at least eliding many of the spoilers that he proceeded to share.

90. André Tchelistcheff was "a winemaker, a research oenologist, working for BV, as everyone called the large Beaulieu Vineyards. In fact, André had years before developed the Cabernet Sauvignon which became the valley's principal wine, and was of course Adam and Frances' favorite beverage. They sometimes consumed too much of it." Harington, Donald. *The Nearly Complete Works of Donald Harington*, Volume 2 (Kindle Locations 26079–26081). AmazonEncore. Kindle Edition.

91. Head of Toby Press.

92. Walter's first wife.

93. As with Harington's description of *With*, what follows condenses the author's extremely detailed, spoiler-filled mapping-out of the novel's plot.

94. Or possibly "sure." (The pronunciation isn't completely clear here.)

95. Who had lived in Clarksville from 1996 to 1998, where Harington and his wife visited twice for readings.

96. Actually, Cagney plays Bottom the Weaver while a young Mickey Rooney plays Puck.

97. Frank Capra's beloved 1934 screwball comedy actually pairs Colbert with classical Hollywood's other favorite CG-initialed matinee idol, Clark Gable.

98. At the end of Chapter Nineteen, and the end of the present tense in *The Pitcher Shower*, the narrator records Sharline's variant on Hoppy's happy bugle call: "Nearing his hometown, which is golden beneath that fabulous red sky, his ladylove lifts the bugle and puts it to her lips and blows. *From far yonder down the road here they come again, folks, Hoppy and Sharline, the happy moving showmen of moving pitchers to show you a bunch of good'uns.*"

99. As it turned out, Harington's prediction in this late 2006 interview was a little optimistic. He finished *Enduring* in 2008, and it was published by Toby Press in September of the following year, shortly after the author had entered hospice and about two months before his death on November 7, 2009.

100. Actually, to 145.

101. Not that such ignorance would keep Harington from serving up the French delicacy to characters in his early story "A Second Career" (*Esquire*, January 1967, 117ff.).

102. Asked during the final round of interviews, in June 2007.

103. Another reference to Pilar Ternera, a character whose complicated story does include her becoming the madam of a brothel and who eventually dies at the age of 145.

104. To interview Walter, Harington not only donned a pair of shorts but also a grey T-shirt with the warning, "Careful, or you'll end up in my novel."

BIBLIOGRAPHY

ESSAYS, ARTICLES, AND SPEECHES

"Arkansas' One and Only Hero." *Arkansas Democrat-Gazette.* October 4, 1997.

"Chicken and Dumplings." *Oxford American* 49, "Southern Food, Vol. I" (Spring 2005).

"Donald Harington Accepts the *Oxford American* Award." October 10, 2006.

"First Dates, Blind Dates, Fan Dates, Last Dates." *Soiree,* February 14, 2009.

"Guestroom Novelist, The." 1990.

"Let Us Become Arkansawyers." *Arkansas Gazette,* June 6, 1983.

"On the History of the Porter Prize." August 12, 2004

"Searching for 'Cities' That Didn't Make It." *Arkansas Gazette,* July 31, 1983.

"Songs of Sunlight and Water." *Arkansas Times,* July, 1989.

REVIEWS

Note: Unless otherwise noted, all reviews appeared in the
Arkansas Democrat-Gazette.

Annotated Huckleberry Finn, The. December 9, 2001.

Balthus. November 10, 1996.

Black House. September 16, 2001.

Essential Duane Michals, The. November 9, 1997.

Home Grown Stories and Home Fried Lies. July 30, 2000.

Library of America Nabokov, The. November 24, 1996.

Lives of Kelvin Fletcher: Stories Mostly Short, The. October 6, 2002.

Parthenon and its Impact on Modern Times, The. September 1, 1996.

"Three for Christmas." December 6, 1998.

Truth about Celia, The. July 20, 2003.

Winter's Bone. Atlanta Journal-Constitution. July 30, 2006.

INTERVIEWS

"Brian Walter *with* Donald Harington." *Arkansas Democrat-Gazette,* April 11, 2004.

Linda Hughes and Larry Vonalt with Donald Harington. May 1979.

"Stay More Interviews, The." Brian Walter and Kim Harington with Donald Harington. 2006 and 2007.

NOVEL TEXT

Harington, Donald. *The Nearly Complete Works of Donald Harington.* 3 vols. AmazonEncore. Kindle Edition.

INDEX

15, 16; common names like Smith,
Taylor, Williams in, 18, 20
Cooking with Southern Celebrities, 177
Cooper, James Fenimore, 63
Coover, Robert, 17
Corner of Rife and Pacific, The
(Savage), 11
Cottingham, Robert, 35
Cotton Lane Press, 22
Counterpoint Press, 251
Courtemanche-Ellis, Anne, 207
Cubism, 223. *See also individual artists*
Culkin, Macaulay, 235
Cultural Olympiad, 243

Daphne (goddess), 36
Darconville's Cat (Theroux), 10, 24
Darragh, Fred, 43
Daumier, Honoré, 93
Davis, Lowell, 74
Dawny, 4, 183–84, 219, 288; compared
to author, 245, 247–48, 249; invok-
ing name of Every Dill, 171; longing
for Latha, 175; lost in the woods,
106, 195; narrating *When Angels
Rest*, 243–50; part of Harington's
own self, 173; possible double for
Every Dill, 122; reader cautioned
about D. with his bugs, 104; reader
hoping he's found, 155
De Havilland, Olivia, 265
De Niro, Robert, 236
De Rola, Count Balthasar Klossowski.
See Balthus
Deane, Ernie, 27
Death in the Family, A (Agee), 165
Death of a Salesman (Miller), 13
Deering, John, 39
Defense, The (Nabokov), 64
Defoe, Daniel, 159, 258. See also
Robinson Crusoe
Degas, Edgar, 169

Delacorte (publisher), 193
Delacroix, Eugène, 220
Descartes, René, 104, 125, 286
Dew, Bettye, 21
DiCaprio, Leo, 236
Dillards, The (band), 73
Dogpatch (Arkansas), 28, 213
Don Quixote (character), 256
Donadio, Candida, 193, 195–96; on
vacation, 195
Dostoevsky, Fyodor: in list (as "Fedor
Dostoevsky") proving that all the
greatest writers have fifteen letters
in their names, 91
Doubleday (publisher), 14, 24
Down in the Holler (Randolph), 163,
180
Drakes Creek (Arkansas), 208, 212;
buildings of, 200; creeks of, 170,
186–87; Harington retreating to
after hearing loss, 186; inspir-
ing character names, 138; loss of
affecting young Dawny Harington,
184–85; model for Stay More, 138;
robbed by Jesse
James, 154; setting for Harington's
first reading of *Huck Finn*, 82; storytelling traditions of, 75; traveling
picture shows, 264, 266; visited by
Leary Ball, 170–71; visited by editor with Haringtons, 162; visited by
Peter Straub with Haringtons, 78
"Dreaming, The," 198–99
Driskell, Leon, 21, 23
Drunks, The (Newlove), 10, 24
Durant, Will and Ariel, 7
Dürer, Albrecht, 33
Dutton (publisher), 24
Dvořák, Antonín, 127, 128, 175–76

Eakins, Thomas, 36
Eastwood, Clint, 294

7

(Harington), 3, 204, 206–13; "Harrigan" in, 176, 207, 209; lost towns vs. ghost towns, 211–12; love story, 211; *No Need of the Sun* as original title of, 4; nonfiction novel, 183, 210–11; photographs in, 209, 210; too autobiographical at first, 207

Lewin, Esther and Albert, 174

Life of Albert Pike, A (Brown), 285

Library of America (publisher), 53, 54; excluding short stories of some writers, 65; publishing Nabokov, 60, 63–65

Life on the Mississippi (Twain), 83, 114

Lightning Bug (Harington), 122, 132, 155, 171, 179, 181, 188, 193–95, 200, 223, 225; allusions in, 119; author's favorite, 194; epigraphs of, 104; John Playford as main musical inspiration for, 128; least-researched of Harington's novels, 131; longing in, 175; naming of Latha Bourne in, 118; origins of, 193–95; Ozarks definition of a virgin, 55; reviewed favorably in *Time*, 193; structure of compared to Dvořák's "New World" Symphony, 127; title of, 193

Lincoln, Abraham, 221

Little, Brown (publisher), 11, 12, 23, 24, 92, 196, 197, 203; as publisher of book on Balthus, 61

Little Rock Nine, 99

Lives of Kelvin Fletcher, The: Stories Mostly Short (Williams), 84–88

Livingstone, Marco, 66–67; commenting on Duane Michals' *Things are Queer*, 67

Lolita (1960 film), 65, 236

Lolita (1997 film), 60, 65, 236; writer, director, and stars of, 65

Lolita (Nabokov), 12, 16, 63, 228, 231;

allowing author to retire in comfort and ease, 54; *Annotated Lolita, The*, 81; author's screenplay of, 65; compared to *Ekaterina* and *With*, 158, 159; inspiration for *Ekaterina*, 202, 226–27; notoriety of, 60; research for, 159; title character making room for a scholared-up Huck Finn, 81

Look at the Harlequins! (Nabokov), 65

Look Homeward, Angel (Wolfe), 118

Loomis, Robert, 190–92

Loring, Charles Elliott, 39

Lortz, Richard, 22

Lost Sister, The (Taylor), 20, 24

Lowell, Robert, 16

Lowry, Malcolm, 159

Lytle, Andrew, 8

Malamud, Bernard, 16, 18

Make Believers, The (Fleming), 7–8, 23; as author's and publisher's favorite, 22

Macchu Picchu, 28

Magritte, René, 66; as Duane Michals' idol, 67

Malcolm (Purdy), 13

Malin, Irving, 15

Man Who Cried I Am, The (Williams), 18

Marble City (Arkansas), 28

Marquand, J. P., 8

Márquez, Gabriel García, 132, 202, 220, 269, 274. See also *One Hundred Years of Solitude*

Mars (god), 240

Martin, Philip, 47

Marvell, Andrew, 220, 292

Maryat, Frederick, 29

Mathews, John Joseph, 294

Matryoshki, 231. See also Russian Dolls

DONALD HARINGTON was born in Little Rock, Arkansas and lost much of his hearing at age twelve due to meningitis. He taught art history in New York City, New England, and South Dakota and, finally, for twenty-two years, at the University of Arkansas. He was the author of fifteen novels and the winner of the Oxford American Lifetime Award for Contributions to Southern Literature, the Robert Penn Warren Award for Fiction, and the Porter Prize for Literary Excellence. Harington achieved more critical than commercial success in his career while always attracting a devoted cult following. The poet Fred Chappell once told the *Arkansas Democrat-Gazette*, "Don Harington is not an underappreciated novelist. He is an undiscovered continent."

⚡⚡⚡

BRIAN WALTER is professor of English at St. Louis College of Pharmacy and the director of *Stay More: The World of Donald Harington* and *Farther Along: The World of Donald Harington, Part 2*. He also appears as an "old coot" interviewer in the last chapter of Harington's final novel, *Enduring*.